The Forgotten Colony

BY THE SAME AUTHOR

In Spanish:

Tiempo de Tragedia, Argentina 1966–1971
(De la Flor, Buenos Aires, 1972)
Tiempo de Violencia, Argentina 1972–1973
(Granica, Buenos Aires, 1974)
Lancelot Holland, viaje al Plata en 1807
(Eudeba, Buenos Aires, 1976)
Arthur Koestler, del infinito al cero
(Altalena, Madrid, 1978)
La Censura en el Mundo – Antología
(Libros de Hoy, Caracas, 1980)

In English:

The Press in Argentina, 1973–1978
(Writers & Scholars, London, 1979)

Poetry:

Se habla spanglés (De la Flor, Buenos Aires, 1972)
Day to Day (Buenos Aires, 1973)

The Forgotten Colony

A History of the English-Speaking Communities in Argentina

Andrew Graham-Yooll

HUTCHINSON
London Melbourne Sydney Auckland Johannesburg

Hutchinson & Co. (Publishers) Ltd
An imprint of the Hutchinson Publishing Group
17–21 Conway Street, London W1P 6BS

Hutchinson Group (Australia) Pty Ltd
30–32 Cremorne Street, Richmond South, Victoria 3121
PO Box 151, Broadway, New South Wales 2007

Hutchinson Group (NZ) Ltd
32–34 View Road, PO Box 40–086, Glenfield, Auckland 10

Hutchinson Group (SA) (Pty) Ltd
PO Box 337, Bergvlei 2012, South Africa

First published 1981

Set in Linotron Sabon by Computape (Pickering) Ltd

Printed in Great Britain by The Anchor Press Ltd,
and bound by Wm Brendon & Son Ltd,
both of Tiptree, Essex

British Library Cataloguing in Publication Data

Graham-Yooll, Andrew
The forgotten colony.
1. British in Argentina – History
2. Argentina – Social life and customs
I. Title
305.8'21'082 F3021

ISBN 0 09 145310 0

To the memory of my father, Douglas Noel Graham-Yooll, a Scot who went to Argentina; to Micaela, my wife; and to Inés, Luís and Isabel, second generation Anglo-Argentines

BOLIVIA
PARAGUAY
River Paraguay
BRAZIL
CHACO
Asunción
Tucumán
Santiago del Estero
Misiones
Corrientes
La Rioja
River Paraná
Córdoba
San Juan
Santa Fe
CHILE
ENTRE RÍOS
Mendoza
San Luis
URUGUAY
San Isidro
Buenos Aires
Montevideo
Quilmes
La Plata
River Plate
Chascomús
ARGENTINA
Bahía Blanca
River Colorado
River Negro
Carmen de Patagones
Puerto Madryn
GOLFO NUEVO
Trelew
Rawson
Río Gallegos
TIERRA DEL FUEGO

Contents

Illustrations

Acknowledgements

Work on this book began in May 1970. I first sought help by writing to several newspapers to ask readers for information. Hence, my first expression of gratitude is to the editors of the *Buenos Aires Herald*, *La Prensa*, and *La Nación*, of Buenos Aires; *La Capital*, of Rosario; *La Gaceta*, of Tucumán; and the *Daily Telegraph*, London, for publication of letters that brought correspondence from around the world. I am therefore also greatly in debt to all those who wrote to me with information.

In 1972 a first draft of the book was lost 'in transit' to publishers in Britain. Rather than rewrite the book, I used the notes collected for articles in the *Buenos Aires Herald*, *Clarín* and *La Opinión*, of Buenos Aires.

Professor Héctor Ciocchini, at the time director of the Institute of Humanities at the University of the South, in Bahía Blanca, offered to make a short book out of some letters from British colonists living in the Bahía Blanca area after 1860. Copies of the letters had been given to me by a descendant of the colonists, Miss E. M. Brackenbury. In May 1973, the Government of Argentina changed and with the new authorities came a faction that equated 'popular culture' with the devastation of much of the established forms of intellectual activity. The library at the Institute of Humanities, which included several valuable collections and had been the home of progressive research in northern Patagonia, was thrown into disorder. What was to be the small volume of letters from the colonists was lost for a time and it was not until a year later that Professor Ciocchini, by then dismissed from his post by the new Government, found the letters among a pile of valuable books which had been ruined. Professor Ciocchini's lifetime work is all but lost. It is very small consolation for him, but I would like to thank him for his efforts first to publish, later to recover, those letters, which are quoted in Chapter 12.

A publication that was completed was that of the diary of the 1807 expedition, written by Lieutenant-Colonel Lancelot Holland, quoted in Chapter 2. A copy of the original manuscript diary was given to me by one of the Colonel's descendants, Philip Holland, in Buenos Aires. The Buenos Aires University Press EUDEBA, published the diary in 1976.

In 1974, a former presidential press secretary, Edgardo Sajón, who had just started a publishing company in Buenos Aires, asked me to rewrite the book in Spanish for inclusion in a collection on foreign communities in Argentina. I finished the translation in 1975, helped by Rafael Noboa, a Uruguayan law student. Edgardo Sajón's publishing company suffered from the economic difficulties of Argentina in 1975 and publication was postponed. In April 1977 Sajón was kidnapped and, it is feared, killed. I would like to pay tribute to him here for his personal courage and to express my gratitude for his encouragement.

In 1978 I started to re-write the original English version. The help of so many people contributed to make this book, including the preparation of the bibliographical list which I unashamedly claim to be among the best on the subject.

Research on the history of the English-speaking communities in Argentina brought me into contact with a vast number of people, too numerous in fact to list here. But some names I must mention. Encouragement came from some of Argentina's leading historians, among them Father Guillermo Furlong Cardiff, SJ, a priest of Irish ancestry who died in May 1974, aged eighty-four. He was one of Argentina's most loved historians and he never ceased to offer whatever information he thought I might find useful. Dr Ernesto J. Fitte, another of Argentina's principal historians, generously gave much advice when I started; as did Dr José María Rosa and the late Dr Arturo Jauretche. Dr Felix Luna, editor of *Todo es Historia* magazine, was kind enough to guide me to sources of reference. I am equally indebted to Alberto de Paula, director of the museum of the Banco de la Provincia de Buenos Aires. For their help and patience I would like to thank historians and researchers Armando Alonso Piñeiro, Jorge Alberto Bossio, Dr Oscar Vaccareza, Dr Vicente Cutolo, Osvaldo Castro, Kenneth E. Brìdger, Alberto Salas, Luis C. Alen Lascano, Mrs Charlotte de Hartingh, Carlos Gregorio Romero Sosa, Dr Nilda Garnelo, Professor Cristina Minutolo, Mrs Courtney Letts de Espil and Ezequiel Gallo, in Buenos Aires; Father Ramón Rosa Olmos, in San Juán; Ventura Murga, Ramón Leoni Pinto and Dr Carlos Paez de la Torre, in Tucumán; Virgilio Zampini, in Gaiman, Chubut, and Dr Rodolfo Terragno, in London.

Many people drew my attention to publications and documents of particular interest. Among this group I would like to express my special gratitude to Dr Allan Murray, for help on British doctors in Argentina; Federico Vogelius, for the use of his library; Frank V. Dobson, for records of British residents in Mendoza; Mrs Gweneira Davies de Quevedo, for information on the Welsh in Chubut; Dr José M. Mariluz Urquijo, for his papers on 'mixed' marriages; Lawrence Smith and William Horsey, for many bibliographical references; Mrs Elsie Rivero Haedo, for records of old farming establishments; Dr George Parsons, for stories on the Irish in Argentina; Eduardo Crawley, for locating old songs and poems; Mr E. R. B. Hudson, for his notes on the British invasions; Miss C. Babington Smith, for notes on John Masefield; Dr John Walker, of Queen's University, Canada, for his bibliography on British writers in the River Plate; Dr Cedric Watts, of the University of Sussex, Alicia Jurado and Lady Polwarth, for information on Robert Bontine Cunninghame Graham; Mr Rex Doublet and Dr Kenneth Dewhurst, for their writings on Dr Dover and the slave trade; Miss Deborah Jakubs, of the Department of History of Stanford University, for notes on British residents; Roberto Vacca, for his diving notes on the *Lord Clive*; Miss Stella Biggs, for her father's diaries and pictures; John Illman, of the British Embassy in Buenos Aires, for help with many contacts; and to Reginald 'Toby' Rowland, MBE, at the *Buenos Aires Herald*, for help with so many details that I would have otherwise missed.

I must also express my gratitude to the staff of the National Library and the Bartolomé Mitre Museum library, in Buenos Aires; to Captain Laurio H. Destefani, at the Institute of Naval

Historical Studies; to Colonel Gabriel Fued Nellard, head of the office of the Argentine Army Historical Studies, in Buenos Aires; to the Gaiman Museum, in Chubut; to the Udaondo Museum, in Luján; to Professor Glyn Williams, of the University of North Wales, Bangor; to Professor H. S. Ferns, at the University of Birmingham; to the staff of the library of the Argentine Rural Society; and of the library of the Jockey Club of Buenos Aires; to the South African Embassy in London; to the South American Missionary Society, in Tunbridge Wells; to the King Edward Horse Association, in London; the library of St Andrew's Scots' Church, in Buenos Aires, St John's Cathedral, in Buenos Aires; the Domingo Faustino Sarmiento Museum Library, in Buenos Aires; the library of the University of La Plata; the British Library, in London, the Newspaper Library, in Colindale; the Public Record Office, in London, the Canning House Library, in London; to Mr R. Fish, librarian of the Zoological Society, in Regent's Park; and to Mr D. M. Henderson, Regius Keeper of the Royal Botanic Garden, Edinburgh.

ANDREW GRAHAM-YOOLL
London

Introduction

The Review of the River Plate, for almost a century one of Argentina's leading commerce and shipping magazines, reported on 14 February 1947, on a nostalgic note, that negotiations for the direct purchase of the British-owned railways in Argentina by the Argentine Government were under way. Among other considerations, the magazine pointed out that such a transfer would mark the end of a chapter in the long and honourable financial association of both countries. For many British subjects resident in Argentina it was more than an end of a chapter: it was an epilogue.

One of Argentina's military and political heroes and the country's President between 1862 and 1868, Bartolomé Mitre, once said, at the time of the building of the first railways, that every stage of the development of Argentina as a nation had British witnesses and participants. The Scots settled, as they do anywhere, and ruled Patagonia and the Falkland (Malvinas) Islands, farming – with a copy of the Bible and a volume of Scott in one hand and a bottle of strong spirits in the other. The English never put down roots, as they seldom do outside of their island; but their influence was everywhere and especially in commerce. The building of the Argentine railways is the best-known symbol of the English presence in Argentina; but they also were strong in the other public services and had a part in most other fields of business. The Irish went as cheap labour, eventually to carve their way into the country's life, from town founders to holders of the highest offices in the nation's government. And then there were the Welsh. They developed their own valley in northern Patagonia as from 1865, to build stone houses with sash windows like the ones they had always known. Although their experiment in the preservation of their cultural heritage and national customs by transplant to another country partially failed, their territory took on the appearance of a little chunk of Cardiganshire. They fostered the memory of Wales and their forbears who landed on the beach of what is today Puerto Madryn, resisted assimilation and tried to keep their language. You can still hear it spoken on buses in the Chubut Valley. They still send a delegation each year to the Welsh Eisteddfod. They also have their own 'Eistedvod' each September in Chubut, with a prize of a bard's chair and a silver crown for the best poem written and recited in Welsh.

The British were, however, among the smallest of the immigrant communities. The conquering Spanish, who in fact had little to conquer but space, supplied immigrants from all of Spain's regions by the thousands. The poverty of the Italians, who also arrived in large numbers, caused their subsequent loss of identity and only a minority resisted assimilation. Spanish and Italians formed the bulk of the 'Argentines'. In 1914, out of a population of nearly eight million, Britons numbered fewer than 28,000 in a registered foreign-born population of 2·3 million. The British stubbornly refused to accept being categorized as immigrants which signified a drop in social class. The British were visitors. The decline in their numbers in the twentieth century is due more to emigration and death than to obscurity through assimilation. Only a minority assimilated, and these were mainly from the lower middle and working class, which included a large proportion of Irish immigrants.[1]

Professor H. S. Ferns wrote in *Britain and Argentina in the Nineteenth Century*[2] that 'between 1860 and 1914 [Argentina] grew into one of the cornerstones of the British economy'. While Britain's economic influence in Argentina was powerful, the British residents reflected some of this influence, but had almost no power. In the first place, Argentina was not officially a British colony. Second, when leading English-speaking merchants in Buenos Aires wanted to expand their interests, capital was not found locally – there was not a big enough money market to support large projects – but in London. And so power was held, in the first instance, by the lender. Third, while it follows that the power of the merchant resident in Buenos Aires grew as his interests expanded, in the case of Argentina the general rule was that as soon as this began to occur, the merchant transferred his profits to London, often leaving Argentina when he had become wealthy. In a British colony, while part of the wealth (understanding wealth as the basis of power) was transferred to the metropolis, some remained behind attracted by colonial enterprises which, though linked to London, had strong local ties. For the British in Argentina there was none of this. In fact there was not even a Spanish precedent, as Spain herself had squeezed every coin from the River Plate colonies to meet the demands of her own insatiable creditors. When the wealth and its holders left, it was a community of managers, not of proprietors, that stayed.

One of the signs of this continuous transfer of wealth and power from the British in Argentina to London is that the sagas of most influential families do not span more than two generations resident in Argentina – the pioneers and their children. The acquired wealth permitted the third generation to move away from the country and escape its unstable politics. And the British community in Argentina generally kept out of local politics – though exceptions are to be found, of course. There appear to have been a number of personal reasons for this abstention; but it may be said in general that it was a matter of racial prejudice: the Latin country's politics were considered unclean, the politicians too corrupt and unpredictable.[3]

It is probably for this reason that the resident British community tends to be forgotten or mentioned only in passing in political and economic studies of relations between both countries.

British influence in Argentina was greatest in four fields: commerce, education, transportation and sports. But there was no British administration, no colonial army to cohese these areas of superiority into institutional domination. British influence was therefore uneven, if widespread.

Although commercial influence is now limited to some banking and a few small entrepreneurial activities, British interests induced the concentration of commerce in Buenos Aires, which led to the laying of a railway network with the port as its terminus, to the growth of shipping and to a share in most public services. Commerce and the railways supported a large number of families, which produced a strong private educational system, still in evidence though long ago forced to abandon the exclusivity of a British-style education for language teaching in the interests of financial survival. Early English education in Argentina was closely linked to the Anglican and Presbyterian churches, which were successful in the establishment of the right to practise a foreign creed, although the churches themselves had no great influence in the country and never constituted any competition for the Roman Catholic faith.

The sporting world of Argentina was practically originated by the British, even if the latter were not thinking in terms of doing Argentina a favour.

With the British railways, British shipping, British meat-packing companies, British-owned farms, British wheat brokers, British importers, British exporters, British banks, British public services, British insurance, British schools, the British community in Argentina was the most numerous outside of the physical boundaries of the Empire.

They were never too concerned with intellectual pursuits, probably in common with many another immigrant community. They were and still are the product of good schools, built on the models of the British grammar and public schools. Education, however, was something sought to pursue commercial advancement.

Often, for this reason, the butt of intellectual irony, this community has nevertheless to its credit that it opened Argentina to the modern world. And Argentina is a far better country for the British drive that pushed through it, from gale-swept Patagonia to the tropics, and from the dirty shores of the River Plate to the magnificent Andean peaks. From pirates to polo players, they were always pioneers.

It is Englishmen's travel books that constituted the first literature of the River Plate; it is an English naval officer's watercolours of Buenos Aires that are still the principal pictorial documents of a city in post colonial years: Emeric Essex Vidal's *Picturesque Illustrations of Buenos Ayres and Montevideo* (London, 1820) are used again and again as an essential source of reference and illustration. The British organized the best schooling in Buenos Aires; struggled to establish their churches and fought, as officers and troops, in the wars of independence. Their hospital made firsts in Argentine medicine all along its century and a half of history; and with it came the city's most sophisticated health service. They had the best clubs – after all, they introduced most sports to Argentines – and built the railways to suit their own plans for commercial gain. In the second half of the nineteenth century unlimited profit was the most respectable aspiration of a Protestant existence and no short cut to gain was frowned on. They were, nevertheless, also responsible for engineering works on those railways which it is doubtful could have been made as fast or as vast by any other. The crossing of the Andes by a railway tunnel, which linked Argentina and Chile in November 1909, ranks on a par with such feats of engineering as the Panama Canal.

The community existed and expanded with a pioneering spirit up to the First World War, which changed not only their but much of the world's way of life. They left their mark everywhere. The British in Argentina celebrated the coronation of Edward VII in 1902 like many an Empire bureaucrat might have wished he could have done. Those were the days of the British in Argentina. North American influence would come later.

The life of the British and of other English-speaking communities seemed to lose some of its adventure and its pioneering element after the 1914–1919 war. The effect of the Great War on these groups could be seen in figures. Almost 5000 British and Anglo-Argentines volunteered to fight for Britain after 1914, giving an idea of their strength. Only one-quarter of that number returned to the country. Influence did not end overnight, of course, but it declined after that and the curtain fell with the nationalization of the railways.

The transfer of the railways was, perhaps, the unkindest end. Nationalization, on 1 March 1948, by President Juan Perón made that army general, in the eyes of resident Britons and of those who lived by them, an evil dictator. Others who imposed order by steel were acceptable disciplinarians in all but the excesses that might affect members of the British community. The uncertainty about their security, being outside the realm, made the British in Argentina enthusiastic supporters of strong-arm rule if it favoured their interests, with nary a thought for democracy as viable beyond Westminster. Authoritarian administration was explained as justified in Latin America where the British communities considered democracy was impossible.

The English-language newspaper *Buenos Aires Herald*, which became 100 years old in September 1976, tries to instil politically democractic and economically liberal ideals of tolerance and understanding into its readers, who are more worried about staying out of the country's turbulent politics in case they might be affected.

Some vestigial features of British influence remain.

The St Andrew's Society of the River Plate pipers' band meets regularly and to play at every Scottish event of importance, which includes the annual Caledonian Ball, in July, the Burns' Night Supper, and the Gathering of the Clans, in the spring. At the end of the music the players usually speak in the metallic-sounding Spanish of the Anglo-Argentines, without a trace of a Scottish burr. Their Scotland is very far away.

Until the mid-1960s the Queen was still toasted at the Boer War veterans' lunch held each year at the Retiro railway terminal restaurant, once the meeting place for the elegant of Buenos Aires and originally a lavish expression of the wealth of the British-owned Central Argentine Railway. But old soldiers decline and die – at the British Hospital, in Buenos Aires, probably in the charitable care of the British Community Council in Argentina.

Hurlingham Club still stands, as exclusive as ever since its foundation in 1898 – exclusive to wealth if not always to nationality – with immaculate golf course, a splendid polo field, a cricket green for the summer and an Argentine military garrison and a rubbish tip for neighbours. A terrorist's bomb destroyed one of the club's older store sheds in 1975 but it hardly moved a hair on the stiff upper lip.

And Harrods winks at shoppers, with an imperial gleam of opulence in its display windows, at the elegant end of the Florida pedestrian shopping street.

In far-away Britain, and in the United States too, though to a lesser degree, the English-speaking residents in Argentina are remembered for their feats, vanished influence and remoteness. The legend is assisted by the contrasts that the British in 'South America' always provided. On the one hand there were the vast investments (worth £125 million, according to *The Times* in June 1902, when Britain was called in by Argentina and Chile to mediate in a dispute over the border line in the southern Beagle Channel) and enterprise and their attendant social subsidiaries; on the other, the opposite extreme, the English down-and-out in Buenos Aires or the Scottish tramps in the provinces – who, unlike the Polish and Russian tramps, refrained from joining the anarchist movement. Many were 'remittance' men, the unwanted or disgraced relatives sent away with a small allowance to avoid embarrassment to their families. Not a few had titles; Eton, Harrow and Oxbridge educations; some became teachers, others alcoholics; still others redeemed themselves by a discrete and respectable existence and a few discredited themselves for all time by marrying a 'native' girl. Some made fortunes; others lost what little they had including their identity and their language in remote parts of the country.

They were rogues and tramps, victors and victims; but as a group they managed to make Argentina an exciting adventure.

The Bibliography shows the multiple angles from which the story of British interests in Argentina might be approached. From the economic relations between the two countries, to travels in Patagonia, the story of one church to the story of a club, all have been dealt with separately. This book aims to give an overall chronological view and tell the story of the English-speaking communities in Argentina through the many individuals who, in the words of President Mitre, were the witnesses and participants of every stage of the development of Argentina as a nation.

1
The Earliest Visitors

Don Pedro de Mendoza sailed from Spain in August 1535 with fourteen ships and over 2000 men and women to found the town of Santa María de los Buenos Aires on the banks of the River Plate in February of the following year. This first town, of houses with mud walls and roughly thatched roofs, surrounded by a wooden palisade and a ditch and occupying no more than the equivalent of two city blocks in what is now the capital of Argentina, was a disaster. The white inhabitants were not prepared for the rigour of survival in the new land. They died of sickness and starvation, the stronger cannibalized the weaker and their town was set ablaze and destroyed by the native indians who had at first appeared to be friendly. In Don Pedro de Mendoza's crew were John Ruter, of London; Nicholas Colman, of Hampton; and Richard Limon, of Plymouth.

Previous to this, there had been Britons in the crew of Ferdinand Magellan, a Portuguese mariner in the service of Spain, when he sailed round the Horn and through the Strait to which he gave his name, during a voyage of circumnavigation – the first ever – 1519.

One Robert Thorne, of Bristol, was among the men who financed the journey of Venetian mariner Sebastian Cabot, who sailed from the Spanish port of Sanlucar in 1526, in search of a passage round or across the newly discovered continent to the 'spice islands'. Aboard his four ships, mostly manned by Spaniards, were Christopher Burbusley, from Worcester; Richard Cork, of Essex; Henry Patimer, of Colchester; Thomas Ternan, of Norfolk; and Cabot's close friend, master gunner Thomas Barlow, of Bristol. Cabot reached the River Plate in February 1527 and founded the first settlement in what would be Argentina, the Fort of Sancti Spiritus, soon destroyed by the indians, on the banks of the River Paraná.

Even at these earliest of 'Argentine' dates there were Englishmen in the land.

At one time a British sovereign reigned over the Spanish colonies. In 1554 Mary I married Philip II, who became King of Spain in 1556. It was because of this marriage that Juan Perez de Zurita was ordered to travel from Perú to found the town of Londres – or, rather, to rename the town of San Juan Bautista de la Rivera to become San Juan Bautista de la Rivera de Londres – in Catamarca, in 1558, in honour of the royal wedding. About 400 English colonists were to be sent there; but the plan came to nought because the queen died that same year. The town was overrun on more than one occasion by the Diaguita indians, and was founded several times in different places. But Londres, Catamarca, still exists and remains today a place of formal pilgrimage for British diplomats.

Sir Francis Drake first sailed to the Spanish colonies with Sir John Hawkins on a slaving voyage from Guinea in 1566. He spent the next few years as one of the most successful corsairs plundering the Spanish Main. In December 1577, Drake left England to sail in the path of Magellan and circumnavigate the world. In September 1578 he passed through the Strait. Drake was in the River Plate between these two dates – not long before the second, and definitive, foundation of Buenos Aires, by Don Juan de Garay, in June 1580. Drake coasted Patagonia where, according to the Reverend Thomas Fletcher, he stopped for the trial and execution of Sir Thomas Doughty, his second in command, accused of conspiring to mutiny.[1]

Drake weighed anchor in August 1578 at San Julián – where he had lost a ship's gunner, named Oliver, who had been beaten to death by exasperated indians after a bout of drinking and excessive teasing – and went on to the Pacific to continue with his exploits against the Spaniards and plunder Valparaiso. Eventually, he crossed the Pacific and arrived back in England in 1580, to be knighted by Queen Elizabeth, in spite of Spanish protests.

After Hawkins and Drake there was Edward Fenton, who entered the River Plate with Sir Francis's cousin, John Drake, in command of one of the ships in the small fleet. John Drake's ship ran aground off the coast of what is today Rocha, in Uruguay, on a sandbank that has since been named on all charts as Banco Inglés.

The man who, according to Jesuit research, was the first Irishman in the River Plate was Thomas Fields, a Jesuit priest and son of a Limerick doctor, who reached Brazil in 1577. He later travelled to San Miguel de Tucumán, finally to work in Paraguay up to 1625.

Thomas Cavendish left Plymouth in July 1586, coasted Patagonia, stopped at Port Desire to rescue a few Spaniards from an ill-fated settlement in Magellan's Strait started by Pedro Sarmiento de Gamboa, and explored the southern islands. John Davis sailed in 1592 to spend two years between Port Desire and Santa Cruz, on the Patagonian coast, finally to return to Cork with only fifteen of the seventy-six men he had set out with.

One century after Columbus had discovered what was by then known as 'Land of Américo' (Vespucci) – based on the accounts of Vespucci's voyages, published in 1507, part of which were found to be a fabrication three centuries later, but which nevertheless gave his name to three continents stretching from Pole to Pole – the Spaniards had a firm hold, whereas the British remained visitors. Spain sent religious missions, founded inland towns, and started trading posts. In 1617 she created the River Plate province, giving it government and boundaries – what is today Uruguay, central and northern Argentina and Paraguay – within the Viceroyalty of Peru.

Having visualized Spanish America mainly in terms of plunder, Britain was ready for a more peaceful settlement. Charles II of England commissioned John Narbrough in 1669 to establish a settlement at Port Desire; but the venture was plagued by misfortune and low morale and eventually abandoned. John Strong, commissioned in 1690 to travel to the Falkland (Malvinas) Islands and open trade with Chile, was also charged with studying the possibility of establishing a settlement on the Patagonian coast to act as a base for trade on the mainland and a staging post for traffic to the Pacific. But Strong's Patagonian mission was a failure, mainly due to bad weather, and he returned to Britain after one year.

Throughout the sixteenth and seventeenth centuries Britain looked on the Spanish colonies with more than passing interest. However, it was the wealthy ports of the Pacific that drew aggression; Buenos Aires, lacking the much sought-after metals, was a poorer colony and so suffered fewer raids. Nevertheless, a suggestion that Britain should invade the River Plate was made in a booklet, *A proposal for humbling Spain*, written, the publisher said, 'By a person of distinction', in 1711. The booklet was attributed to Governor Pullen of the Bermudas, who submitted his project for invasion to Robert Harley, Earl of Oxford, whose principal act as Lord High Treasurer was to be the Treaty of Utrecht. The invasion proposed by Pullen did not take place until almost one century later.

In September 1711, Harley, interested in gaining access to trade – rather than plunder – in the Spanish Americas, pushed through Parliament a bill to set up 'The Company of Merchants of Great Britain trading to the South Sea and other parts of South America'. Creation of this South Sea Company was as much a commercial venture as a political move by the Tory Government to match some of the power of the East India Company, which contributed large sums to the Whig cause.

The South Sea Company was inspired by what has been described as the most successful privateering voyage in British maritime history, financed by a syndicate of Bristol merchants and city dignitaries and commanded by Captain Woodes Rogers, with Dr Thomas Dover, a physician, as the owners' representative.[2] They had a commission from Prince George of Denmark (consort to Queen Anne) to 'cruise on the coasts of Peru and Mexico, in the South Sea, against Her Majesty's enemies the French and the Spaniards'. Dr Dover's expedition captured several ships off Chile, attacked the port of Guayaquil and held it to ransom, and then sailed further north to more prizes.[3] Dover, who had invested £3000 in the expedition, collected £6600 as a result of his exploits, on his return to Bristol. Such excellent gain in business was bound to encourage others.

In March 1713, the Treaty of Utrecht, which concluded the war of Spanish Succession, gave Britain her first trade link with the River Plate and Harley the opportunity to exploit the slave trade in South America. One of the Treaty's many agreements was the 'Asiento de Negros' which awarded Britain the contract, previously held by the French as from 1701 and by the Portuguese before that, to supply slaves to Spanish America. Such 'Asientos' with other countries were a necessity to Spain because war had so impoverished the nation that the Crown could not keep its colonies supplied with cheap labour.

The slave-trade agreement was for thirty years and the South Sea Company took over trading posts at Buenos Aires, Vera Cruz and Cartagena. The contract was to supply 4800 African slaves a year to Spanish America, of which 1200 were to go to Buenos Aires. A price of 33⅓ pieces of eight was agreed for every slave that was delivered alive, 'not being old or defective'. As a result of his success as a privateer, Dr Thomas Dover was elected president of the 'factory' at Buenos Aires in September 1714, with a salary of £1000 per annum. His enthusiasm led him to invest in the Company all that he had made on the privateering voyage. But it was not a happy association. There were disagreements with the ship's captain, with the shippers, with the rules about how many servants and how many Europeans could accompany him to Buenos Aires – among them was William Toller, an unauthorized passenger, invited by Dover to keep a historical record of the Buenos Aires venture – and about the expenses necessary to instal the warehouses, offices, homes and 'barracoons' to accommodate the slaves, at what is today Buenos Aires' very elegant Plaza San Martín, on the north side of the city. And there was also a battle between Dover and the Company over the supply of medicine for the Africans.

Dover arrived in Buenos Aires in September 1715, just ahead of the first five slaving ships. The installations he received from the French were minimal; one of the ships arrived with 100 cases of smallpox aboard and Dover exhausted his expense allowances almost immediately in caring for them. At this point he went to ask for help from the Jesuits whose mission was next to the San Ignacio Church, on the south side of Buenos Aires, and such was the trust he had won by his diplomacy – on arrival he had gone to greet the governor, the bishop and other church authorities – that he was lent 150,000 pesos by Father Herran almost on the spot and without interest. The Jesuits asked for no guarantees, trusting, they said, the honesty of the Britons to repay the debt. Some time later the British slavers indeed returned the money and in so doing enquired why it was that the building of the church had been delayed. They were told this was due to a shortage of funds. As a mark of gratitude Dover advanced the Jesuits a sum for the completion of the San Ignacio church – and this church still stands today. It is some irony that the Jesuits, while helping to finance such a miserable trade as slavery in Buenos Aires, were actively resisting enslavement of the native indians of Paraguay by the Spanish at Asunción and by the Portuguese Mamelucos in what is now southern Brazil.

The Spanish had imported nearly 23,000 slaves up to 1680, the Portuguese and the French another ten thousand up to 1712; the British took over a further 10,000 during the Asiento agreement.[4] Slaves were paid for mainly in hides, which were an attractive commodity to the British. The trade in slaves was soon supplemented with the smuggling of British manufactured goods into the River Plate colonies – such goods were banned by the Spanish monopolists because of the competition they represented. Thus South Sea Company slaving ships – and others not authorized to trade in the area – set sail from Buenos Aires loaded with hides, the product of deals with local merchants assisted by corrupt functionaries.

While Dover was a successful manager, reports of how much he had bribed local officials – to allow quick passage of British manufactured goods and an increased supply of hides to Britain, or to make sure that Customs overlooked the transfer of hides from South Sea Company ships to privately chartered merchantmen – and complaints about the volumes he and the half-dozen Britons at the 'factory' were smuggling, as well as his own complaints to the directors of the South Sea Company, decided his dismissal. Dover was replaced by another 'factor' and he returned to Britain in the middle of 1717. In spite of the indecorous manner of his parting from the South Sea Company, Dover can be considered an important early pioneer of British trade links with the River Plate countries.

As a result of the excessive overpricing of slaves, the South Sea Company collapsed suddenly in 1720. The 'bubble' had burst. The Company had spent over one million pounds in bribery, had suffered theft and fraud, and had lost public confidence. Following the crash, Dover, considerably poorer, returned to his medical practice. His life work was *The ancient physician's legacy to his country, being what he has collected himself in forty-nine years of practice*, published in 1733. He died aged eighty-two and 'drifted into our modern life on a powder label', according to Sir William Osler, one of his biographers. The powder – a mixture which included opium, saltpetre and liquorice, to be taken with white wine, against fever – kept his memory alive for many years.

Despite the agreement with Britain to supply the Spanish colonies with slaves, Spain made it only slightly easier for foreigners to reside in the territories of the Empire. Britons, other than the 'factory' managers, were given forty days in which to complete business on a shipment of Africans and leave. But, as with all other practical relations between the Britons and the Spanish, bribery could overcome any rule. Among those who stayed were a few of the slaving ships' physicians who, being educated men, left written accounts by which they could be traced. In 1715 there was a John Burnett, a graduate of Edinburgh, and in 1718 a Dr John Mylam was faced with coping with a smallpox epidemic. Another, Robert Fonteyn, was described as a doctor 'of whom it has been seen that he has conducted himself with the greatest charity and unselfishness in the care of the needy'. London-born Dr James Ross Pringle is recorded as being the first British settler in Mendoza.

Dr Pringle abandoned his ship, sickened by the 'cargo', and from Buenos Aires made his way overland, with the intention of going to Chile. In Mendoza he found that the Andes pass was snowed up and he waited there for better weather. But good weather was too long in coming: Pringle had settled. In August 1721 he married and changed his name to Diego Ruiz Pringles, because 'castillanizing' his name made it easier to be a permanent resident. He had nine children. A ship's assistant surgeon, describing his journey to the River Plate with the South Sea Company's ship *George* and overland to Chile (1752–6), reported finding Pringle in Mendoza established as a vintner and keeping a large family in comfort.

One of Pringle's daughters, Manuela, married one Thomas Innes, 'native of the Kingdon of England', according to the marriage entry, in November 1750. A great-grandson of James Pringle, Juan Manuel Pringles, reached the rank of colonel in the War of Independence, to be murdered in March 1831 by one of *Caudillo* (chieftain) Facundo Quiroga's followers.

The most famous of all the River Plate slave ships' doctors was Thomas Falkner, writer and Jesuit priest. Falkner was born in Manchester, in October 1702, of English Calvinist parents, and studied at the Manchester Grammar School. Trained as a physician, the Royal Society commissioned him to go to the River Plate to work as a botanist and physicist. He arrived in 1730 on a South Sea Company ship.

Shortly after his arrival, he fell seriously ill; but being a Briton, and therefore a 'heathen' in those intolerant times, the doctors of the town would not assist him. In fact, many Spaniards believed that associating with a Briton was tantamount to dealing with the devil. A priest eventually came to his aid and during his convalescence he was converted. Falkner entered the Jesuits' Company in Córdoba in May 1732. He was not the only Briton to become a Jesuit in the River Plate at that time: over a dozen others followed his example in the next few years.

As a missionary and medic, Falkner won widespread recognition. Most of his three decades in the colony were spent in the city of Córdoba, but he was not restricted to that one place. In 1743, with another priest, he founded the settlement of Nuestra Señora del Pilar, on the Lake Padres, a short way from what is today the city of Mar del Plata.[5] Though as a priest he moved freely, he must have found it lonely as a Briton. In 1744, a census ordered by the Governor of Buenos Aires, Domingo Ortiz de Rosas, showed that there were seven British residents, although there may have been others who had disguised themselves by 'castillanizing' their names and accepting the Roman Catholic faith. This same census showed that the overall population of Buenos Aires was

10,056 with another 6035 in the outlying areas.

Falkner's scientific investigations led to the identification of new botanical species, and also to the discovery of the skeleton of a giant armadillo, in 1754, while he was employed as administrator of an *estancia* (ranch) at Caracarañá. On leaving Carcarañá he returned to Córdoba, where his renown as a doctor kept him fully occupied. He was often sought by Britons in need of assistance. During the week of 17–24 March 1763, Falkner received thirteen Britons into the Jesuit Company, most of whom were English.[6]

In 1767, when Charles III of Spain ordered the expulsion of all Jesuits from the Empire, Falkner had to leave. He was back in Britain in 1771. The record of his travels into the provinces of the colony and his Patagonian experience is to be found in *A description of Patagonia, and the adjoining parts of South America: containing an account of the soil, produce, animals, vales, mountains, rivers, lakes, etc. of those countries; the religion, government policy, customs, dress, arms and language of the Indian inhabitants; and some particulars relating to Falkland's Island* (London, 1774). In this book Falkner suggested that Britain could make an excellent and safe port on the Patagonian coast, from where much of the South Atlantic could be controlled. The comment prompted the Spanish authorities to found a settlement at Patagones, in 1782.

Though the age of piracy and plunder was now over and Britain sought to trade with rather than raid the colonies, there was always a fear of an attack or attempt to seize the Spanish possession. In fact, the eighteenth century in the Spanish colony was one of near constant fear of British invasion, an after-effect of the frequent attacks against ports on the Pacific during the previous century. On the Atlantic the potential invaders were merchants or smugglers, the latter a business in which the British and Portuguese were the masters on the eastern coast of South America. British designs on the colony were reported regularly and the sighting of phantom invasions announced frequently. These fears were all justified, however, although not until 1806 and 1807 did such invasions take place.

2

The Invasion that Failed

I

Britain's long-term, formal influence in Argentina began with a military invasion that failed. The military expeditions to the River Plate in 1806 and 1807 and their failure were of passing importance in Europe, although *The Times* on 14 September 1807, described the disaster as 'perhaps the greatest which has been felt by this country since the commencement of the revolutionary war'. Nevertheless, these military expeditions broke the commercial stranglehold that Spain kept on her River Plate colonies. And they would open Buenos Aires to popular action and political expression that would lead, in time, to rebellion against the Spanish Crown.

Buenos Aires, Paraguay and Uruguay with Patagonia (the last of these in name only, as it was inhabited only by a few nomadic indian tribes) had been made into one province of the Spanish Empire in 1617. The province had been separated from the Viceroyalty of Peru and made a viceroyalty in its own right in 1776. To the European, even to the Spaniard, it was a vast, largely unknown and exotic territory. Britain never ceased to see the Spanish colonies in South America as a very desirable base from which to command new markets as well as hold naval supremacy in the South Atlantic.

There were a few English-speaking people in the Spanish colony in the early days of the nineteenth century. Some were long-time residents who had evaded the forty days' residence limit for all foreigners. The Britons who had worked with the South Sea

Company and settled were generally assimilated and there is little trace of them. 'Foreigners' were understood to be non-Spaniards, but more specifically non-Catholic. The Irish, for instance, were welcome, being Roman Catholics. Non-Catholics were 'heathens' usually associated with the enemies of the Spanish Crown. 'Heathens' in Buenos Aires were avoided, suspected of conspiracy and, among the most ignorant, thought to associate with the devil. Many of those who stayed on in Buenos Aires were recorded as having expressed agreement to convert to Roman Catholicism, theoretically the only way in which they could be allowed to remain in the colony. Religious conversion or 'castillanization' brought changes of names such as in the case of Hill, which became Gil; Williams became Guillón or Guillán; Corry turned into Correa; and Bond was cut to Bon.

This adaptation of names was aimed at avoiding the native fears and suspicions of foreigners who, in addition to being called infidels, were suspected of being spies for Spain's enemies. A register of resident aliens was part of the colonial administration because Crown laws barred foreigners from the Empire. However, all laws were evadable and bribes, 'castillanization', or, in some cases, religious conversion, were the loopholes chosen.

Smuggling was one occupation for the few Britons in the River Plate – the profits of which were equally, often not even secretly, sought by many Spanish merchants in and out of the Buenos Aires Government. Smugglers used as a base the Portuguese-held town of Colonia del Sacramento, across the River Plate from Buenos Aires.[1]

Ingleses – the name usually given to any 'heathen' from the British Isles, North America and, sometimes, even Germany – were seen officially, however, as useful, if suspicious members of the colonial society. In 1748, the *Cabildo* – the town's principal authority, a form of city council which answered directly to the King's representative – asked the Governor not to expel two English carpenters, because there were too few in the colony. In 1778, a group of Irishmen had travelled out under contract to work in beef salting; and in 1785 several butchers had been imported from Ireland. A hide-tanning expert had followed; and there are government memoranda from 1794 proposing the immigration of 100 Irish beef salters. In 1801 six experienced tanners had been employed from the United States.

Some of the arrivals had been accidental. A small fleet led by the British ship *Lord Clive* had left about eighty men alive, but many more dead, in the River Plate when fire engulfed the *Lord Clive* in an attack on Colonia del Sacramento. What was left of the ship is still under four metres of sand and mud at the bottom of the river, off the coast of Uruguay. The tragedy of the *Lord Clive*, a ship of sixty guns, supported by two frigates and accompanied by five merchantmen, was the result of optimistic reports for an assault on Buenos Aires written by one John Read, a slave trader who had settled in the town in 1759. The ships entered the River Plate on 2 November 1762, and Captain John MacNamara, formerly of the East India Company, decided to take Colonia first. The battle, on 2 January, lasted four hours. Two hundred and seventy-two men, including MacNamara, were killed on the ships. Four men died at the Fort of Colonia. An unknown number of British officers were taken prisoner while they still splashed about in the shallow water of the river. Sixty-two members of the crew saved their lives by leaping into the muddy Plate as the *Lord Clive* burned to the waterline. They were interned in Córdoba. Among them were said to be the founders of the Carrel, Todd and Sarsfield families in South America.

There had been other rough arrivals. In 1797, the French crew of the *Lady Shore*, which had left London in August carrying seventy-five British women and forty-four men to convict settlements in Australia, mutinied off Brazil. The crew hoisted the French flag and, after putting the captain ashore, sailed for Montevideo. The ship was seized by the Spanish and all aboard were interned. Some of the women married and returned to respectability; others became prostitutes and vagrants.

In 1804 there were forty-seven men and ten women with English names – at least, names that could be connected with British origins and could be recognized – in Buenos Aires. They were registered as aliens. However, the actual number was no doubt higher, but others must have avoided the listing or 'castillanized' their names to go unnoticed. Of the fifty-seven people, the forty-seven men included twenty-seven Britons (twenty-four

English and three Scots), according to the aliens' register up to October 1804. The other twenty men and ten women included ten Irish and twenty North Americans. Nationalities may have been an accident of birth or of registration; civil servants were unreliable scribes and often wrote down what they thought was best or what they thought they had heard. Also, contemporary political alliances made some nationalities more acceptable than others and therefore places of birth were changed for convenience. The forty-seven men included a variety of professions: four physicians, four cobblers, three tailors, three carpenters, seven boatmen, two sailors, two teachers, a leather craftsman, one blacksmith, as well as a number of import and export merchants – and suspected smugglers.

Very few of the *Ingleses* were of a high social standing, and when a foreigner did rise in society he became a suspect spy or smuggler, or both. The Spanish fear of spies led officials to suspect, for instance, a novice at the Santo Domingo Convent, John Constanse Davie, who was later to become known to historians as the author of two volumes of letters on Paraguay, Buenos Aires and Chile. It is true that many did try to enter the lucrative business of smuggling, but the label of 'spy' was more often a mistaken exaggeration of the activities of those who were primarily on the look-out for trade opportunities and became informers by virtue of the knowledge they had assimilated.

One such man was William Pius White, an American, born in Boston in 1770, who reached Buenos Aires in 1803. He arrived as a supernumerary and built his fortune as a slave trader and smuggler. White is understood to have been one of the correspondents who lured Sir Home Riggs Popham to the River Plate for the first invasion, in 1806. Popham is reputed to have owed White a sum of money from an earlier association with the North American in India. And White found no better way to collect his money than to persuade Popham that the River Plate was a good source of booty. The North American's contacts with William Carr Beresford, the officer who led the 1806 landing, and the intelligence he offered him won him the hatred of the Spanish officials and a prison sentence after Beresford's surrender. But the town's captain general (a rank equivalent to that of interim viceroy), Santiago de Liniers, later pardoned White, to whom he had sold a large estate on the outskirts of the town. In 1809 White was to go into business with Bernardino Rivadavia, a rebel against the Spanish Crown, married to a former viceroy's daughter and a future president of the republic in 1826. Rivadavia ended the partnership on the grounds that the North American's commercial practices were questionable.[2]

Another such story centres on one of the British officers' principal hosts, Ana Perichon, an attractive Caribbean-born woman of French ancestry who combined glamour with a fancy for officers, thus becoming the gossip of the colony. She had arrived in Buenos Aires in 1796 with her husband, Thomas O'Gorman, an Irish merchant. Thomas was the son of a prominent physician, Michael, established in Buenos Aires since the early days of the viceroyalty, when he had been appointed administrator of the colonial hospital system.

Thomas O'Gorman was a discredited merchant and cuckold. For a time he tolerated his wife's flirtations; but when she became the most regular visitor to the apartments of Captain General Santiago de Liners at the Fort and gossip reached every home in the town, they separated. The scandal that resulted forced Liniers to send her to Rio de Janeiro in 1808 and there she again became the centre of rumours as the alleged companion of the British minister, Lord Strangford. Members of the Portuguese court took a dim view of this intrusion and she was ordered to leave Brazil, finally to be allowed to return to Buenos Aires, in November 1810, through the mediation of a British naval officer.

Thomas O'Gorman was expelled from Buenos Aires in 1807, for the support he had given the British during the invasion. He too was allowed to return, but in 1809 he left the River Plate for good and settled in Lima.

White and O'Gorman were marked as spies; but it seems more likely that they were only acting as informers to some commercial houses. It was another Irishman, James Florence Burke, who really filled the role of 'spy' when he travelled out with orders from the British Government to supply information on the colony, ranging through all aspects of local life, from geographical detail to commercial and social customs, armament and attitudes to Spain.

The time was that of Pitt and Britain was still coming to terms with the loss, almost three decades before, of the North American colonies. Europe was closing its ports to English goods, the fear of invasion from France was strong – and would be only partly allayed by Trafalgar – and equally strong was the need to find new markets and new sources of supply. South America was one possibility as was southern Africa.

Burke was first in Buenos Aires during 1804, aged thirty-three, and visited the town again in 1808. The first visit by Burke came before the British invasion; the second amid conspiracy against Spanish rule. In 1804 he made his way around Buenos Aires as 'the colonel', announcing an interest in various commercial ventures. He was a tall, elegant man who at first impersonated a Prussian officer, although he later shed the disguise. Burke took rooms at the *Posada de los Tres Reyes* ('Three Kings' Hostel'), which stood on a site on what is today 25 de Mayo Street (then called Santo Cristo). This was held to be the best hotel in town – a low building, cold and damp, with small rooms and thick walls. It had barred windows with crochet curtains, which were the only thing that softened the fortress-like appearance of much of the building in the town. From Buenos Aires, Burke moved to Spain, all the time keeping a correspondence with members of the British Government, which later refused to reimburse his expenses. In Spain, Burke introduced himself as a merchant and scientist, long resident in the River Plate area.[3]

The accounts of flashy conspirators in addition to the alien status of Britons did residents nothing but harm. Whatever influence they achieved was looked upon with suspicion that they were well paid agents of 'heathen invaders'. The fear soon reached government officials who interned six men and three women, because they were British, in March 1805.

In 1806, Buenos Aires had a population of between 25,000 and 50,000. Its army was a small force and lacked training. For example, the *El Fijo* regiment, Buenos Aires' own local guard, had seventy-five soldiers and ninety-four officers; their discipline was non-existent. The fifteen Corps stationed in and around Buenos Aires and the main cities in the interior, including Montevideo, totalled 6300 men.

The town was a village and not a very big one. The only paved streets stretched no more than two present-day city blocks, fan-like from the *plaza* in front of the Fort, a sprawling building which had undergone a metamorphosis from mud and wattle barricades to Government House and garrison in the course of three centuries. All the other streets were earth; deep and stinking swamp when it rained. Many streets had saints' names. The town spanned about fifteen present-day blocks along the river front, with the slave market at El Retiro on the northern outskirts and with several cattle slaughter, meat and hide salting concerns to the south and south-west on Buenos Aires' natural southern limit, the Riachuelo river. The town had a cathedral, standing on the north side of the main square, *Plaza Mayor*, which was used as public meeting place and as an open market. The *Cabildo* building spanned the west end of the square; while across the square, on the south side, was the main shopping area running the length of the *plaza*. Behind this cluster of buildings was a large fortress-like building occupying an entire block. There was the San Ignacio Church, built thanks to the British slavers, an orphanage, a convent, an armoury and a high school, all of which was to be known a few years later as the *manzana de las luces*, the 'block of lights', the 'illuminated' in this case being the town's intellectuals. The Fort was on the east end of the square, its walls washed by the River Plate. Beneath all the buildings ran a network of tunnels, their use still not explained.

The town had three main cafés which doubled as meeting places for the exchange of information and the reading of European – mainly Spanish – newspapers, in lieu of the erratic local publishing of news.

This was the town that Sir Home Riggs Popham found when he invaded the River Plate province in 1806.

Popham, an adventurer as well as an explorer, astronomer, navigator and astute diplomat, sailed from Britain under General Sir David Baird in August 1805 with 6600 men and with orders to capture the Dutch colony at the Cape of Good Hope. They sailed first to Madeira, then to Salvador, Brazil, and from there to the Cape which was taken after a single battle on 18 January 1806, five days before Pitt died in Putney.

The expedition was aimed at making the trade routes to the East Indies safe for British shipping as well as securing a base from which to conquer the River Plate. However, there was no urgency to invade the Spanish colonies and no order from the British Government for the start of this second stage of the expedition.

But Popham, who knew of the British Government's aims and had received information that showed the River Plate colonies to be poorly defended, decided that he would not await orders, assuming that his action would be approved in the end. Popham enjoyed a degree of popularity in the Navy because 'he looked carefully to the interest of the men and officers under his immediate command, particularly in the matter of prize-money, which was frequently the main object of his operations . . .'[4]

And this interest in the booty probably decided Popham to get to Buenos Aires first.

He knew of Pitt's inclination to support South American emancipation movements to end Spain's control of the continent. He had discussed such support and even the possibilities of invasion of South America with Castlereagh and General Francisco Miranda – then resident in London but who would return to Venezuela in 1810 to lead the country to independence with Simón Bolivar's help. And in October 1804 Popham had written to Viscount Melville proposing an invasion of the River Plate colonies, though he assured that occupation could not be permanent and the country would have to be won, following initial military intervention, by the establishment of trading posts along the coast.[5]

II

Early in 1806 Popham convinced Baird of the possibility of invading the Spanish colonies of Montevideo and Buenos Aires. The success at the Cape was a little dizzying and troops were available. Popham had sought information from travellers and seamen and they had told him what he wanted to hear. Montevideo, he had been advised, was without defences other than a crumbling fort. Buenos Aires, the capital of the viceroyalty, was an equally unprotected city where the *Criollo* – the native-born white descendants of Spaniards – population was becoming increasingly embittered at the incompetence of the Spanish administration. Popham's informers were to be proved inaccurate, though not totally wrong. A North American captain, merchant and slaver had claimed that Montevideo would be the easier target. Other information had come from a Scot at the Cape, who had been a pilot in the River Plate for fifteen years, 'though his intellect was not effective whenever he found access to the bottle'. He had painted a picture of the River Plate political situation such that occupation was a matter for no more than three Scots in a boat.[6]

Baird approved the adventure. He gave Popham 922 men and thirty-six officers of the 71st Highland Light Infantry regiment – accompanied by sixty women and forty children – a small artillery detachment, a few dragoons and a Royal Marine battalion. The then Colonel William Carr Beresford was placed in command of these forces and promoted to brigadier-general, the same authority as Commodore Popham. This was Baird's form of insurance against disobedience of his orders. These were that Beresford should take possession of the colony and proclaim himself governor. Baird was of a political school that considered Spain an enemy but not one he wanted to see defeated by 'revolutionaries'.

Popham sailed with eleven ships, five transports escorted by six battleships, for the River Plate on 12 April. He called at St Helena where he took aboard another 300 men and some field artillery; and arrived off San Felipe de Montevideo on 8 June. The accommodating informers had showed themselves to be of little value: Montevideo was fortified and would require strong and prolonged fire to overcome it. He looked to Buenos Aires. Aboard he was running short of food. Rumour reached him that there was treasure in Buenos Aires awaiting shipment to Lima and Spain: all appetites could be satisfied in Buenos Aires, a town of which the principal defence was its isolation. It stood alone on the edge of vast open plains on the banks of a shallow and muddy river.

Popham took his ships south, where the river was less silted. On 25 June Brigadier-General Beresford went ashore at Quilmes, twelve miles south of Buenos Aires, with a force of 1635 men. He entered the town on 27 June and the next day raised his flag at the Fort. Resistance amounted to only a few token shots. The troops were not prepared for battle and, however outrageous this sounds, 'not interested', according to Manuel Belgrano, later to become one of the leading independence officers and politicians. In fact, the officers of two companies argued with the Viceroy that it was their duty to defend the town and not to go into the field.[7] Most of the troops were Spanish veterans – because the creoles were not allowed under arms – grouped according to the provinces of origin. The Viceroy, Marquis Rafael de Sobremonte, had been attending his daughter's wedding when informed of the British landing. He soon realized that Buenos Aires had no defence, that his troops were useless and that he had no inclination to organize them. He fled the town with the colony's treasure to establish a new capital in Córdoba. Beresford sent a party after Sobremonte who was caught, but allowed to continue to Córdoba, without the treasure. Beresford did not wish to deal with the problem of holding captive the King's representative in case this should precipitate public reaction or diplomatic confrontation that he was not prepared for. The treasure that the British forces seized was said to be only part of vast wealth hidden in Buenos Aires and never recovered. This story remains a matter of speculation. From Córdoba, Sobremonte started to organize an army to resist the British.

From aboard HMS *Narcissus*, off Buenos Aires, Popham wrote on 6 July:

> To the commerce of Great Britain it [Buenos Aires] exhibits peculiar advantages, as well as to the active industry of her manufacturing towns. And when I venture in addition to assure their Lordships of the extreme healthiness of the climate, I trust that I only hold out a consolation that the friends of every person employed on this expedition are justly entitled to, and which I am satisfied will be equally gratifying to the feelings of every British subject.

Popham's report dismissed the native forces as incompetent although it exaggerated the size of the enemy. 'The enemy was posted at the village of Reduction [now Quilmes], which was an eminence about two miles from the beach, with the appearance of fine plain between the two armies, which, however, proved on the following morning to be only a morass in a high state of verdure', said Popham's report published in the *Gazette* on 13 September. The first edition of *The Times* that Saturday morning had sluggishly recorded on the second page that 'no accounts had been received of the expedition'. But the type grew in size and leapt out of the page on column four of the same page in a later edition which announced:

> By an express, which we have just received from Portsmouth, we have to congratulate the Public on one of the most important events of the present war. Buenos Ayres at the moment forms part of the British Empire, and when we consider the consequences to which it leads from its situation, and its commercial capacities, as well as its political influence, we know not how to express ourselves in terms adequate to our ideas of the national advantages which will be derived from the conquest.

Popham's adventure had become a matter of national interest, an outlet for trade and for public concern as an alternative to the problems created by an Europe closed to Britain by Napoleon. 'By our success in La Plata, where a small British detachment has taken one of the greatest and richest of the Spanish colonies, Buonaparte must be convinced that nothing but a speedy peace can prevent the whole of Spanish America from being wrested from his influence and placed forever under the protection of the British Empire,' exulted *The Times*.

But exactly one month and a day before this publication Buenos Aires had ceased to be a British possession.

Popham's report, when it arrived, delighted the British public, anxious for demonstrations of success.

> The able and excellent disposition of General Beresford, and the intrepidity of his army, very soon satisfied the enemy that his only safety was in a precipitate retreat, for we had the satisfaction of seeing from the ships near four thousand Spanish cavalry flying in every direction, leaving their artillery behind them, while our troops were ascending the hill with that coolness and courage which has on every occasion marked the character of the British soldier, and has been exemplified in proportion to the difficulties and dangers by which he was opposed. On the 27th, in the morning, we saw some firing near the banks of the River Chuelo . . . Early on the 28th, a royal salute was fired from the castle of Buenos Ayres, in honour of His Majesty's colours being hoisted in South America, and instantly returned by the ships lying off the town.

Beresford sent his first full despatch from the Fort on 2 July. He described the landing in more moderate terms:

The troops which had opposed us during these days appear to have been almost entirely provincial, with a considerable proportion of veteran officers. The numbers that were assembled to dispute our passage of the river, I have since been informed, were about two thousand infantry. I had no reason from their fire to suppose their numbers so great; the opposition was very feeble; the only difficulty was the crossing of the river to get at them.

In a ten-point proclamation of terms granted to the Buenos Aires inhabitants, Beresford made all Spanish troops prisoners of war, while the few native officers were freed. He assured that there would be respect for the Catholic religion and promised protection for the Church. Private property was not to be touched, which won Beresford immediate acceptance among most local business.

With the promise of such rigid protection to the established religion of the country and the exercise of its civil laws, the major-general trusts that all good citizens will unite with him in their exertions to keep the town quiet and peaceable, as they may now enjoy a free trade and all the advantages of commercial intercourse with Great Britain, where no oppression exists, and which he understands has been the only thing wanted by the rich provinces of Buenos Ayres and the inhabitants of South America in general, to make it the most prosperous country in the world.

On 16 July Beresford detailed the money put aboard HMS *Narcissus*. Some of the booty was shared by the troops. Of the near £300,000 seized, General Baird received £23,000; Beresford took £11,000 and Popham collected £7000. *The Times* of 19 September reported that:

Six wagons were filled with the treasure taken in Buenos Ayres and landed from the 32-gun *Narcissus*, Captain Ross Donnelly (at Portsmouth). The procession was followed by vast numbers of seafaring persons in this port, the population of the town turned out to witness it, rending the air with their patriotic acclamations in honour of bravery of their countrymen and of the triumph and treasures they had gained from the foe.

The chorus of one of these songs, 'The dollars of Buenos Ayres', ran:

Suppose for fun we just knocked down
This town of Buenos Ayres.
Then drink away with a hip-hurra
For the dollars of Buenos Ayres.

and:

We said Boney might be damn'd
Since we'd got Buenos Ayres
Then drink and sing to George our King
And the dollars of Buenos Ayres.[8]

In the colony the flight of Viceroy Sobremonte had disheartened the Spanish establishment; while the native population and their leaders saw their political opportunity begin to take shape. A scant number of people swore allegiance to the British Crown. Fifty-eight people, most of whom were British residents, gave their oath; but there were also several of the town's merchants to whom their commercial interests were more important than a change of monarch and a different flag.[9]

British influence was soon to be noticed in many ways. The most immediate change was in commerce where there appeared a more sympathetic attitude to liberal trade. There also grew an interest in British politics and culture. In Montevideo and Buenos Aires certain preferences for British goods began to be noticed in the shops. On a far more trivial note, as winter ended and spring grew nearer some women began to follow what they had heard were English fashions and did not cover their arms. Of course, baring so much flesh, even in the warm weather, brought vituperation and even the occasional adjectives linking the ladies to the more disreputable professions.

Beresford was harassed in his efforts to reduce evidence of colonial rule. His very presence was portrayed as a threat. Martín de Pueyrredón, a tough leader of the unruly *gauchos* and the pacified Indians; Martín de Alzaga, head of the Spanish merchants and an enemy of free trade and of the 'heathen' British; and Santiago de Liniers, a clever politician and leader with personal ambitions; each presented the invader as the perpetrator of terror. In addition, Sobremonte's flight, the ineptness of the local Spanish troops, the rapid change of allegiance of a few merchants and civil servants, including the *Consulado*, were all factors which favoured increased *Criollo* political influence which would in turn contribute to the decline of the Spanish monopoly.

While Beresford pleaded with Popham to secure the presence of a larger military force, Liniers transferred troops from Montevideo. The small British fleet, with little experience in navigating the rivers that flow into the Plate, failed to intercept him. Liniers did not attempt to organize a complete army, but a fairly disciplined part of one. For numbers and effect he depended on the reaction of the civilian population and the *gaucho* cavalry, which had managed to inflict serious casualties on the British the previous June by picking off stragglers and escaping unimpeded. These fighters and the townspeople were organized into militias who elected their commanders – usually the wealthier members of the local establishment – giving them an unquestionable political strength.

On 10 August, Liniers, Pueyrredón and Alzaga assembled a large force outside Buenos Aires and launched their attack the following day. Beresford found himself trapped in a town where every house was a fortress, every flat roof a nest for snipers. From the rooftops, boiling oil and water, stones, shots and a variety of projectiles fell into the narrow streets, where the men of the 71st desperately resisted. By midday on 12 August the situation proved untenable and Beresford surrendered.[10] The townspeople called the occasion the 'reconquest' – *La Reconquista*.

Beresford, an officer of one of Europe's strongest armies, considered his surrender to a ragged citizens' force to be conditional and that all members of the invading force would be allowed to leave Buenos Aires, as soon as an exchange of prisoners could take place. Liniers initially agreed to this, but he was fiercely opposed by the *Criollo* leaders who invoked their new-found power and on the basis that as it was their victory it was therefore for them to decide the settlement. The public feeling was that over 1000 foreigners should not be allowed to return to their ships and be given the opportunity to prepare another invasion.

On 7 December Viceroy Sobremonte – then only a figurehead and the target of rude slogans and songs – approved the internment of prisoners, sending 200 to Mendoza, 200 to San Juan, 200 to San Miguel de Tucumán, 100 to Santiago del Estero, 50 to La

Carlota, 50 to San Luis and 400 to Córdoba. The last group had left Buenos Aires for Córdoba on 13 October. The Viceroy's approval was thus no more than a formality.

In fact, the distribution of prisoners was different from that detailed: 188 men had gone to Tucumán and not as many as 100 were sent to the other northern destination, Santiago del Estero. A total of 309 went to Mendoza. This group included 240 men, forty-one women and thirty-seven children. Many of the people in the Mendoza group were not held there but farmed out to towns north in San Luis and San Juán, partly because of the limited capacity of the villages, but also because of ill-feeling against the Britons. This antipathy was not only the result of their part in the invasion of Buenos Aires but also for their immoderate drinking and unruly behaviour. The expense of the internment of such a large number of people had persuaded the local government to put most of them in the custody of private persons – summoned to hold them as a patriotic duty – which seems to have resulted in free access to the bottle and general disfavour.[11]

Beresford and his second in command, Colonel Denis Pack, and another seven officers, were transported to Luján, eighty miles from Buenos Aires and held in the *estancia* Los Barbones, near Salto de Areco. Beresford felt cheated by the Government which had broken its pledge to a conditional surrender. Pack's record as a prisoner was not one of good conduct. He was repeatedly offensive to the people in the town of Luján, which prompted them to attempt to kill him one day while he was out riding. Instead they ambushed and killed Pack's companion, Captain Ogilvie. The murdered officer was seen by historians as representative of many of Beresford's men, generally considered to be well educated. Ogilvie held a long correspondence in Latin with a local priest, Father Castañeda, one of the colony's leading political theorists and intellectuals.

The suspicion that the officers at Luján were conspiring to escape and would not accept captivity, as the Spanish assumed that officers should, decided the Government to order their transfer to far away Catamarca. Faced with such a prospect Beresford and Pack planned their escape. In February 1807 they left the *estancia* Los Barbones with the assistance of a Peruvian of dubious reputation, and of a man named Saturnino Rodriguez Peña, Liniers' secretary. His reasons for assisting such a flight have never been clear, but perhaps he was paid or even he was given some kind of an assurance of future British support for an independence movement in the River Plate, which Rodriguez Peña was known to sympathize with in spite of the office of his master. If indeed Beresford had given such an assurance he would no longer have been following Baird's orders. In Buenos Aires the escape was thought to be a plot engineered by Liniers because his own plan for a settlement with a conditional surrender had been overruled.

Beresford and Pack were hidden in a house in Buenos Aires and then taken back to the British transport ships which had brought the force from the Cape. Beresford remained on the ships; but Pack immediately prepared to go back into action.

The officers scattered in the district near Buenos Aires were said to number sixty-three, according to an account published in Buenos Aires on 13 January 1807. There were nine at Villa de Luján, eight at Capilla del Señor, six at the *estancia* of a man named José Otarola, two on the *estancia* of the Zavaleta brothers, fourteen at San Antonio de Areco, five at the Guardia de Luján, three at Fortín Areco, ten at Salto and six at Rojas. These were all outposts which would later show British influence in farming and railways. At that time the existence of those officers was comfortable and their custodians treated them kindly. The inconvenience of an invasion apart, the arrival of these visitors was the most exciting thing to happen in the dull life of the colony in years. The families welcomed the prisoners, who had a noticeable influence on their captors. Cricket in Argentina had its origins in those districts of Buenos Aires province where the officers were held. The officers were able to tell their captors' families about the life and culture of England and Europe and its refinements. Some officers used the opportunity to explore the countryside and make notes on the area which were later to become the basis of articles and learned papers when they returned to Britain. It was not altogether wasted time.

While he had been Commander of the Fort, Beresford too had been widely accepted. Then aged not quite forty and the son of the Marquis of Waterford, his guests and hosts in Buenos Aires came from the best of local society. He had received many gifts and attentions and his officers had enjoyed the parties to which they were invited in all the homes of the colonial aristocracy. Colonel Pack was thirty-three at the time of the first landing and had commanded the 71st Highlanders, and he too had been well received in the best houses. His escape embarrassed the friends he had made in Buenos Aires society who thought that an officer should not reduce himself to breaking away.[12]

While Beresford's defeat was still not known in Britain, General Sir Samuel Auchmuty sailed from Falmouth with a reinforcement of 6300 men. Brigadier-General Craufurd was given 4000 men and ordered to invade Chile and 'establish an uninterrupted communication with General Beresford, by a chain of posts or any other means' – 750 miles separate Santiago de Chile from Buenos Aires. Popham's success had dawned on everybody as a marvellous opportunity.

'By such a union we should have a never failing market for our commodities, and our enemies would be forever deprived of the power of adding the resources of these rich countries to their own means of annoying us', *The Times* had written on 15 September 1806.

The South American success unleashed widespread interest in Buenos Aires. An advertisement in *The Times* of 16 October announced that a gentleman who was to be on 'one of the first ships to Buenos Ayres (offered) to act as commercial agent' to anybody desirous of his services. This notice was the first of a flood of such offers and applications for jobs.

On 23 December *The Times* published rumours of Beresford's defeat: 'We do not consider them entitled to the least credit.' The rumours were confirmed on 17 January.

Reinforcements from the Cape of Good Hope were ordered to Buenos Aires by Baird. But Lieutenant-Colonel Backhouse, in charge of the fresh forces, arrived in the Plate some time after Beresford's surrender and found that he was the senior officer in command without orders or anybody to report to. Backhouse and Popham attacked several points on the coast of the Banda Oriental [Uruguay] and took the town of Maldonado. At one point they decided to rid themselves of the burden caused by 200 prisoners by leaving them on the Isle of Lobos, off what is today the resort of Punta del Este. Faced with starvation, some of these prisoners managed to swim to the mainland. Their story aroused such anger when it reached Buenos Aires that several British prisoners were publicly beaten to death.

Auchmuty arrived in the Plate in January and, with Popham and Backhouse, put siege to Montevideo, which surrendered and was occupied on 3 February. Popham was then relieved by Admiral Sterling, who had arrived with Auchmuty. Pack, who had joined them after escaping from arrest in Luján, was ordered to take the town of Colonia. Pack's raid was marked by success. An extract from general orders, dated 10 June 1807, in Montevideo, stated that:

> The commander of the forces congratulates the army upon the brilliant achievement performed by the troops at Colonia, under the immediate command of Lieutenant Colonel Pack who, on the morning of 7th instant, attacked the enemy in a very strong position twelve miles from Colonia and, with a spirit becoming British soldiers, destroyed, captured and put to flight double their numbers . . .

Meanwhile, in London, Lieutenant-General Whitelocke had been ordered on 5 March to travel to Buenos Aires, as Governor General of South America with a salary of £12,000 a year, and recapture the capital of the River Plate. Whitelocke took command of the forces in Montevideo on 11 May.

But in Britain, before the news of the second attack had been received, there were signs of apprehension. On 27 August *The Times* was a little less than optimistic:

> Whatever difference of opinion may exist with respect to the value of the object which we are solicitous to recover, there can be but one sentiment in regard to the issue of the attempt to regain possession of this settlement. But the subject should perhaps be viewed in connection with our military character, rather than in relation to our commercial prosperity . . . The commercial advantages to be derived from the vice-royalty of Buenos Ayres should, perhaps, be regarded as of far less comparative importance. The inhabitants have hitherto manifested no disposition cordially to embrace an English interest. To retain possession of it would always require a very considerable force, and these are not the times when this country with any sort of prudence or forsight can thus strip itself of a garrison requisite for its own defence.

However, to those who witnessed it, the River Plate territory was an attractive commercial proposition. The Banda Oriental, over which the British troops imposed their authority, was not a place for booty, but it may well have made a merchant's dream. A member of Whitelocke's staff, Lieutenant-Colonel Lancelot Holland, entered in his diary for 24 June:

Soon after we were on shore we got on horseback and rode to a village called Real de San Carlos, about three miles from Colonia. The country is quite open, the ground not quite flat but undulating, the sod very fine. We did not see such immense herds of cattle as I expected, but the officers told us by extending our ride a little we should have seen the face of the country cover'd with bullocks. There were a great number in sight.

An indication that the British planned to stay for some time was given by publication in Montevideo of a news-sheet, *The Southern Star*, a four-page foolscap-size weekly published in English and Spanish and sold between 23 May and 11 July 1807.

Whitelocke went ashore south of Buenos Aires on 28 June. 'The place fixed upon for the disembarkation was about three miles from the village called Ensenada de Barrangon [Barragán], between it and a point of land called Point of Lara,' Holland wrote in his diary. The English commander had a force of 7000 men, including those ashore and those who remained in the ships, while 4000 men stayed in Montevideo. He had every right to think that such a force was enough to take Buenos Aires: Beresford had done so with one-tenth of the number.

The attack on the town was launched on 5 July. By the afternoon of that day the defenders, disorganized, rushing from one point of contact to another, crowding to hit the enemy, leaving sections of the town deserted after one onslaught, had nevertheless proved that they could hold the invaders. And then, just as fast as it had started, the invasion came to an end. Holland's entry in his diary later recounts:

Colonels Guard and Pack having agreed with General Craufurd that we were reduced to the necessity of surrendering, General Craufurd settled with this Illio that we should give ourselves up as prisoners of war. We were ordered to march out without arms. It was a bitter task, everyone felt it; the men were all in tears. We were marched thro' the town to the Fort.[13]

Nothing could be more mortifying than our passage through the streets amidst the rabble who had conquered us. They were very dark-skinned people, short and ill-made, covered with rags, armed with long muskets and some a sword. There was neither order nor uniformity among them.

The people of Buenos Aires called the event the 'defence' – *La Defensa* – of their town.

Liniers had taken over the Viceroy's rooms in the Fort since the previous September and there he became the English officers' host; Viceroy Sobremonte had been suspended from all his duties, the *Cabildo* resorting to the grounds that he was in ill health.

The civility of relations between victors and vanquished is remarkable. Contacts appear quite casual and hardly possible in perspective. Whether or not it was due to a real liking for one another among the foes or a need by the Spanish to strike an early bargain and be rid of the invaders is difficult to gauge. An example of the comfortable coexistence – and some dislike for the invaders – is given in Holland's 7 July entry in his diary:

In the morning a pushing Irishman, a Captain Carroll of the 88th, who speaks Spanish and contrived thro' this to get intimate with the Spaniards, seeing me in a dirty uncomfortable state, offered to procure me a shirt and a razor; this was not a proposal to be neglected. I followed him not knowing where he was leading. To my astonishment he brought me to a room where Liniers, just got out of bed, was dressing. He very coolly told him what he had brought me there for and Liniers immediately fetched me a razor, shirt, etc., after which he was half an hour looking for a new toothbrush for me. He talked all the time, fast and to little purpose. Whilst I was with him, not less than ten ill looking Spaniards, some military, some civilian, passed into his room without ceremony, with loud complaints about the English. Their manner is that of a people on a footing perfectly equal.

A cessation of hostilities was agreed upon between General Liniers and General Gower, till twelve o'clock; all was therefore quiet till that hour, excepting some firing from the gunboats, who did not know of the treaty. A 24-pounder from one of them went thro' the building we were in, into Liniers' apartment; had they continued some of our own officers would probably have been hurt. At twelve o'clock a flag of truce arrived, bringing General Whitelocke's acceptation of the terms agreed on the last evening; great and universal was the joy of the people, firing, shouting, etc.

General Leveson Gower has been blamed, along with

Whitelocke, for the failure of the attack on the town, although the former avoided responsibility. Gower, then aged thirty-three, has been described as a hypocrite and an incompetent sitting-room strategist who was responsible for the issue of orders which no officers could understand and without consultation with Whitelocke, because they were constantly at odds. Holland had expressed his impatience with both officers, when writing in his diary, and sounded particularly annoyed with the fastidious and inadequate Whitelocke. Holland, in turn, played a part of his own in the luckless invasion – which he had been reluctant to join because it had meant postponing his wedding – by failing fully to transcribe the orders dictated by Gower. The orders that officers received omitted several crucial sentences referring to the advance through the town.[14]

'The terms [of surrender] were that the prisoners should be restored on both sides, and the Plata evacuated by the English in two months. The field officers dined again with Liniers. In the midst of dinner some of the townspeople came to demand Pack, and Liniers had the greatest of difficulty in getting them out of the room; there was a vast bustle and confusion. Liniers was in a prodigious passion', wrote Holland of the evening of 7 July 1807.

Pack was bundled off 'disguised as a Spaniard' to avoid the public's 'excessive irritation against him'. Barring this incident, contacts between both sides were generally friendly, quite out of proportion with an unprovoked attack by a foreign army on the quiet town.

The following day the first British troops began to embark.

On the day that the British South American adventure ended, General Whitelocke wrote:

> The result of this action left me in possession of the Plaza de Toros, a strong post on the enemy's right, and the Residencia, another strong post on his left, while I occupied an advanced position towards his centre; but these advantages had cost 2,500 men in killed, wounded and prisoners.
>
> This was the situation of the army on the morning of the sixth, when General Liniers addressed a letter to me offering to give up all his prisoners taken in the late affair, together with the 71st regiment, and others taken with Brigadier General Beresford, if I desisted from any further attack on the town and withdrew His Majesty's forces from the River Plate, intimating at the same time, from the exasperated state of the

population, he could not answer for the safety of the prisoners if I persisted in offensive measures. Influenced by this consideration (which I knew to be founded in fact), and reflecting on how little advantage would be the possession of a country the inhabitants of which were so absolutely hostile, resolved I to forego the advantages the bravery of the troops had obtained, and acceded to a treaty which I trust will meet the approbation of His Majesty.

Why Whitelocke did not withdraw from the town to reorganize his far superior forces and attack again is very difficult to explain at this distance. But perhaps it should be borne in mind that Whitelocke had been chosen on the strength of personal influences, not for any known political qualities, by men who had little idea of where he was going, but who thought they were giving him an easy mission and a chance to do well. An uproar followed his defeat later that year and accusations pointed to his incompetence and his cowardice and the disastrous effects of appointments by favouritism. The reaction was all the more fierce from a commercial community in Britain which had been led to believe that South America was the answer to many trade problems. On the other hand, at least one writer hints that Whitelocke might be seen as a sensible man who became aware of the hopelessness of military control of the Spanish colony, because no more than the capital on the river could ever be taken and held.[15] However, Whitelocke found no better way of drawing attention to his discovery than by disgracing himself and his army.[16]

There was not one good word for Whitelocke anywhere. On Wednesday, 30 September 1807, *The Times* thundered:

It being clearly understood that the late disastrous affair at Buenos Ayres is to be thoroughly investigated and the conduct of the commanders to be judicially scrutinized, the purpose for which we so zealously called the attention of our countrymen to their apparent mismanagement is now fully answered; they are to be put upon defence and we shall therefore say not one word more of General Whitelocke, till that defence is before the public . . .

On 28 January 1808, the trial of General Whitelocke by nineteen officers opened at the Royal Chelsea Hospital. He was charged on four counts of incompetence and that he had 'unnecessarily and shamefully surrendered all such advantages, totally evacuated the town of Buenos Ayres, and did shamefully deliver up to the enemy the strong fortress of Monte Video, which had been committed to his charge . . .'

The Press had a field day. Whitelocke became the target of the angriest pens, the fiercest cartoons and the most cutting commentary. Satirical poems, in varying lengths and venom, were frequently directed at Whitelocke and Popham.[17] After a trial lasting fifty-one days, in which every fault was dragged through the court to satisfy a public and a commercial community for the failure to give them the promised prosperity of a new colony, Whitelocke was declared totally unfit and unworthy to serve His Majesty in any military capacity.

King George commanded that the sentence 'be read at the head of every regiment . . . with a view of its becoming a lasting memorial to the fatal consequences to which officers expose themselves, who, in the discharge of the important duties confided to them, are deficient in that zeal, judgment and personal exertion which their sovereign and their country have a right to expect from officers entrusted with high commands.' Pamphlets on the trial and the expedition, accounts of the failure and humiliation of Whitelocke became best sellers for a short time.[18]

The other principal personality in this adventure, Sir Home Popham, got off lightly. He was tried aboard the HMS *Gladiator*, in Portsmouth, on his return to England. He alleged that he had not acted against orders because he had proceeded on a proposal which was accepted and without orders; and his action, in first instance, had met with general approval. Beresford and Pack – who married General Beresford's sister in 1816 – both continued into distinguished careers in the Peninsular Wars.

Whitelocke's invasion cost over 300 killed, nearly 700 wounded and over 200 missing. He reported that 170 deserters of the 71st had not been traced and referred to desertion as a disease. 'The more the soldiers become acquainted with the plenty the country offers and the easy means of acquiring it, the greater will be the evil, as the temptation is irresistible.' Which must have sounded as good as an invitation to return.

It is now, of course, impossible to trace all the men who could not be rounded up and returned within the two months after the

7 July surrender. One story, however, tells of a man who was among twelve stragglers on the day of that disastrous assault. They went to the home of Martina Céspedes to ask for water. The woman, an unattractive, middle-aged widow with three daughters, captured all twelve by luring them into a *patio* at the back of her house and then barred the doors. She reported her catch to Liniers and agreed to return eleven men, the twelfth having been claimed by her youngest daughter, Petrona. She is said to have given her English husband four children; but records do not show his name.[19]

The many men, soldiers and officers, who stayed behind make a colourful group. One who stayed in Buenos Aires was Patrick Island, who some Argentine chronicles describe as a nephew of Beresford. He was shot by a slave of the Gómez Farías family, on 27 June 1806, and was then nursed by them until fully recovered. Island changed his name to Islas and married one of the Gómez Farías girls, Bartola, at Arrecifes. He later became a militia captain at San Antonio de Areco during the civil war after 1820, in the *Unitario* army of General Juan Lavalle. He eventually got his throat cut by the enemy group, the *Federales*, led by General Juan Manuel de Rosas, in November 1840.

There was a doctor who was held in San Antonio de Areco. When a transfer of prisoners appeared to include the doctor, the townspeople appealed to the Viceroy and they were able to retain him and his much appreciated services.

Artillery Major Alexander Gillespie was taken with other officers to Chilecito, in La Rioja, in the Andes foothills. Gillespie only returned to Britain about ten years later and published a book about the provinces. In his *Gleanings and remarks collected during many months of residence at Buenos Ayres and within the upper-country* (Leeds 1818) he assured that: 'No city of the globe has such a glorious future as Buenos Ayres.'

In some respects the dispersion of the prisoners could be said to have laid the foundations of the British community in Argentina. Of the 188 men sent to San Miguel de Tucumán, thirteen men remained when the prisoners were released in 1807. This may not have pleased the provincial authorities, because the terms of the armistice demanded the return of all prisoners under the threat of annulment of the pact. The thirteen therefore went into hiding when their release was announced, apparently in fear of punishment by their compatriots for celebrating with the townsfolk when the news of the defeat of the second landing reached the northern provinces. Eleven of these thirteen have been traced in Tucumán, through the cathedral's archives recording their conversion and marriages.[20]

3

The British Merchants of Buenos Aires

The conspiracy for revolution

Spanish colonial policy had ruled that goods required by Buenos Aires could only be imported from Spain via Lima and then carried south overland. This imposed a severe limitation on the economic and political growth of the River Plate. It had meant that northern cities such as Córdoba, Tucumán and Salta became more important than Buenos Aires in the colonial network. The situation changed, however, when Buenos Aires became the capital – because of its position on the coast – of the Viceroyalty of the River Plate in 1776, and a few years later the Viceroy opened the port to neutral foreign traders. They were allowed to unload their goods on payment of Customs duties, to help the crisis-ridden treasury. Merchants, or smugglers, who entered the estuary for these benefits were ordered to leave after unloading; but there was no consistent drive against contraband. Spanish monopolist traders, however, pressed for and won the reimposition of import restrictions after a few months. Between 18 November 1797 and 20 April 1799, the Spanish Crown, in answer to the appeals from Buenos Aires, authorized the opening of the port again to neutral ships. Duties were lowered in January 1798 and Customs revenue that year rose by five times the average for preceding years. But free trade was opposed by the merchants of Cadiz and Buenos Aires was closed again to all but ships from Spain.[1]

The British military invasion of 1806 brought the previously unheard of state of free trade. General Beresford, during his forty-seven days as Governor, established this by three decrees in

June, July and August. He imposed a twelve per cent duty on British goods and a seventeen and a half per cent duty on those from other parts of the world. The decision spurred into action the real victors of the British expedition, the merchants. Contemporary reports show that there were 2000 merchants with over 100 ships to unload outside Buenos Aires and Montevideo between the time of the first landing and the capitulation the following year. George III, pleased with the success that in some measure reversed the loss of North America, declared Buenos Aires an open port on 17 September 1806 – but by then the city had been reconquered.[2]

So Beresford was welcomed by those who saw in him a clear commercial advantage. Spanish manufactured goods, almost free of import taxes, were usually more expensive than the smuggled British goods. Even the North Americans, strong in commerce, including smuggling, on the Rio de Janeiro–Buenos Aires route, but always faced with arbitrary rates set by transatlantic traders, still managed to place their freight in the River Plate ports at better prices than those of the Spanish.

The success of the 1806 landing caused a fever of activity among Britons with an eye to doing business with Buenos Aires. Anybody who had ever had any information on the Spanish colony was called on to share it. Pamphlets and books were rushed to the printer. Among these, the most important was one titled *History of the viceroyalty of Buenos Ayres, containing the most accurate details relative to topography, history, commerce, population, government, of that valuable colony*, by Samuel Hull Wilcocke, published in London in 1807. Wilcocke had never been in Buenos Aires, according to his own admission. He nevertheless had a wealth of information to offer. He said that the Spanish Viceroy was not paid much, but accused the Crown's representative with doing better by other means, such as by accepting bribes and by blackmailing opponents. The author said that the only respectable groups in the many-class society in the viceroyalty were the residents who had come from Spain, known as 'old Spaniards' or 'old Christians'.

When the British occupied Montevideo in February 1807, merchants unloaded over one million pounds sterling in goods, with no fear of saturating the market since they expected much of their goods to go on to Buenos Aires. While the success of Whitelocke's operation was awaited, however, smugglers were already active, moving the goods from Montevideo to Buenos Aires. Martín de Alzaga, prominent in Buenos Aires society and one of the leaders of the militia against Beresford, reported to the *Consulado* in May 1807 that a farmhouse outside the city, as well as most shops and stores in town, were stacked high with English goods.[2]

Whitelocke's capitulation in July 1807 precipitated a crisis among the British on both sides of the River Plate and many were forced to sell at a loss. A small number stayed on. The next four years were to be difficult for the members of this group, often living in doubt from one day to another, and fearing reprisals, despite the measure of support they received from those of the *Criollo* community who favoured a liberalization of commerce. However, this local support would soon make them appear to be political, and not just commercial, conspirators against Spanish rule.

When the Supreme Central Junta of Spain declared war on Napoleon on 6 June 1808, it announced its desire for friendship with Britain. The British crown ordered an end to hostilities against Spain in July. Merchants in Britain assumed that trade with Spain also meant commerce with her colonies. The greater volume of potential trade was commercially ideal for the consignees in Buenos Aires but the instability of the market made the responsibility for more shipments a hazardous affair. However, as has been mentioned before, Britons did have an ally of sorts in the interim Viceroy, Santiago de Liniers, who had a tendency to overlook illegal business by foreign residents – an attitude which was the bane of Spanish monopolists – in the very realistic necessity for even the smallest sums of cash that might flow from such trade to the treasury.

By 1808 this unofficial policy made Britons doubly suspect; in addition to being thought of still as spies who were privileged by Liniers' whims, they were also considered supporters of *Criollo* conspirators. In July of that year, Percy Clinton Sydney Smythe, Viscount Strangford, appointed British representative to the Portuguese Court in Brazil, arrived in Rio de Janeiro. Strangford, a cunning junior diplomat, was to be called on for help by the British in Buenos Aires – when they felt that the authority of the Royal Navy commanders, occasionally visiting the River Plate, was not sufficient – and was to have some influence on the *Criollo* revolutionary movement, mainly through his advice about European attitudes to such action, even though he considered independence efforts premature.[3]

Events leading to the revolution built up rapidly from early 1809. In January, the *Cabildo*, encouraged by Martín de Alzaga, tried to force Liniers to resign, on the pretext that he had allowed his daughter to marry without first seeking the King's consent. Liniers, though disliked by many in Spain and Buenos Aires because of his French origins and because, even as a Frenchman, he had won so much influence, was a good court conspirator and defeated the drive against him. However, his easy-going politics, which were of benefit to foreign residents, were doomed. Spain did not like such liberalism.

In that first month of the year, Spain signed a new treaty of friendship – following the announcement made in the previous year – with Britain. As a result of this, on 20 January, Spain, aware of Britain's interest in the River Plate market and of the plight of the colonial treasury, authorized all British goods that had entered Buenos Aires during the invasions to be cleared and to pay the same duties as those paid for Spanish manufactured products. But it was only a bureaucratic gesture by then. Merchants who had paid anything in excess of the duties had little chance of ever seeing a refund and many who had not paid had left long ago. Nobody was satisfied.

The newly appointed Viceroy, Admiral Baltazar Hidalgo de Cisneros, arrived in Buenos Aires on 29 July 1809. At Montevideo, a few days before, he announced that he planned to enforce the laws of the colonies. The statement put the fear of ruin into many foreigners. Others, accustomed to the whims of viceroys, thought the threat of only relative importance and something that could be resisted.

Within three weeks, Cisneros faced his first test. John Dillon and Joseph Thwaites, two Britons who had lived in Buenos Aires for some time, wrote to Cisneros for authorization to unload goods aboard the Cork-registered ship *Speedwell*, anchored in the Plate. The two men had been unable to unload at Rio de Janeiro and claimed that if they were prevented from doing so at Buenos Aires they faced bankruptcy. It was a humanitarian appeal, in a way, but with a strong political and commercial content. The Dillon–Thwaites letter was the first of a series the Viceroy was to receive in the next few months, each letter asking for relaxation of import restrictions. The correspondence coincided with representations made by farmers outside Buenos Aires who asked for the reduction of export duties on their produce and an end to the privileges granted to Spanish traders in the town.

Cisneros recommended that the *Consulado* approve the Dillon–Thwaites request, more concerned with the shortage of public funds than with the complaints by the Spanish traders against his decision. It saved Dillon and Thwaites from ruin and their success encouraged the placing of more orders of British goods for the River Plate. Six other ships were allowed to unload immediately after the *Speedwell*. The ships were anchored in the river and probably had been sailed there on their captains' information from shippers in Europe who were convinced of the imminence of change, given events in Spain and France.

But the dying regime was still kicking. The Viceroy introduced a form of 'free trade' ruling which loosened restrictions on imports. But just four days before publication of this ruling he decreed the enforcement of all other laws of the colonial system, which meant that foreigners not registered as residents could only remain in the city for forty days. Rumours of the decree reached the resident foreigners the moment that it was drafted. The few French and Portuguese and some North Americans were the first to be told to leave. On 18 December, district mayors went to the homes of Britons and advised them that they had eight days in which to pack and leave: not even the established forty. It seemed a last-minute attempt to reverse foreigners' influence on the political opposition from the *Criollo* intellectuals to colonial rule, an opposition which had grown in strength since the defeat of the British invasion.

On 20 December, a committee of British residents – most of them Scots – led by Alexander Mackinnon, sent a letter to

Cisneros through Captain Boyle, of HMS *Lightning*, anchore nine miles off Buenos Aires, asking for a reprieve. Mackinnon, a tough character with a capacity for political manoeuvre, was a Scot who had been banished from Naples for his involvement with the lady friend of a nobleman and from there had made his way to Buenos Aires. He obviously was not prepared to risk being thrown out of this town too.[4]

On 28 December Cisneros authorized the unloading of goods from recently arrived ships, but said that the British ashore had to wind up their business as soon as possible and leave. No deadlines were set; but there seemed to be little time. Mackinnon and his group confidently protested to government officials about such a loose-ended statement. Their efforts were rewarded on 5 January when Cisneros – allegedly acting on the advice of aides who were in fact revolutionaries – gave the Britons a reprieve of four months, as from the original eviction date, 18 December. They had to leave by 18 April.

Mackinnon, apparently the community's natural leader, kept George Canning, treasurer of the navy until Pitt's death and as from 1807 minister for foreign affairs, informed of all events in the River Plate. One of the residents, Robert Ponsonby Staples, would report later that British goods worth £1,133,000 had been unloaded at Buenos Aires in the year between November 1808 and November 1809, which admittedly gave Britain an interest in what happened in the Spanish colony. However, it is difficult to put Staples' figures in a reasonable perspective; while the Spanish authorities insisted that Buenos Aires should be a port at least partly closed to goods other than those from Spain, the British were entering the market with manufactured goods, cheaper than Spain's products, traded for hides and salted beef, or cash.[5]

In the next three months Britons formed their club, the British Commercial Rooms of Buenos Aires. Alexander Mackinnon was the first chairman. It was not, however, until 1811 that it found a permanent address – at the home of Mrs Clarke, on what is today 25 de Mayo Street. From the earliest times the Rooms were supplied with British newspapers, journals, and information of commercial interest, and a set of telescopes to watch shipping on the river, so merchants could have early warning of the arrival of freights – but which inevitably gave rise to further rumours of conspiracy.[6]

On 8 April 1810 Alexander Mackinnon and four members of the Rooms wrote to Viceroy Cisneros to ask for an extension of the 18 April deadline, alleging that newly arrived goods would not be cleared in time. Cisneros ignored the appeal and remained adamant in his correspondence with Lord Strangford, in Rio de Janeiro, who on 23 February had also asked for an extension. Finally, Captain Charles Montagu Fabian, of HMS *Mutine*, and in command of three other Royal Navy ships in the River Plate, wrote to Cisneros on 12 April. Fabian attached to his own letter a 10 April petition from the British residents asking him to intercede. Cisneros kept Fabian waiting until the eve of the deadline; then he replied that the Britons could have another month, up to Friday 18 May, but not without remarking on their use of the Royal Navy for support.[7]

In the first four months of 1810 the British community in Buenos Aires grew to an estimated 124 people, a growth in contrast with their apparent peril. As soon as Mackinnon and his friends had achieved the extension to 18 May, they set about having this date extended. Unfortunately there are no records about the way in which the Britons lived as each successive deadline approached – whether the group lived with their bags packed, in hotels, in their homes, or quite sure that something would change to allow them to stay as long as they thought necessary.

On 18 May, Cisneros informed the Commercial Rooms that Britons had only up to 26 May and he would not change the deadline any more. But the day before the latest deadline Viceroy Cisneros was deposed and replaced by a *Junta* of pro- and anti-Spanish *Criollos*. They announced that they would govern in the name of the King of Spain until they could negotiate acceptance by the Crown of autonomous rule for the colony. Shortly after the event, which would become a historic day in the Argentine calendar, Alexander Mackinnon led his fellow Britons to visit the *Junta* secretary, Mariano Moreno, to congratulate him on the change and receive assurances that their commercial interests would no longer be subjected to any interference.

There has always been speculation as to the exact role of the Britons in the downfall of the Viceroy; but there is no evidence of any direct participation other than consultation and moral support. The British invasion had undoubtedly set the trend towards independence in motion and Spain was ripe to lose the colony, just as the colony was ready for change. The speculation centres upon assumed assurances secured by the conspirators that four Royal Naval ships in the River Plate would not assist the Viceroy in their capacity as representatives of a European monarch assisting the representative of another monarchy. However, none of this appears to be documented. The British ships are also suspected of supplying the revolutionaries with ammunition.[8]

But British support for the revolution cannot be doubted. Indeed, the British South Atlantic station detachment in the River Plate, formed by the *Mutine*, *Pitt*, *Nancy* and *Mistletoe* – many of whose officers were, surprisingly, ashore in Buenos Aires at the time – greeted the event with a gun salute.

The Times reported on 7 August

> the important information that the inhabitants of Buenos Ayres, after the example of those of the Caracas, had deposed the Viceroy and established a provisional government.[9] We are enabled to lay before our readers some interesting documents concerning this event. It will be seen from these that there is nothing of a revolutionary spirit, no intention of casting off their allegiance to the parent state and assuming independence, in the proceedings of these colonists: on the contrary, they profess inalterable fidelity to Ferdinand VII or any government lawfully representing him. It is evident, however, from the military measures they have adopted, that they are determined to assert their independence, should the state of the mother country, or any other circumstances, render it necessary and advisable . . . In consequence of this change in the government, some regulations favourable to commerce were established.

For the liberals and intellectuals in the *Junta* the 25 May revolution was the culmination of much sitting-room conspiracy and that autonomy could be declared without bloodshed was for them a special victory – a victory which marked the beginning of a new, *Criollo*, élite. *Junta* member Manuel Belgrano recalled in his autobiography that General Craufurd had discussed with him the chances of independence in the River Plate in negative terms.[10]

The *Junta* secretary, Mariano Moreno, had been given a similar opinion by Lord Strangford. In June 1810, however, Strangford warned Canning to respect free trade in the River Plate and avoid taking sides, at least in the early stages of the change. Such a policy, Strangford argued, did not require commitment but would nevertheless earn the revolutionaries' gratitude for the simple fact of non-intervention.

Strangford's mission in Brazil ended in 1812. In February 1811 the Buenos Aires *Cabildo* issued a decree in which His Majesty's minister to the Portuguese court in Brazil was thanked for his services to the River Plate provinces, made a citizen of Buenos Aires and offered one square league of land. Strangford, who had never been in the River Plate capital, refused both on political grounds. Such honours were proffered mainly to win sympathy with Britain and reinforce the impression of a favourable attitude towards British interests. Strangford's services had been limited to counselling members of the *Junta* against breaking with Spain, while simultaneously appearing to be sympathetic to the cause of change.

The first British subject to be granted Buenos Aires citizenship was Robert Billinghurst. He is thought to have arrived in Montevideo at the time of the invasions and crossed to Buenos Aires after May 1810 to offer his services as an officer – which he had been in Britain, before he had gone to South America – to the revolutionary government. It was in recognition of this that he was granted citizenship by the *Cabildo* 'for his distinguished merit', on 3 December 1811. James Paroissien, born in London in 1773, applied for citizenship on 25 November 1811, a few days before Billinghurst; but it was granted a few days after Billinghurst's was awarded. Pariossien, a physician graduated in London, would later serve in South American liberation campaigns with General San Martín. The third Briton to take out citizenship was James Winton, whose new status was reported by *La Gaceta de Buenos Aires* in February 1812.

Britons tried to win acceptance and overcome suspicion of being subversive heathens in a variety of ways, other than offering to serve with the revolutionary forces.[11] In the first days after the May revolution, Britons made a considerable impact by their show of generosity. Donations were made following a government appeal in *La Gaceta de Buenos Aires* on 18 September 1810 for support for a public library. 'Good patriots' were called on to cover the costs. One month later the newspaper published a letter from British residents praising the idea to set up a library, with a list of the gifts of sixty-seven contributors, showing that about fifty per cent of British residents supported the plan. Among the names were Mackinnon and Staples, already mentioned, but others too such as Thomas Fair, James Brittain and James Wilde, who were founders of great families that would be notable through the length of the century.[12]

Britons also contributed to the building of a school. *La Gaceta* of 14 August 1812 reported that donations were pouring in, and the first were from 'three foreigners, virtuous lovers of humanity'. The figures were high: John Thwaites gave 5000 pesos, Robert Orr and Frederick Heathfield gave 1000 pesos each. *La Gaceta* of 1 September 1813 published a list of Britons who had contributed money to a fund for widows of the battle of Salta, where Manuel Belgrano had defeated the Spanish General Pio Tristán on 13 February 1813. This time the list gave thirty-four British names, including Billinghurst. The British were seen to be supporting the 'cause'.

The Honorary Consul

A name already mentioned, and one which appeared among the contributors to the library fund, is that of Robert Ponsonby Staples. He may have arrived with the British invasions or shortly after to import cloth and buy hides, and is thought to have claimed to be a representative of the house of Montgomery, Staples & Co., of Belfast. Staples appears to have been a member of the Commercial Rooms from their beginning and among the correspondents who advised Lord Strangford, on 23 July 1810, that British interests would not be affected by the revolutionary *Junta*. Staples had also written to Castlereagh, the War Minister, about the relaxation of import restrictions, while the Spanish authorities had been in control, and had added the remark that a

British invasion might still be successful. If this glimpse of Staples shows him as a shady individual, he was also one of the more colourful members of the English-speaking group in Buenos Aires during the independence decade.[13]

Staples' principal weakness was his desire to be a consul. However, Britain did not name representatives in the newly independent South American nations for some years, which thwarted Staples' deepest wish.[14]

He first reached public notice with an announcement in the *Correo de Comercio*, on 13 October 1810, advertising his new beef-salting plant at Ensenada de Barragań, south of Buenos Aires, in partnership with a Scot, John MacNeile. Business was good and Staples tried to expand, applying to Castlereagh, in August 1811, for help to obtain a licence to sell salted beef to the British West Indies. But the Buenos Aires Government's high duties on exports and failure to get any big orders forced the partners into difficult times. They were officially cautioned in November for the haphazard way in which they were running their business. The caution changed nothing; in fact the business declined further and on 9 September 1812 MacNeile advertised the sale of the plant; explaining that the decision to sell was prompted by export duties that were too high. There were no buyers and the plant was closed. It was reopened a few months later when the Buenos Aires Government, fearing a Spanish royalist invasion and in need of food for the troops, ordered salted beef in bulk from MacNeile. Staples had left the partnership by then.

In the meantime, Staples had written to the Foreign Office to ask for authorization to act as British representative in Buenos Aires. He was appointed on 16 March 1811. It was good news for Buenos Aires to have one of the world's major powers recognize the revolution – and such was the interpretation given the appointment. But the Buenos Aires Government remained cautious about such informal recognition. When Britain informed Spain of the appointment, the reaction was one of intense displeasure, even though Britain said that it did not mean recognition of Buenos Aires. Although the River Plate capital was no longer her colony, Spain had not abandoned plans to reconquer the area, and under colonial law diplomatic representations could only be posted to the capital of the Empire. Spain officially rejected the appointment in June.

Staples' letter of credence reached him by the slow boat of bureaucracy and on 21 March 1812 he delivered it to the authorities in Buenos Aires. Bernardino Rivadavia, Secretary for Foreign Affairs, was upset by the informality of what he had thought should have been an important event. Three days later he sent the papers back to Staples demanding that they should be sent with a formal covering letter, requesting their acceptance. Staples let a few more days go by and then sent his papers back to the Secretary, with the required covering letter. But in it he asked for an urgent reply so that he might put his report to London on the ship that was due to sail imminently. The reply was delayed until 4 April, and then Rivadavia again rejected the appointment papers on the grounds that Britain named a consul but said nothing about the recognition of the new administration. A few months later, in June, Staples returned to London and there tried to have his papers renewed, but in vain.

With financial difficulties looming, Staples stopped working on the post of consul and, on 13 April 1813, proposed that the British Government should send him to Buenos Aires as a confidential agent. Castlereagh, who by then was launched on his career as Foreign Secretary in the Lord Liverpool government, appears to have liked Staples' proposal because it did not entail recognition of Buenos Aires in any way. However, on second thought, he rejected the idea, because the Government had a sufficient number of confidential agents in the new countries who were not pestering all the time with matters of appointments and acknowledgements. They just wrote their letters.

Staples, with no official support, returned to Buenos Aires in November 1813, when he rejoined his old partner, MacNeile. To his surprise, he found that political and business circles in Buenos Aires viewed him as a diplomatic representative. Far from trying to explain the misunderstanding, Staples tood advantage of it. Most people of any importance who were travelling to Britain went to Staples for letters of introduction. This was also the case with Rivadavia and Belgrano, who visited him on 4 December 1814, the eve of their departure on a mission to seek support for the revolutionary government in Europe. From each of his visitors he elicited information about local affairs, which he then transmitted to the Foreign Office.

Staples was in a peculiar situation. Rear-Admiral Sir Manley Dixon, of the South Atlantic naval station, in the River Plate at the time, ordered one of his officers going to Valparaiso to send all mail to the station through 'Robert Staples, Esq., H.M. Consul in Buenos Aires'. Staples was also called on by politicians and officials during the very fluid political life of the new country. On one occasion he was asked to act as official interpreter during mediation by Captain Josceline Percy, of the HMS *Hotspur*, anchored in the Plate, when a politician, Alvarez Thomas, rebelled against the local government on 15 April 1815 and deposed *Director Supremo* Carlos de Alvear.

Whatever he did, Staples was cautious; but he missed no opportunity to gain public attention. On 3 July 1816 he took in hand an issue over a British ship which had broken port rules. In a letter to the authorities he said that he was acting as 'Chargé d'affaires'. On this event, *The Times* of 11 October reported:

> With the few letters that reached town yesterday, there came also a protest relating to some trifling irregularity of a British vessel in landing her goods. This document is authenticated by Mr P. Staples, who signs himself Consul of His Britannic Majesty. This latter circumstance occasioned much speculation on 'Change, as the merchants trading to Buenos Ayres knew of no person there who has of late officiated in that character; they therefore suppose that some change may have taken place in the principles and conduct of the government to induce this gentleman to so announce himself. Some time ago Mr Staples was sent out to Buenos Ayres in the character of British Consul, but not being able, consistently with the amicable relations and friendship which subsisted between the Spanish and British governments, to recognise the insurgent governments, he obtained his passport and returned home. The British government deeming it, however, expedient to have some person at Buenos Ayres to watch over the British interests, sent out Mr Staples in his private character, to purchase dollars & Co., on account of the government, in order to be ready to act according to the circumstances in the event of any change of politics of the government. It was therefore supposed that Mr Staples was acting only as the private agent of the government, and that he would continue to act in that capacity until the Buenos Aires government assumed a new character by declaring in a formal manner its independence.

Staples' action cannot but raise a smile, when it is considered that it caused speculation about British government policy in such places as the London stock exchange.

One of Staples' successes with the local population was when, on 26 July 1816, he advised the British press and, therefore, that of the rest of Europe, that the United Provinces had declared their independence from Spain at San Miguel de Tucumán, on 9 July. How he managed to be ahead of all others in posting the news is not known. Whoever gave him the information in Buenos Aires did so in the knowledge that he could use it well.

During that July, Alexander Mackinnon and a group of members of the Commercial Rooms, confident of Staples' connections and influence, asked the local government to accept the 'consul' as the merchants' representative. They set his payment at one and a half per cent of the volume of British goods cleared at the port of Buenos Aires, plus one *Real* for each ship in which those goods arrived. Trade was not enough to make Staples wealthy but, in addition to his own import and export business, it gave him a comfortable income. There were several British-owned trading companies in Buenos Aires then, most of them with small turnovers. An 1817 list showed that the principal British merchants in that year were George MacFarlane, James Brittain, William Miller, James Buchanan, W. Parish Robertson, Thomas Newton, Adam Guy, John Higginbotham and Thomas Barton.

Most of these men had rebuilt their businesses after the near catastrophe following the British invasions. Staples, who kept careful records of trade, reported that totals for British goods sold in Buenos Aires during 1806 reached £881,451 and only £40,567 in Montevideo. The following year, when far greater volumes had been concentrated in the River Plate, Montevideo took the lead, but with only £153,905, while in Buenos Aires sales made a mere £23,469. But by the time of the 1810 revolution, British capital in Buenos Aires was estimated at between £750,000 and £1 million.

Staples was known to military officers and became an occasional confidant of the man who was to become the liberator of a large part of the continent, General José de San Martín, a man who admired the liberal establishment and thought that the best form of government for the River Plate was a limited monarchy with a republican constitution. His contacts with Britons in Buenos Aires and abroad often led to a debate on the right European to start a *Porteño* (the name given to the Buenos Aires resident) royal house. The frequency of meetings between Staples and San Martín became greater during 1817, and each was faithfully reported to the Foreign Office. All descriptions of San Martín by Britons draw the reader's attention to his strong personality, combined with modesty and great charm. Even those who took a dislike to him for political reasons admitted their admiration for the man.

Staples acted in his assumed capacity of 'consul' in the Banda Oriental [Uruguay] when the provincial leader or *caudillo*, José Artigas, signed a treaty assuring protection of all British subjects operating in or out of Montevideo. Artigas needed the duties that their trade brought him. The agreement as a formal document was rejected when it reached London; but rejection was never so official or so public as to render it completely useless. As his influence extended to Uruguay, Staples wrote to London in June 1818 to propose that a vice-consul be named in Chile. But this letter, like so many others of his, was not answered – perhaps a bureaucratic slip or perhaps a sign of sheer exasperation.

While Staples had his problems, the Government of the United Provinces of the River Plate had them too, and it was tired of Europe's delay in recognizing independence. This led to friction with foreign residents – irritation at their presence and at their reluctance to give financial assistance to the independence armies. *Director Supremo* Juan Martín de Pueyrredón complained publicly that the British were not being co-operative when he asked them for funds for San Martín's army in Peru in April 1818. Merchants, in turn, complained that the economic situation was bad. Staples, summoned by the Government in Buenos Aires, said that he would ask them to give funds voluntarily. Pueyrredón set the British community's share at 141,000 pesos, but only 6700 were raised. On 16 September, Pueyrredón threatened to seize their property if they refused to give more. The chief officer of a naval ship patrolling the River Plate, Commander Bowles, in a letter to the Admiralty, put the whole incident down to Staples' incompetence, although such a reaction may have been more an cxpression of pique over the attention that Staples received. The government in Buenos Aires perhaps showed an understandable preference for dealing with a civilian rather than with the Royal Navy, which often assumed British consular and diplomatic representation. Staples wrote to London complaining about the double representation and asked for an appointment. On 2 January 1819, the Foreign Office finally wrote to him rejecting his demands. Staples, probably in a state of dejection, wrote on 12 May to say that he was no longer acting as a 'consul'. But one month later he wrote to the Under-Secretary for Trade at the Foreign Office to advise that British merchants in Buenos Aires had confirmed him in his job as their representative.

On 16 September Staples is mentioned in what must have been one of his last jobs 'in office'. Bernardino Rivadavia, in a letter to Pueyrredón, said that Staples had introduced John A. Barber Beaumont to the government to present a proposal for British immigration to set up farming colonies on the west bank of the River Paraná. In the correspondence, Staples was referred to as the 'consul'.[15]

In 1820 Staples returned to London. There he applied for the consulate in Lima, Perú, but failed to get it. His story for the present purpose should end here. But it is interesting to follow him just a few more years; in 1822 he became a partner with one Thomas Kinder to launch a £1 million bond issue for Peru. In June 1823 he was reported to be in Calcutta, but on his way back to South America. Finally, on 10 October 1823 Robert Ponsonby Staples' dream came true. Canning signed a list of consular appointments: Staples was included as Consul in Acapulco.[16]

4
North Americans

Early Merchants

Mariners from the New England ports of North America had sailed south for over a century before the independence of the United States. Sealing vessels had long travelled the Argentine coast, their captains operating as masters of land and sea. Their crews sometimes went ashore at Buenos Aires, although Rio de Janeiro was used more often for its greater hospitality and fewer restrictions on foreigners. The North American community in Buenos Aires was small and at times amounted to not many more than the crews of the few ships in port.

Their fortunes varied.

William Pius White, a Bostonian, born in 1770, travelled to the River Plate when aged thirty-three, in pursuit of a local tradesman who owed him money. He made large sums as a merchant and gun-runner for the Buenos Aires revolutionary government; but he died in poverty in Dolores, in January 1842. Although his house had been used by British officers during the 1806 invasion, in the battles for commerce he tried to be a neutral middleman. He was called on by the revolutionary government in December 1813 to help finance over 200 guns, a thing he soon managed to do. In spite of his efforts, the government failed to pay him. As part compensation for the delay in the payment, he was awarded a licence to operate as a privateer in partnership with a group of Buenos Aires naval officers, though the income which he derived from the gains of corsairs was erratic. Moreover, he complicated his own matters by retaining what he received instead of sharing with his partners in an attempt to put pressure on the authorities to pay their debts. He squabbled over this with the naval chief, Admiral William Brown – who came out in defence of his fellow officers – and White was imprisoned. He was harassed by successive governments for persisting in his claims and had his property confiscated – to pay his partners – while his demands for payment were ignored. In 1835 he was granted a subsistence pension; it was only in 1863 that President Mitre ordered payment of the State's debt to White's heirs.[1]

One of the few early North Americans in Buenos Aires whose life is fully recorded – through diaries and correspondence held at Yale University – was David Curtis De Forest. As a commission merchant in Buenos Aires he became a wealthy man and was to the Americans what Staples was to the British: he wanted to be named United States consul.

De Forest was born in Huntingdon, Connecticut, in January 1774, into a wealthy family. He started his career at sea and reached Montevideo in July 1801. His diary reports the sight of ships aplenty and flourishing trade, even though the port was 'closed'; this scene was what probably tempted him to try his fortune in the River Plate. He was not allowed to go ashore because of a Customs scare as a result of recent large-scale smuggling, and because he had no papers. He went to Brazil and from Rio Grande made the 400-mile journey south overland, arriving back in Montevideo in February 1802. He crossed to Buenos Aires in March and lodged at the *Hostería de los Tres Reyes* at first, before moving into a monastery of the Franciscan order to learn Spanish. His diaries do not explain how a non-Catholic such as he was came to reside in the monastery. He did say that he was very comfortable, however, and he invited fellow-travellers and merchants to walk with him in the orchard and to dine.

He started business in trade across the River Plate, with Montevideo. Buenos Aires, De Forest said, was very European and had 40,000 inhabitants. He disliked the then fashionable bull-fighting at El Retiro, which he referred to as the 'bull-baiting circus'. His first stay in Buenos Aires lasted nine months; in December he returned to the United States. In January 1805 he asked the government in Washington to make him a consul or commercial agent in the viceroyalty. In June he was once again in Montevideo, without the appointment or even permission to enter Buenos Aires. He tried for the consul's post again in February 1806. However, although there was private interest in trade with the viceroyalty, officially there could be no consulate, because Spain did not admit such postings in her colonies. Nevertheless, if not a diplomat De Forest was a respected merchant and so was offered four ships to take to Buenos Aires. He sailed from Boston in May, in his own brig, the *Jane*, which anchored outside Montevideo in September. Buenos Aires had just staged the 'reconquest' – *La Reconquista* – of the town held by the British. De Forest failed to get any form of assurance or date for entry to Buenos Aires from Popham, who was still in the River Plate planning a new landing on the Spanish colony. After sixteen days at anchor, De Forest sailed the *Jane* south, waited another six weeks and then slipped through the British line to anchor in the shallow water in front of the Fort of Buenos Aires on 21 November. It had taken him six months to get there.

One interesting aspect of De Forest's papers is his description of Buenos Aires life in those months of the British invasions. He found a great anti-English mood in the town; more in the nature of sports fans delighted with their team's victory than an actual hatred for the British. Public venom and contempt were reserved for the Viceroy Sobremonte who had fled from the British attack.

The feeling was exacerbated in February 1807 when Liniers – who had led the defeat of Beresford – returned to Buenos Aires to report that Montevideo had been taken by the British. The public gathered in the main square, in front of the *Cabildo*, chanting anti-government songs and shouting 'Hang the Viceroy'. Liniers replaced the Viceroy a few days later, though with the rank of captain general. De Forest praised Liniers, a sympathy that may have suffered some deterioration at the end of February when the North American spent two days in prison because he spoke English, and all such persons were detained at some time.

After the defeat of Whitelocke by Spaniards and *Criollos* in the 'defence' – *La Defensa* – of Buenos Aires, De Forest was able to clear the cargo of the *Jane*. His papers hint at contacts in business with the Buenos Aires *Criollo* intellectuals who then spoke of the need for change in the Spanish system of government and who would later become revolutionaries. De Forest, like the British who were always suspected but never proven allies of the *Criollo* revolutionaries, never admits to being more than sympathetic towards the independist movements and certainly not conspiratorial. He settled in a house on the northern side of the city (the residential Vicente Lopez district today), bought from a Dr Philip Roubles. His servants included 'two Englishmen' and nine negroes, but he gives no indication as to the terms of employment.

When Viceroy Cisneros arrived in July 1809, De Forest joined all foreigners in their apprehension, which in his case proved well-founded as he was ordered to leave in December. He threw a farewell party on Christmas Eve and on Christmas Day boarded a British ship in the Plate, not leaving, but changing ships three times between then and February to give himself time to wind up his business.

At the age of thirty-eight and back in the United States, he married a girl of sixteen whom he promptly took back to Buenos Aires. They reached the River Plate in February 1812 and because of his uncertainty about landing permission, ventured up the coast at night. The ship ran aground and De Forest and his wife, eight months' pregnant, waded ashore with mud up to their waists. His fears about the reception he would receive in Buenos Aires proved unfounded: in August *La Gaceta de Buenos Aires* reported that he had been granted citizenship in recognition of his support for the revolution. His fortune grew from then on, in partnership with a *Criollo* of Irish descent and an American resident. As from 1815, thanks to a corsair's licence and ten per cent of the prize gained by the four ships that he operated, he joined the circle of the wealthiest men in Buenos Aires society.

In February 1818, he returned to the United States and was asked to serve as consul for the United Provinces of the River Plate in his country. The United States Government rejected his credentials; but he acted with the freedom of an accredited representative. The parties which he gave at his home in New Haven, Connecticut, to mark each anniversary of the 25 May revolution were a 'must' in the diaries of diplomats and senior civil servants.

He died in February 1825, his widow aged nearly thirty. She died in 1873, in poverty.[2]

The United States did have representatives in the River Plate long before formal diplomatic recognition. The names of Joel Roberts Poinsett, William G. Miller, Thomas Lloyd Halsey – who, in 1813, was described as an Irish sheep farmer – and John B. Prevost, figure in records as 'delegate agents'. During the years after the change of government in the River Plate, an American agent's job was especially difficult since it was his task to plead with the local authorities for protection for United States shipping against the threat of roving Royal Navy ships.[3]

The appointments of 'delegate agents' ended with that of John Murray Forbes, who arrived as a non-accredited agent before relations were formally established. Forbes, a descendant of Scottish immigrants to the United States, was first posted to Buenos Aires in October 1820, to prepare for the opening of a legation. He had been a member of a special mission to South America formed by Caesar Augustus Rodney, Theoderick Bland and John Graham. Forbes and his colleagues had reported to President Monroe in Novevmber 1818 'on the critical and revolutionary state' of the provinces of South America. Rodney and Forbes had shown some optimism for the political evolution of the River Plate provinces; Graham and Bland had thought the country a hopeless mess.[4]

Forbes' work in Buenos Aires during his initial and unofficial days included presiding at what is believed to have been the first 4 July United States Independence Day anniversary celebrated in Buenos Aires, in 1823. The event was reported in the *American Daily Advertiser* of Philadelphia, in its 5 September issue: 'The fast sailing brig *Dick*, Captain Woodhouse, arrived New York 3 September, in forty-eight days from Buenos Aires. The citizens of the United States to the number of thirty were celebrating the anniversary of our Independence at Mrs Thorn's Hotel, Mr Forbes presiding assisted by Captain C. Prince, of New York, as vice-president.' At the banquet, revellers were informed that a 'preliminary treaty' had been signed between Spain and Buenos Aires to end the war of independence. Peace between the former ruler and former colony was the foundation for diplomatic relations between Buenos Aires and the United States – and Britain – because the United States would not recognize the new republics of South America until Spain had definitively and formally relinquished them. In *An Englishman's impressions of Buenos Aires, 1820–1825*, the author said that the place where the feast was held was a 'hotel kept by a respectable North American female, Mrs Thorn, a widow . . . much resorted to by the Americans'.[5]

Caesar Augustus Rodney was appointed to be the first minister plenipotentiary posted by the United States to Buenos Aires. He held the post from 2 August 1823, with Forbes as his assistant, to 22 May 1824. He arrived in Buenos Aires in November 1823, shortly before the Monroe Doctrine was announced. Rodney, born in 1772, had a successful career as a lawyer, assisted by an inheritance from an uncle, before his posting to Buenos Aires with his ten daughters and three sons. He was ill most of the time that he was in Buenos Aires and died in the town in June 1824.[6] Forbes took over from him and also died in Buenos Aires, in June 1831.

Apart from having to persuade North American residents to support him in his work on behalf of the United States, one of Forbes' early problems was dealing with both sides in the tense situation leading to war between Buenos Aires and Brazil in December 1825, a time when he was called on to show sympathy for each of the two nations. The war was the final expression of an antagonism long felt between the Imperial Court of Brazil, which since 1810 had watched the independist movement in the River Plate with distrust, and the Buenos Aires Government. To the political rivalry of the two different systems was added the dispute for possession of the former Spanish colony which is today known as Uruguay. It was then called the Banda Oriental (or eastern fringe) by Buenos Aires, and Cisplatina province by Brazil. The Emperor of Brazil, Dom Pedro I, also used the tardy excuse that he would defeat the revolutionaries and restore Spain's lost colonies to the Spanish Crown. By then Spain had accepted the existence of the United Provinces of the River Plate as an independent Republic and its authorities had been recognized by the United States and Britain. On 11 November 1825 Forbes addressed his first letter on the subject of the approaching war to the United States mission in Rio de Janeiro:

You will probably have knowledge of the note of the Ministry of Foreign Affairs to the Minister of H.I.M. the Emperor, by which is announced the important measure of the [Buenos Aires] national congress receiving into the national family the Oriental [Uruguay] province and pledging themselves to maintain the inviolability of her territory. We are now to contemplate the consequences, the first of which will probably be the blockade of these rivers (or at any rate of this road) by the Brazilians, who have undisputed maritime superiority.

The Emperor of Brazil declared war and the blockade of Buenos Aires on 10 December, a few days after the birth of his son and heir.

Foreign residents, excepting those who participated in the fighting, looked gloomily on the conflict. It forced the accumulation of stocks of goods for export and prevented currency remittances; government debts to merchants and suppliers went unpaid, and austere living was imposed on the town's inhabitants. However, the war did help merchants sell off existing stocks on the local market. North Americans returned to trade in the River Plate faster than the British towards the end of the fighting, in 1827. British diplomacy was responsible for the settlement that ended the fighting and created the independent state of Uruguay as a buffer between Brazil and Argentina; but Britain was not as successful in trade at that time having accepted the 'full blockade' doctrine – against the protests of British merchants and their representatives in Parliament – which meant that siege-busting was not officially encouraged if the blockade was seen to be effective and brokers would not therefore insure freights for the River Plate.[7] North Americans had no such policy; each merchant and master risked capture on his own and made whatever deal he could with insurers, blockade officers, traders and the governments involved.

The participation of a number of North Americans in fighting on both sides in the war encouraged the Buenos Aires Government to try to recruit foreigners into the army. Forbes' later official business included trying to prevent the recruiting of North Americans. In August 1829 he wrote to the government complaining that 'According to reports made to the undersigned, several citizens of the United States have been lately taken by force from the peaceful pursuits of the industry of the country into military service.' The British representative had been involved in a similar complaint before this and the French agent was asked repeatedly to complain on behalf of fellow-nationals. Forbes won the release of most of the recruits with the exception of a few who stayed in the forces of their own will.[8]

The Buenos Aires that Forbes lived and worked in was a town which was trying to change rapidly to incorporate as many advances from Europe as possible. Before the war with Brazil the United Provinces of the River Plate had entered a period of progress. This period had begun with an attempt to draft a national constitution – subsequently changed many times – in the early 1820s.

It incorporated rules of respect for individual freedoms and tolerance for foreign religions and, among other things, gave the country the name of Argentina (from 'Land of Argentum', or 'Silverland', or 'Land of the Plate', the origins of the actual decision to impose such a name not being clear). The government tried to put order into the urbanization of Buenos Aires, even though for most of the century the 'city' was regarded as a 'Big Village', *La Gran Aldea.* The town got better roads, the legislature was improved, the university was created in 1821 and so was the Academy of Medicine. The *Plaza* Mayor, in front of the Fort, was cut in half by a shopping arcade, known as *La Recova*, running from north to south. The eastern half of the square, nearest the Fort and the River Plate, was named *25 de Mayo*, after the date of the 1810 revolution; the western half, in front of the *Cabildo*, became the *Plaza de la Victoria.*

North Americans resident in the town at that time are not easy to trace. *The British Packet and Argentine News* published information about people 'in the parish', without giving their nationality. The Spanish-language journals occasionally gave the place of a person's origin; but more often reference was limited to a surname. However, *The British Packet and Argentine News* occasionally reported events specifically concerning the North Americans and this allows the drawing of some thumbnail sketches of the community and of some of its members. For example, on 10 July 1830 the paper said that 'The citizens of the

United States resident in this city celebrated the fourth of July at several private dinner parties; the incessant rain prevented any exterior display.' The death of one Captain William Appleton, reported on 11 September 1830, was marked with respect, the United States flag being hoisted to half-mast at the Washington Hotel and on all North American merchant ships in the port. The death of Dr Henry Bond, aged thirty-three, of Maryland, on 2 May 1831, was reported because he was a brother-in-law of the Governor, Juan Manuel de Rosas. The newspaper was a strong supporter of Rosas. While this might show how close the government and the English-speaking community could be at times, Bond is not a good example as the Governor took little notice of any members of his family other than his wife and daughter. Another Dr Bond, Joshua Bond, was mentioned on 11 August 1832 because he had challenged George Washington Slacum, the United States consul, to a duel, which was prevented by police. The paper did not mention the reason for the duel; but it may be assumed that Slacum might have insulted Dr Bond, as Argentine historical documents concerning the consul do attribute him with a disagreeable manner.[9] In February 1835, the North Americans were reported to have organized their first community ball in Buenos Aires, in the 'central law courts building', to mark Washington's birthday. It was described as one of the great social successes of the times.

News items in the English-language Press most often concerned the community's more prominent members, and these were businessmen. Among the more notable was John C. Zimmermann (1786–1857), born in Germany but taken to New York in 1802. He travelled to Buenos Aires as a supernumerary on a ship from Baltimore – a sixty-day voyage – with a consignment of guns for the Argentine authorities. He went into partnership with De Forest; later dissolved that arrangement and went into a more lasting company with Benjamin W. Frazier, from Philadelphia, who married Zimmermann's daughter. Other contemporary North American firms in Buenos Aires were those of Samuel Hale, Danna, Carman and William Passman. Zimmermann, Carman and Passman are names of families which have remained in Argentina to this day.

Samuel B. Hale was one of the early merchants who won considerable power and wealth. Born in Boston in March 1804, he also arrived in Buenos Aires as a supernumerary, in 1830. Within three years he formed his own import and export company, which became one of the strongest in the local market, with forty-six small craft operating in the coastal trade and three large ships to span the world. From a start in trade he became a contractor for the Buenos Aires waterworks, a director of the Bank of Buenos Aires, of the Buenos Aires Commercial Bank, of the British-owned Primitiva de Gas Company and of the Western Railway. He became vice-president of the cattlemen's Rural Society in 1868. He also acted as a Buenos Aires town councillor, which made him one of the very few English-speaking residents who used his commercial power to gain access to political positions. The English-speaking community generally stayed in business and out of politics. Hale's quiet manner kept him out of the limelight, a manner to emulate for the many people whom he hid in his port depots or shipped into exile on his vessels during many years of dictatorship and political uncertainty for government opponents. He died in Buenos Aires in 1888.[10]

One of the most prominent of North Americans in Argentina was William Wheelwright, shipwrecked off Buenos Aires in 1822. This event in effect put an end to his career at sea, which had begun at the age of twelve; although it was the starting point of a successful career as a shipowner. Born at Newbury, Massachusetts, in 1798, he died in London in September 1873, but spent much of his life and made his money in South America. He was, above all, an ambitious businessman; his activities being those of the prototype of successful nineteenth-century financial adventurer who started with nothing yet had a 'nose' for the right enterprises. He went to Chile in 1824 and bought a ship to trade along the Pacific coast. Though he tired of this and stopped at Guayaquil, as United States consul, he returned to Chile in 1829 to start a shipping line, running between Valparaíso and Cobija. He searched for North American or local capital to back several investment plans but, failing to attract enough money, he went to Britain. There he started the Pacific Steamship Company in 1840 with two ships, the *Perú* and the *Chile.* By 1875 the renamed

Pacific Steam Navigation Company had fifty ships. In Chile he invested in mining, started water desalination, installed the street lighting in Valparaíso (where a monument to Wheelwright was built in 1877, in his lifetime). In Argentina he raised British money for the Grand Central Argentine Railway; planned a railway line to Tucumán through northern and central Argentina; masterminded the Buenos Aires–Ensenada railway, trying to convince the government to make the latter city Argentina's main port. He left vast sums to charity and a fortune to his widow and daughter. A town in Santa Fé was named after him.

Among the very few foreign residents who left their names on commercial empires was Melville Sewell Bagley, born at Bangor, Maine, in July 1838. He arrived in Buenos Aires in 1862. With the help of a local apothecary he produced an aperitif based on oranges which he called *Hesperidina*. The drink became the foundation product of what was later to be the Bagley biscuit company. He became well known in Buenos Aires for his advertising campaigns, as he used large print notices in the papers, breaking with the custom of small-print publicity, and introduced brightly coloured carts to make delivery of his products. He died in July 1880.

One North American name that has gone down in Argentine history is that of William Rawson, an Argentine-born doctor and politician. He was the son of a physician, Dr Aman Rawson, of Massachusetts, who arrived in Buenos Aires in 1818, lured by a colleague, Dr William Colesberry, of Philadelphia. Colesberry had established a successful practice in Mendoza five years earlier and had joined the revolutionary expedition to Chile to fight against the Spanish colonial authorities. He had also worked in Tucumán, Salta and Jujuy; but returned to the United States where he died.

Aman Rawson followed Colesberry to Mendoza, then moved to San Juan, where he opened his practice, under the impression that the healthy, dry climate of the Andean provinces would help both his own health and his career. His two sons were born in San Juan: Benjamin Franklyn [March 1819] who became a successful landscape and portrait artist, and died in a yellow-fever epidemic in March 1871; and William Colesberry [June 1821] who became a physician, then moved into politics and became a senator and a cabinet minister. William was the founder and first president of the Argentine Red Cross. He died in Paris in February 1890. While the Red Cross and his political career make him a historical personality in Argentina, it is in Patagonia where his name lives on.

It was Rawson's efforts that introduced European colonization to the southern territory, most notably the Welsh colony in the Chubut Valley.[11]

Missionaries and Methodists

Between 1823 and 1827 three North American Presbyterian ministers, J. C. Brigham, Theophilus Parvin and William Torrey, of the North American Bible Society and the Board of Missions, arrived in Buenos Aires. Parvin, who had been ordained in 1826 by the Presbytery of Philadelphia, was married to a daughter of United States diplomatic representative Caesar Rodney. Brigham went to Chile; Parvin and Torrey remained in Buenos Aires, where they were responsible for the foundation of the first North American church in South America. Missionary reports and church records had estimated that there were seventy-five North American families resident in and around Buenos Aires, apart from a large temporary population of seamen, who justified the posting of missionaries to that city. However, there were soon plans under way to take missionary work for the purpose of conversion much further afield.

One of the first North American missions to Patagonia, in 1833, was inspired by a mariner's book.[12] The book was by Captain Benjamin Morrell, who, having sailed the *Wasp* out of New York in July 1822 and gone south, had kept records of everything he saw and of a few things he did not see but was told about. He appears to have added to his notes some exaggeration as to the extent of the welcome he had received at the places where he called. The richness of the soil and the friendliness of the inhabitants may have even been decided according to the state of his own mood. He returned to New York, after ten years at sea, and the following year published a book on his travels. The volume included a section on Patagonia, where Morrell said that he had found docile natives who could be fertile ground for a missionary's seed. This was inaccurate because Morrell obviously had not had enough contact – other than for trading – to establish such sophisticated communication with what were a nomadic and primitive people.

The age was one in which all denominations sought to spread their gospel and take the relief of their religion to those which they considered spiritually doomed races.[13] The North American Board of Commissioners for Foreign Missions became interested in sending an exploratory mission to the land Morrell wrote about and sought confirmation of his remarks. In letters dated 24 and 25 February 1833, the seaman confirmed that all his book was reliable. Two students were selected by the Board for a voyage of missionary exploration and ordained in Boston in July 1833. They were Titus Coan, of Auburn, and Mr Arms, of Andover. Early in August they boarded the south-bound *Mary Jane*, whereupon they were informed by the master that Patagonia was not the friendly place Morrell had written that it was.

On 19 November 1833, the *Mary Jane* sailed away from two very lonely men on the shores of what were called the 'Eastern Patagonias'. It took them several days of walking and calling to contact the natives and ask them for food. Members of the tribes did not come loaded with gifts as Morrell's book had assured they would, largely because they were men and women whose own search for food was a constant struggle. The missionaries' supplies were therefore provided by ships that anchored in the natural ports of the Patagonian coast. Coan reported meeting two English seamen, early in January 1834, who had lived with the natives for several months after deserting their ship; the two sailors had now decided that they preferred shipboard hardships to the wilderness ashore. The North American missionaries established some form of communication with the natives, using signs and a few words; but they never knew when, if at all, they had made themselves understood. The weather was warm so the missionaries did not suffer the rigours of the climate, although they did learn from the English seamen about the winter living conditions of their near-naked hosts. The natives dressed in the briefest of rags, these being made of Patagonian rabbit skins or, occasionally, *guanaco*. They used sealskins and the hides of wild cattle for their huts, which were generally leaky and unsteady; but above all they were people who had enormous resistance to the cold. They traded furs for food and alcohol with the masters and crew of passing ships. The Patagonian soil gave them little natural food and they planted none.[14]

When, towards the end of January, a French and two North American brigs anchored in the Bay of San Gregorio, the two missionaries asked the sailors they had met to advise that they had decided, in view of the limited results of their mission, to take such an opportunity to leave. Their decision threatened to put an end to the few hard-won and precarious contacts with the natives who, although not informed of the departure plans, immediately became suspicious of the preparations they saw. Suspicion grew into anger to the point where they refused to allow their visitors to go to the coast. The white men's presence had offered them a bridge of contact with the passing ships. Captain James Nash, of the North American ship *Antarctic*, was notified that the missionaries wanted to see him and when they were delayed thought this was not due to an accident. When an indian woman, named María, who by virtue of marriage to an indian *cacique* or chief was regarded as holding authority, went aboard for a supply of spirits, Nash made her his prisoner.[15] The hostages were exchanged on 25 January after Nash offered an increased volume of food and drink. The following day they set sail.[16]

Coan and Arms were back in the United States in May 1834 and years later Coan published a book about their journey.[17] However, the book lacks much in description of the Patagonian natives, possibly because of the time elapsed between the journey and the writing or because of the writer's ignorance of the land he had travelled to. Other missionaries followed, of course; but their expeditions were not successful and only a few hardy men spent any length of time in the exploration of Patagonia.

The North American Presbyterian enterprise was eventually absorbed by the Methodist Episcopal Church in Buenos Aires. John Dempster was the founder of the Methodist church there in December 1836.

Dempster was not hindered in his preaching; but as with other foreign denominations he was advised by the government to restrict this to his few countrymen in the town and was ordered to hold services in English only. The congregation grew, nevertheless, with the addition of several European residents and, in 1839, became big enough to support the construction of a church. A plot of land was bought and a grant of 10,000 United States dollars was advanced by the church in New York, although construction was temporarily stopped when further payments from the Missionary Society were suspended due to financial difficulties caused by other commitments. However, the church was completed and in January 1843 the Reverend William Norris held the dedicatory service, one year after Dempster had left Buenos Aires. Little is recorded of Dempster's activities after that but an announcement in *The Standard* of Buenos Aires on 5 March 1864 quoted *The Christian Advocate and Journal* which reported that on 28 November 1863 Dempster had died in Chicago, aged sixty-nine. Norris was replaced by the Reverend Dallas D. Lore – founder of a newspaper called *The Buenos Ayres Herald* – in 1846. The last nineteenth-century superintendent of the Methodist church was Dr Charles Drees, who was best-known in Buenos Aires as the author of a book on his community, *Americans in Argentina*, published in 1922. The history of Protestant churches in Argentina becomes easier to follow after 1857, because in October of that year the Buenos Aires municipal authorities ruled that all churches should keep records of births, marriages and deaths reported to their ministers.

5

Mercenaries and Heroes

A majority of the officers in the earliest days of Argentina's navy were Britons, recruited from merchant vessels or simply 'bought' with ships docked at Buenos Aires. The ships were acquired by the government to organize a fleet which would resist harassment of international shipping by Spain, intent on regaining her old colony. The number of *Criollos* in crews grew during the war with Brazil in 1826, though the officers were in their majority Britons. The army, with fewer English-speaking men in its ranks, still had many, as well as just about every other European nationality.

Money, quick promotion and adventure were the lures that enticed foreigners into the armies and navies of the South American provinces which had decided to be independent from Spain. Buenos Aires had declared its autonomy in 1810; the Spanish Crown had rejected the idea and was determined to recover her River Plate colony. The revolutionary authorities of 1810 had almost no forces for defence, they had to create them.

To organize an army there were a few officers who had been trained and had served in Spain and who could be summoned to use their experience to train others. The most famous of these was José de San Martín. After serving in the Spanish army and spending one year as a prisoner of the English at Gibraltar during the Napoleonic wars, San Martín went to Britain. There he secured for the South American revolutionary cause the sympathy of many officers and the services of others, including those of Lord Cochrane, an impoverished, proud Scottish aristocrat, permanently embattled with his superiors, yet renowned as a naval tactician.

San Martín, a mature, well-educated and well-connected officer aged thirty-four, sailed from Britain for Buenos Aires in January 1812. He was by then regarded as a traitor by Spain, where he had lived from the age of seven and in whose forces he had fought and had been decorated. In Buenos Aires he recruited and trained men for a grenadier regiment to fight in the war of independence. A Scot, John Parish Robertson, who watched from a bell tower as the grenadiers fought their first battle at San Lorenzo, north of Buenos Aires, in February 1813, described the regiment as extremely effective in his *Letters on South America*, in which he left one of the best eyewitness reports of any of Argentina's independence battles. After the defeat of the Spanish troops, who had arrived from the Banda Oriental, Parish Robertson supplied wine and food for the wounded.[1]

San Lorenzo was only a rehearsal for battle within the plan San Martín had charted for eventual emancipation. Assisted by the more distant view of the continent which he had been able to take from Britain, he saw that it would not be enough to fight the Spaniards within the United Provinces of the River Plate. A far vaster plan was necessary. This was to attack the Spanish in Chile and Perú, in combination with the liberation movements of the north of South America, led by Simón Bolivar. San Martín moved his army to Mendoza, where he was appointed governor, and from there prepared his assault on the Spanish in Chile.

Lord Cochrane was called to the Pacific by San Martín, later to be commissioned by the Chilean revolutionaries to defend the coast against Spanish ships as well as to support San Martín's march north to Peru.

Cochrane disliked San Martín. The cause of disagreement, apart from personal differences, centered on the Scot's distrust of San Martín's tactics, reflected in a slowness in seeking a clash with the Spanish forces in Peru. Captain Basil Hall, commander of HMS *Conway*, an admirer and friend of San Martín as well as chronicler of the revolutionary attack on Peru, found San Martín's slow advance to be more reasonable for South America in the long term, as the Argentine commander sought not just a military victory, but political penetration.

Cochrane's expedition in the Pacific and San Martín's march overland attracted large numbers of foreign volunteers and sympathizers. War against Spain in the River Plate would be another source of attraction. While Cochrane organized the naval force in the Pacific, Buenos Aires had no such human resources to build a navy or money enough to buy more than a few ships. So foreigners were attracted with the promise of high wages, sums which were often never paid. However, as soon as this deficiency became apparent to all, the government introduced privateering licences, by which ten per cent of enemy ships and goods captured would be awarded to the captor. Guns seized would be bought by the government. This created an interest among international merchants and adventurers, some of whom travelled to Buenos Aires carrying guns to sell to the authorities. Some stayed, putting their ships into service with the infant navy, sometimes applying for officers' commissions or offering to act as privateers under the ten per cent arrangement. There is no fixed pattern for these careers. Some retired in Buenos Aires, some retired to their countries, having made large sums of money, and some entered the services of other countries. A few have streets and squares in Buenos Aires named after them, in recognition of their services: Drummond, Beazley, Seaver, among others.

By far the leading personality among these men was an Irish seaman; his exploits and leadership were to become a source of attraction which brought foreigners to the River Plate. He was William Brown, a fortune-hunter who decided to settle in trade in the River Plate; as Admiral Guillermo Brown he has been raised to the rank of national hero and star of the Irish community.

Brown was born at Foxford, near Castlebar, County Mayo, in June 1777. When he was nine years old his parents moved to North America, where his father died soon after their arrival. He joined the United States merchant navy, signing on as a cabin boy; but in 1796 was taken by force on to a British ship and during the Napoleonic Wars was taken prisoner by the French. He escaped captivity, was recaptured and fled again. In July 1809 he married Eliza Chitty and together they made the journey to South America, intending to settle in commerce in Montevideo. In April 1810 they moved to Buenos Aires in Brown's own ship, which he planned to use in coastal trade. His plans were dashed and his finances imperilled when he lost the ship to a Portuguese raider.

Later, after borrowing money to obtain another ship, he was wrecked trying to get through a Spanish line – by 1814 Spain was blockading Buenos Aires without formal declaration of such action. Brown's cargo was rescued with the help of William White, the North American merchant, and profitably disposed of. Brown and White became closely acquainted as businessmen with similar interests, although they fell out a few years later.[2]

With his profits Brown went on a trading journey to Chile and, back in Buenos Aires, bought the *Industria*, which had been the first regular packet between Buenos Aires and Colonia. This time the boat was captured by a Spanish frigate.

By then Brown's losses threatened to damage his credit beyond repair. So with a group of Irish sailors, aided by some Scots and North Americans, all recruited in the seediest corners of the riverfront, he went out with two small, borrowed boats and, under cover of darkness, boarded a Spanish ship. His band overpowered the crew, who were forced into the boats to tow the ship back to Buenos Aires. With much ceremony and publicity he recorded the ship as his own prize. The Irishman's daring action naturally aroused public and official interest. The Buenos Aires governor or *Director Supremo*, Gervasio Posadas, saw his chance to recruit a useful officer for his feeble fleet and offered Brown the post of commander of the Buenos Aires navy in March 1814, which he accepted and, with a ship named *Hercules* as his flagship, Captain Brown set out for the battle for the River Plate.

On 15 March, after four days' fighting, he took Martín García, an island in the River Plate roughly halfway between Buenos Aires and the Banda Oriental coast. From there he went to Montevideo, the last Spanish colonial stronghold on the Atlantic coast of South America. In a series of historic battles, he lured the Spanish vessels out of the port to destroy what he could not capture.

Brown returned to Buenos Aires a hero. He was cheered in the streets and his portrait went up on the walls of many homes. The authorities set him apart from the British community as their own personality; the British looked upon him as their own, a man of courage whom they had given for the Buenos Aires cause and whom they needed for assurance in such a distant and troubled land. The stories about Brown became popular currency, with fantasy mixed into events to the point where legend and reality have become difficult to distinguish. Stories, typical of those about popular figures, include one that held that Brown had once run out of ammunition during a battle. As the enemy closed in to board his ship, sure that he could not fight, the Spanish came under a fearful cannonade: the balls used were old, very hard cheeses kept in the galley store-room. . . . Another story of the early days of the Buenos Aires navy held that Brown had to train local soldiers to be sailors. They were men who could not read or write and Brown could not trust their memory, so he used the one thing at which they were experts, Spanish playing cards or *barajas.* Every part of a ship was named after a card, and no time was wasted in teaching sea lore. . . .

Brown was said to have been an expert seaman with a feeble fleet. But he used the light craft he had to great advantage: he sailed into shallow, poorly charted water where the bigger ships of the enemy ran aground. The story is told that he once grounded a ship in this way and then boarded it with a group of infantrymen. He marched the soldiers along the flat bottom of the ankle deep River Plate under the cover of darkness and, below the angle of the ship's guns, he went aboard and made the crew his prisoners.[3]

After an initial bruising of Spain in the River Plate, Brown went ashore for a time and lived in a house at Barracas, on the town's south side. Not suited to this, he prepared a private fleet, applied for a privateer's licence from the Buenos Aires government to operate in the Pacific and sailed from the Plate in October 1816. The life he found in the Pacific combined profit with the support of the Chilean emancipation movement. The Chilean navy was by then under the command of Lord Cochrane. Brown was captured by the Spanish, but ransomed in an exchange of prisoners. On his return to Buenos Aires he found the town blockaded by Spanish and Portuguese fleets and he sailed to Barbados, where a British naval station had him arrested, charged him with piracy and ordered him to pay a heavy fine before he was freed. He returned to Buenos Aires in 1818 when Spain had been all but defeated in the River Plate. He had to face a government inquiry into the operations in the Pacific and was accused of leaving the country when he was most needed. The accusation of desertion may have been justified in a military context. His personal finances were another matter. Although a popular hero his income consisted of what the government paid him for his services – with great delay. The revenue came from the capture of enemy ships which he had to share with fellow-officers. So it was natural that he should have sought the rich pickings of the wealthier Spanish colonial ports in the Pacific. In 1819 Brown announced that he was retiring from service in the navy.

He opened a grocery two blocks south of the Fort, on the banks of the river. He is said to have lived there quietly for the next six years as a 'gentleman shopkeeper'. But grocery in retirement was not to be a permanent occupation. The entries in his diary just before the war with Brazil over possession of the Banda Oriental, reveal a certain amusement at the inevitability of conflict:

> 8 November 1825: The *Argos* of Saturday contains a letter from the Minister of Foreign Affairs of the United Provinces to His Excellency the Ambassador of Brazil. . . I have heard that the Emperor has promised to give up all claim to the disputed country on receiving five million dollars; but as most of the province is already in the hands of the patriots, this is a measure which is not likely to be accepted. . . As the Buenos Aires government have not a single vessel or gunboat, it will be very easy for the Brazilians to blockade the river and stop their revenue, which is entirely derived from the Custom House and Post Office, but eventually they must be defeated. Bolivar is said to be marching to the assistance of patriots and, of course, will sweep everything before him, and the temporary blockade may enable people to sell off their old stock of goods, which is much overgrown. The Brazilians have at present a large squadron in the Outer Roads, in front of the town, but they are unable, on account of the little water, to come within gun shot. The ordnance from the Fort, if they were a little nearer, would play upon them in fine style. They practice firing every morning, hinting in this way to their opponents that their reception will be a warm one.

The diary recorded rides into the country to visit English landowners and, on 15 November 1825, described the first journey of a steamboat off Buenos Aires. The steamboat, the *Druid*, was owned by two Scottish brothers named Parish Robertson – one of whom had been the witness at the battle of San Lorenzo.

War with Brazil, declared in December, gave rise to many social occasions to raise funds for the war effort. Brown, who had been promoted to admiral and called out of retirement to lead the tiny Buenos Aires fleet against the Brazilian blockade, had one of those engagements nearly every day. Brown's diary recorded his disapproval of or admiration for the appearance of some of the leading ladies of the British community. The dresses, arms, faces and other features of Mrs Hardesty, Mrs Cartwright, Mrs Barker, Mrs Sheridan, etc., were described by the Irishman.

The Press announced bazaars, parties and theatre performances. For example, *The British Packet and Argentine News* announced on 12 August 1826 that 'The English performance will take place this evening.' Seven days later the paper commented,

> The second representation of the English amateur performance took place on the 12th inst. for the same charitable object as the first, viz – to afford relief to the widows of those killed and for the wounded of the national [Buenos Aires naval] squadron. The audience was numerous, but not so crowded as on the first night [22 July]. We noticed several high diplomatic characters. Admiral Brown and his family occupied a box near the stage. The gallant chieftain seemed to court privacy and sat at the back part of the box all the evening. A number of his hardy seamen were dispersed in different parts of the house, amusing the audience with their jokes and criticism. . .

In the early weeks of the war Brown sustained some of his most famous battles among the twenty-nine that he fought during the two-year conflict. He started the war with eleven ships against Brazil's thirty-one. The Buenos Aires fleet was formed with ships bought from Chile – which sold off its fleet as soon as the government thought that Spain could no longer be a threat on the Pacific and once enough shore batteries were installed. However, several of the ships had been in a state of disrepair and were lost in Magellan's Strait. Privateers were recruited later. Recruitment was inhibited at first because Buenos Aires had been forced to cancel all corsair licences in 1821 under pressure from the United States as one of the pre-conditions for the establishment of diplomatic relations. Britain had argued that privateering, like slavery, had to be abolished as a symbol of progress and civilization. Eventually, the war and the poor local fleet made a return to privateering necessary, in defiance of international pressure.[4]

Every battle that Brown fought in the River Plate was watched by the population of Buenos Aires which flocked to the riverside, to await news of the battle and to try to see Brown, often battered and broken, hold, out-manoeuvre and sometimes defeat or escape the enemy.

In the end, there were no victors in the war, although Buenos Aires suffered severe economic difficulties as a result of it. Britain, alarmed by the conflict between two customer countries, mediated to create the buffer state of the Banda Oriental (Uruguay) in 1828.

Although he preferred the military to the political turbulence of the River Plate, Brown was installed as Governor of Buenos Aires by military chiefs who were anxious to use his prestige as a front to their own contests for power. He held the post from August 1828 to May 1829, shortly before the start of civil war between the political factions in the city and the chieftains in the provinces. Brown's sympathy lay with the educated liberals of Buenos Aires and with the European-oriented élite that favoured centralized government. Those he favoured were defeated. He went back to his home in Barracas, where he remained, while many took refuge in Uruguay to escape a wave of terror unleashed in Buenos Aires by General Juan Manuel de Rosas, the chief of the victorious provincial leaders.[5]

Brown was called back to his ships yet again when a French fleet commander declared a blockade of Buenos Aires as from March 1838. The blockade was declared on what, in perspective, appears to have been a minor issue. Admiral Leblanc, commander of a French fleet ordered to Buenos Aires to protect French residents from arbitrary seizure of property and conscription into the army, was ignored for several weeks by the Buenos Aires Government. Finally he gave the authorities forty-eight hours' notice that he would blockade Buenos Aires until he received assurances that French nationals and their property would be given treatment similar to those of the 'most favoured nation' – which at that time was Britain – until such time as a treaty could be signed. The government refused to give way arguing that no resident could be given special status above any other. After two and a half years of minor battles in which Brown saw only occasional action, the blockade, which reduced British trade with Buenos Aires by half, was lifted. The French won only what the Buenos Aires Government was prepared to give in a bilateral accord – that was, terms which offered some guarantees of respect for private property and foreign residents; but made all conditions subject to circumstances – and under British arbitration.[6]

Yet another important clash in Brown's career was still to come.

Brown defeated Giuseppe Garibaldi at Costa Brava, on the Paraná river, in September 1842, when the Italian, having been condemned to death in Genoa, fled to South America and took up the cause of the Montevideans, once again under threat of annexation from Buenos Aires. However, Brown and Garibaldi met as friends later in Montevideo. Soon after, in July 1845, Brown was pressed to retire, aged sixty-eight, definitively this time, by Admiral Inglefield, who was commanding a British fleet in an Anglo-French blockade of Buenos Aires that lasted nearly three years. This new action, agreed by Britain and France, was a result of a decision by Buenos Aires to close the River Paraná and bar commercial access to Paraguay.[7]

In his last years, Brown limited his activities to trying to breed horses without much commercial success and to a social life within the circle of British residents in Buenos Aires. He died on 3 March 1857, attended by a fellow-Irishman, Father Anthony Fahy, who would become famous in Argentina for his work on behalf of Irish immigrants.

Three generations of Brown's descendants joined the navy, starting with his son, William. Brown's daughter, Eliza, had died early, heartbroken after the death of her betrothed, Francis Drummond, of Dundee, who had served in the Brazilian navy, then had joined the Buenos Aires navy. There he had met Eliza Brown to whom he was to become engaged. Their romance was known to her father in January 1827, when Drummond, aged twenty-four, was promoted to captain. In action at Monte Santiago in April 1827 – where Brown's fleet of four ships met sixteen Brazilians – Drummond's ear was shot off. Under heavy fire, his ship, the *Independencia*, was battered useless and Drummond transferred to the *Sarandí*, commanded by a North

American. As he stepped aboard, his hip was smashed by a shot, and he died a few hours later. When the sixteen-year-old Eliza heard the news she dressed in her bridal gown, walked into the River Plate and drowned. She was buried alongside her fiancé.

While Brown is the greatest hero in the Argentine navy, foreigners on land have not achieved such fame. Generals O'Brien and Miller did, however, become prominent as officers of General José de San Martín, on the Argentine general's expedition across the Andes to Chile and later to Perú.

John Thomond O'Brien, born at Battingloss, County Wicklow, in 1786, the son of a wealthy landowner, was with San Martín throughout his expeditions, in the grenadier regiment. However, fortunes could change and in 1837 the Buenos Aires government ordered the arrest of O'Brien, who spent several months in prison, accused of being an agent buying guns for General Santa Cruz, of Bolivia. O'Brien died in Lisbon in June 1861 on his way back to Buenos Aires from a visit to Ireland.[8] General William Miller (1795–1861), of Wingham, Kent, was San Martín's constant companion, having joined him after the battle of Chacabuco, in Chile. San Martín later wrote that if he had been given six officers such as Miller, war in Perú would have ended much earlier. They remained good friends in their retirement and San Martín, who chose to live in voluntary exile in France, visited the Miller family in Canterbury. San Martín spent only twelve of his mature years in Argentina, and twenty-six in exile, until his death in 1850. It was George Canning who at one time gave him protection in Britain against threats from Spain and France, both angered by San Martín's support for the South American revolutionary cause and by his connections with British Freemasonry – which had helped him with his expeditions.

The letters of Samuel Haigh, a Scottish merchant resident in Mendoza who was in Chile when San Martín led his troops there, describe a close relationship between San Martín and his English officers during the expedition for Chilean independence. Haigh was a supplementary aide-de-camp to San Martín at the battle of Maipú, the Argentine general's third and last battle in Chile, in April 1818, which effectively ended Spanish rule in the country.

Apart from the Britons who accompanied San Martín there

were others who offered him their services as a kind of home guard. When San Martín had recruited almost every available native to take with him to Chile and while he was governor of Mendoza, he received an offer from the British in the province to form a civil defence force. This was to protect Mendoza against the Spanish while all the local men were away. The offer included uniforms and guns. A provincial government official wrote to San Martín to recommend that the volunteer force should be accepted because they were 'accustomed to fatigue and risks as many are former prisoners', who had stayed in the country after the British invasion a decade before. San Martín approved the list of forty-six volunteers commanded by one John Young and his lieutenants, Thomas Appleby and James Lindsay. It was not the only case of the formation of a 'little army' by foreigners – such forces were organized a few years later by Britons in Buenos Aires and in Montevideo – but such cases are rare. Many of the men who fought with Brown or with the revolutionary armies are mere names with a brief service record and are included in Argentina's biographical dictionaries.

One Peter Campbell, an Irish Catholic, stayed in Buenos Aires after the 1806 invasion. He was among the more colourful of the *ingleses* who stayed.

Campbell, who had landed with Beresford, first went into tanning leather for export. Then he worked for a time as a foreman on the ranch of the Parish Robertson brothers in Corrientes province. In their book *Letters on South America* the brothers described Campbell as 'a fierce fellow' who rode everywhere with two cavalry pistols in his belt and a rusty sword at his side. His skin was so darkened by the sun that he often looked black, but for his blond beard and moustache. Campbell rapidly adjusted to the local living fashions of the *gaucho* – the man of the land.[9] He became an officer in the forces of the chieftain of Uruguay in 1814, *Caudillo* José Artigas, and together they led their troops to occupy the provinces of north-eastern Argentina, making Corrientes their headquarters. From there they went south and attacked garrisons held by the Córdoba and Entre Rios chieftains, to annex parts of both provinces. When their ally, the leader of Santa Fé province, was in danger, Campbell led a force of 600 men along the Paraná river, supported by about twenty canoes. They were credited with terrorizing every town on the river. Bartolomé Mitre, Argentine President, military commander and historian, wrote that Campbell invented a new kind of warfare: he would order small bands of his *gaucho* troops, the gangs known as *montoneros*, to charge the enemy and on reaching the opponents' lines they dispersed to form *guerrilla* groups of two or three men. Once this was done, the men dismounted and while one man held the horses, the others fired at random targets. The *guerrillas* then remounted and fled back to their own camp and their action was followed by a bigger *montonero* charge.

Campbell died peacefully in Corrientes, where he returned to tanning, in 1832.

The number of North Americans in action against Spain and Brazil was smaller than that of Britons; but there were many in the River Plate as privateers. Of about forty people who held corsair licences during the war against Spain, thirty of them were North American.

James (Diego) Chayter, born in Baltimore in 1767, arrived in the River Plate in his own ship in 1815. He carried guns and ammunition for sale to the revolutionary authorities. He was granted a privateer's licence and command of the fourteen-gun corvette *Independencia del Sud* in May 1816. With this he harassed ships out of Cádiz and took several Spanish vessels in the Atlantic. He returned to Baltimore for repairs and was forced to surrender two ships that he had captured. From there he went back to the coast of Spain and then sailed to Buenos Aires, with eight captured ships, in September 1817. When Buenos Aires, under pressure from the United States and Europe, put an end to the corsairs in October 1821, Chayter, awarded the rank of lieutenant-colonel in the navy, offered his services to Colombia.

Colonel John Halsted Coe, of Springfield, Massachusetts, started out in South America at the age of eighteen, in Lord Cochrane's crew. After the Chile and Peru campaigns, aged about twenty and on his way back to the United States, he passed through Buenos Aires where he was offered a commission in the navy, in which he served up to 1835. He then went to Montevideo, to join the army, where he fought against Buenos Aires. He was employed again by the Buenos Aires navy in the early 1850s and went on to change sides several times during factional strife and disputes between rival provincial chiefs. He finally went back to Springfield in 1853, yet returned soon after to Buenos Aires and died there in October 1864.[10]

There were several men by the name of King in the Argentine forces. At least two were Irish; both sailed with Brown. Another, a North American, Colonel J. Anthony King, wrote a book about his life in Argentina, *Twenty-four years in the Argentine Republic*, published in 1846. He was born in New York, about 1803, and left a comfortable home at the age of fourteen to reach Buenos Aires in 1817. He started work in a French perfumery and from there joined the army, first in Buenos Aires and later in the provinces, changing sides on a few occasions according to the fortunes of local chieftains.

A name for speculation is that of Irish-born Guillermo Reynafé. The name became well known because his three sons, as soldiers and politicians, dominated Córdoba province for many years. The father's arrival in the Spanish colony is not recorded; but he lived at Tulumba, in Córdoba, where his three sons were born and where he held a minor government post. This is the discovery of Córdoba historians who found documents signed by one 'Quin Fait' and which they assumed to originate in the words 'Queen's Faith', which became *Reyna* (Queen) *Fé* (Faith).[11]

These are a few thumbnail sketches of the dozens of British and North American names that are to be found in the records of every Argentine province. The newspapers at the time of the war with Spain and later with Brazil published long lists of them, with collective praise for their support for the Buenos Aires cause.

They are not a feature of the early part of the century alone. Forty years later there were still Britons in the Argentine forces. For example, in *The Standard*, 5 July 1865, we read:

> We regret to learn that General Paunero has had to shoot some more deserters: among his troops are five Scotchmen, four Irishmen, two Englishmen and a North American. The Irishmen say they have only just arrived in Buenos Aires from County Westmeath when they were entrapped by some crimps under the pretence of hiring to work on an

estancia at San Pedro, receiving each $500 advance money; but when on board the steamer they were told they were soldiers and have since been repeatedly cuffed for not understanding the officers' orders.

And in *The Standard* of 10 September 1865:

The island of Martín García is now defended by Captain Davis's English Brigade. We hope President Mitre feels confident that the Island is now in safe hands; as yet the garrison is rather slender only counting forty-seven men, but the gallant captain has his recruiting flag flying at the Retiro and is expecting a contingent from the camp.

The time was the start of another war, against Paraguay, when Brazil, Uruguay – which then had a puppet government obeying Brazilian orders – and Argentina joined forces in the Triple Alliance, which defeated Paraguay after five years' fighting. There were few British officers leading Argentine troops in that conflict, as there was by then a small professional army. However, English, Irish and Scots from the *camp* and *gauchos* were 'press-ganged' into the army.[12]

6

The Opening of the Colony

Buenos Aires in the 1820s was a village trying to be a European city; attempting to imitate fashions, social customs and political practices, yet failing to achieve a good imitation. However, the effort to modernize and to leave behind the constrained colonial society was a cause for optimism among visiting Europeans. An anonymous traveller and writer who described the town in this way said that:

Many of the Buenos Ayreans of the second and third grade have most confused notions of London. They think that all England is in London; and in speaking of the arrival of a vessel from Liverpool, Falmouth or any other port, they add Liverpool in London, Falmouth in London, and when speaking of English passengers arriving, no matter from what part, they are all from London. Seeing so many Englishmen in their country, gentry of the above description have most exalted notions of themselves and of the superiority of Buenos Ayres over the rest of the world. We must not blame their self-importance; for we have a tolerable share of it ourselves, else the world has terribly belied us . . .[1] The beach is crowded with sailors of all nations, grog-shops, stores, etc. The English sailors idling about the beach would man a ship of war. A stranger, seeing so many English faces, might suppose it an English colony.[2] At night the sailors in the grog-shops dance, to the music of the fiddle and flute, reels and the College hornpipe in perfection, astonishing the Spanish girls.

There are two English coffee-houses or hotels: Faunch's and Keen's. The former is a very superior one and provides the dinners given upon our national days, such as St George's, St Andrew's, etc., besides numerous private dinners of Englishmen, Americans, Creolians, etc. It is situated near the Fort. Faunch, the master, and his wife have had great experience in their profession in London; and the style of his dinners is hardly exceeded there. The King's birthday dinner is kept with great *éclat*:

the room us surrounded by flags of different nations; and they have both vocal and instrumental music. From seventy to eighty persons generally sit down at a table, including the ministers of the country, who are always invited. The Government pay us the compliment of hoisting the flag at the Fort on that day.[3]

The traveller and author said that many Britons, on arrival, chose to reside with Spanish families to improve their knowledge of the language. While he found that the British were welcome – 'A knight of the napkin [waiter] got me into conversation ... declaring that he liked them [the English] better than any foreigner' – he also discovered that they were a nuisance at times: 'In cases of debt [the courts] are very lenient, seldom committing to prison, except for a flagrant attempt at fraud ... The English disputants, it has been observed, are very numerous, causing more trouble than those of all the rest of the town put together.'[4]

The year 1820 was the start of a decade of contrasts. The first stumbling steps towards European-style progress were taken, under what may be called a liberal administration which turned its attention to advancement in Buenos Aires at the expense of the provinces. It was a decade of war, with Brazil first, and civil war later. It was the time of the establishment of diplomatic relations, with the United States and Britain; and of the first attempt at creating a system of presidential government. The British community got its first church, first schools and first cemetery, as well as its first medical dispensary and first libraries. The first – and for many years the only – large group of British colonists arrived in Buenos Aires. These were Scots who settled in Monte Grande, south-west of the city of Buenos Aires.

In his efforts to improve the town, Bernardino Rivadavia, Minister for Government and Foreign Affairs, forbade the storage of hides in the centre of the urban area – a thing which was eventually praised by resident Britons because it got rid of the source of a rather powerful stench, but at first caused much grumbling because they had to find out of town warehouses; he introduced a traffic code and numbered streets and houses. One English traveller, in Buenos Aires in February 1821, praised Rivadavia for 'clipping the wings' of the Catholic Church. A majority of the Church's orders were useless and their strong traditions were a hindrance to liberal progress, the traveller wrote.[5] In 1822, Rivadavia made a contract with James Bevans, a waterworks engineer, to draw up plans for a water supply system and a port for Buenos Aires. Bevans – an English Quaker whose clothes and those of his family were a curiosity in the town – submitted four plans for a port, none of which were used until some years later and then in combination with other projects. But Bevans's is the original design for the water supply and drainage system in Buenos Aires.[6]

Buenos Aires' first bank was started in January 1822, with a Briton, William Cartwright, as president of the nine-man board of a joint stock company registered as *Los Directores y Compañía del Banco de Buenos Ayres Sociedad Anónima.* Diego (James) Brittain and Robert Montgomery were the other two Britons on the board. All three had been in Buenos Aires for some years, having chosen the River Plate for trade in preference to the uncertainty of Europe and the lingering hostility of the United States. In Buenos Aires they were pioneers in business and enjoyed comfortable incomes. Each lived in large estates, or *quintas*, on the western perimeter of Buenos Aires. On 23 February 1822, in the rooms of the *Consulado*, the bank's statutes were drawn up and signed and the event toasted with wine. On a few occasions a majority of shares were controlled by British residents, but this was not the rule in the bank's history. British names such as William Orr and William Parish Robertson, who had been in Buenos Aires since before the independence of the River Plate states, and John Miller – who is said to have imported the first Shorthorn bull to Argentina – and several others were among the first shareholders.

The bank started with a capital of one million pesos, in one thousand shares of one thousand pesos each. Although the shares were not within the reach of the ordinary man's purse – the bank's first book-keeper, an Englishman named Mr William Robinson, was appointed with an income of 1200 pesos a year, while the bank's first cashier, a German named August Thissen, received 3000 pesos a year – the terms for subscription were accessible to European middle-class residents, who were an upper class in Buenos Aires. The bank's statutes allowed operations to start after the subscription of 300 shares, each of which could be purchased with a down payment of 200 pesos, followed by another 200 pesos two months later; with payment of the remaining 600 pesos in instalments to be negotiated between the shareholder and the director. On 15 July 1822 the bank opened to the public. Metal boxes for carrying currency as well as bank notes, 'printed in the Spanish language', were ordered from London.[7]

A short time after this order was placed, the bank acquired its own minting equipment; hence the Buenos Aires mint also was a British private enterprise in its origins. The equipment reached the bank by indirect circumstances. The government had ordered a minting machine from John Miers, who had taken one set of printing equipment and plates to Chile. However, on delivering the second set to Buenos Aires, he found he was not going to be paid. This was because the government had decided that it could no longer afford such equipment and as the bank had placed an order for notes – to supplement the existing government notes, some old over-stamped Spanish notes and United Provinces of the River Plate coinage issued since 1813 – the machinery could be dispensed with. The erratic financial relations with the government were something that foreigners had to live with and while such a hazard discouraged some investment the wealth of the land was an incentive to take such risks in the hopes of making vast profits in trade. Miers sold out to the bank. Miers had first travelled to South America in 1819 to invest in copper mining. The mining venture had failed, so Miers had returned to London, with the order for the minting equipment for Chile. Although his commercial plans were not a success, he later wrote down his experiences in an entertaining and enlightening style. When he published these notes, under the title *Travels in Chile and La Plata* (covering the years 1819–24), these were widely read and became considered basic information on the area for many years.

Among the members of the bank's board there were some interesting personalities. William Parish Robertson, a director of the bank towards the end of 1823 and in 1824, was one of them. He and his brother had been among the merchants who had hoped to make a fortune out of the British invasions of 1806–7 by being among the first British traders in the River Plate. The two brothers arrived in Montevideo in 1806 but were forced to return to Britain the following year when the invasions failed. They were back in the River Plate in 1808 and from then on tried a variety of lines of business. John Parish Robertson was in Buenos Aires in 1809, when trade restrictions were partly lifted. He was a big, handsome Scot with dark hair, thick eyebrows and a thin beard. One of his claims to fame is to have given Argentina an eyewitness report of General San Martín's first vistory over Spanish forces at San Lorenzo, north of Buenos Aires. After exploring much of the country for its commercial prospects, the two brothers opened an imports business which they expanded to Paraguay, for which they had their own shipping service on the River Paraná. At first they were accepted by the Paraguayan dictator, José Gaspar Tomás Rodríguez Francia, known as *El Supremo* (1756–1840), and this won them trading facilities. However, Francia later closed the country to all foreigners and forbade Paraguayans to travel abroad; the brothers were expelled, losing all their property in Paraguay. They next set up a general trading company with offices in Buenos Aires and Lima, which prospered greatly when the brothers were awarded the administration of a British loan to Peru. They extended their interests to mining in north-western Argentina, though they failed in this venture because of a dispute over ownership of the title to the land. Then they entered the Bank of Buenos Aires. While doing this they took part in negotiations for a one million pounds bond issue, through Baring Brothers, for the Buenos Aires government, and also organized land colonization, which had a good start with a colony formed by immigrant Scots at Monte Grande, in 1825.

During the negotiations for the Baring Brothers bond issue William Parish Robertson was in Buenos Aires – as a member of the bank's board – and John was in London. The talks were started by Rivadavia in August 1822. It had become fashionable for the newly independent republics to seek loans by floating bonds through brokers in London. Apart from the element of prestige of such loans, Rivadavia needed the money if he was to see his plans for a modernized city of Buenos Aires materialize. Bevans' plans for the port in Buenos Aires estimated that construction would take eight years at a cost which the town alone could not meet. Rivadavia placed orders for equipment with the government's representatives in London, Hullet Brothers, and cultivated as many British acquaintances as he possibly could towards his target of a loan. He was a regular guest at British community occasions and was never short on flattery. One example was the banquet at Faunch's Hotel, on 23 April 1823, marking King George IV's birthday. One of the British hosts toasted Rivadavia, being the senior government minister present; to which Rivadavia replied in English, raising his glass to the British government and to the world's 'most moral and illustrated nation: England'.

By the end of 1823 Rivadavia had decided to extend use of the future loan to the construction of three towns on the eastern coast of Buenos Aires, between the capital and the north Patagonian town of Carmen de Patagones, the building of a water-supply system for the city according to the plans drawn up by Bevans, and the establishment of several outposts in the country's interior, north of Buenos Aires.

The bond issue was oversubscribed by optimistic British investors, most of them small income holders hoping to get £100 out of each £85 invested within one year. Barings had raised the money by 25 June 1824, after advertising the promise of prosperity of the rich former Spanish colonies in the River Plate. The Buenos Aires Government received a little over £700,000 out of the million, after deduction of advance interest payments for the investors, commissions and charges for Barings, and commissions for the Robertsons.[8] It was the biggest coup they ever made.

The Robertson brothers reported most of their travels and business ventures to their grandfather, who forwarded what he considered of most interest in the letters to the Foreign Office. The old man kept all the letters and from these eventually came the brothers' most lasting claim to fame: two books entitled *Letters on Paraguay, comprising an account of four years' residence in that republic, under the government of Dictator Francia* (1838) and *Letters on South America, comprising travels on the banks of the Paraná and the Rio de la Plata* (1843) published in London.

The money from the bond issue was never used to build a port or any other of the original projects, but to finance the war with

Brazil. And with war repayments lapsed, causing losses to the many investors in Britain. The delay in the repayment provoked a long correspondence between the two governments. Although the British Government did not want to be involved in a direct way in the private financial ventures of individuals, arguing that each had taken risks they had been fully warned about, the Foreign Office was forced for reasons of political expediency to be seen to be claiming payments. In January 1838 the British minister in Buenos Aires wrote to Lord Palmerston, the Foreign Secretary, reporting that the Buenos Aires Government repeatedly argued 'how faithfully the instalment had been paid, and this during a moment when from various circumstances the Treasury was so exhausted that the last payment was made up from the private purse of the Governor and a few of his friends'. This was a plea for time and patience in answer to British claims for compensation for losses caused to British subjects during the war with Brazil. Alternatively, and also in January 1838, the Buenos Aires Government suggested that the Falkland (Malvinas) Islands be formally handed over to Britain – which had occupied them in 1833 – in exchange for cancellation of the debt. Britain decided that the islands were not worth putting the British Government into such debt with private members of the public and, in any case, she was retaining them. The loan was finally cancelled in 1904, though only after it had contributed to plunge Barings into a financial crisis in the 1890s and after British, German and North American institutions had underwritten the Buenos Aires debt.

The Baring loan was part of a growing British presence in the newly independent nation. British commercial influence was to be seen in the city of Buenos Aires itself, where a directory, the *Guía de Blondel*, published by a Frenchman between 1826 and 1834, listed more than eighty concerns run by Britons (and some North Americans) in its section on merchant houses and consignees. In 1829, the British and North American commercial concerns included eighteen grocers, four hotels (Faunch, Thorn, Smith and Keen), nine cabinet-makers, three upholsterers, two warehouses, two livery stables, three blacksmiths, one general brokerage firm, one auctioneer, two printing offiçes, four house decorators, one jeweller, four watch-makers, five apothecaries, eight physicians, six tailors, two saddlers, two bootmakers, three hatters, one tinsmith and one brewer.[9] For the sake of a very general comparison it should be stated that the other largest European community, with the exception of Spaniards, was the German which numbered an estimated two hundred members in the early 1830s. A German traveller to Buenos Aires in 1831 said that most of the men who welcomed him at the Deutscher Club were employed by British-owned trading houses.

Soon after relations with Buenos Aires were established by the United States under the terms of the doctrine of President James Monroe in December 1823, the biggest event for the British in the town was the formalization of relations with Britain. The appointment of a British consul, Woodbine Parish, gave residents a new sense of security. He had arrived in Montevideo on 22 March 1824 aboard HMS *Cambridge*, which also brought his wife, Amelia Jane, and a vice-consul, Charles Griffiths. Parish was soon able to announce that he was confident of success in his negotiations for a Treaty of Friendship between London and Buenos Aires. The announcement was made at the St Andrew's Day banquet, on 30 November 1824, at Faunch's. The consul reported:

> We were a very numerous party, upwards of seventy, and I must say I never saw such a scene in my life as took place after what I told them [of my full powers to treat with the Government] – they appeared all mad and I expected that the tables and chairs would have followed all the bottles and glasses out of the windows, in true Spanish style. Some of the Buenos Ayreans who were desirous to drink Mr Canning's health threw away their glasses and insisted upon having bottles of wine instead of glasses to drink it in . . . and yet, they were sober.

The Treaty of Friendship, Navigation and Commerce, between Britain and the United Provinces of the Rio de la Plata, signed in February 1825, was to govern Anglo-Argentine relations for almost a century. At the time of signing the Treaty marked the end, in theory, of instability for British residents, who feared harassment on religious grounds and, although at all times they had found enough power to deal with the local government almost as equals, there was the spectre of unpleasant conflicts, forcible recruitment and expropriation of property. These fears had hung over the community throughout the United Provinces' dispute with Spain over independence of the former colonies.[10]

The Times had taken up the cause of diplomatic recognition of Spain's former colonies and the cause of commerce with them early in 1824, campaigning vigorously for the establishment of formal links. Every occasion when merchants gathered to give their support to such links was amply reported in the paper. On 31 January 1824, *The Times* launched the subject into public debate with an editorial which recalled that:

> It is now more than fourteen years since the war first sprung up between Spain and her colonies; and so long as the contest continued, we, though solicited by both parties, most religiously abstained from assisting either . . . But the affair has now been long decided; the South Americans have prevailed by their native strength; peace is practically established between the contending parties; independence of the South American States has been acknowledged by Foreign Powers – of whom, be it observed, we were not the first. We are, therefore, as free to form alliances whether offensive or defensive, with those new states, as with any of the old ones of Europe . . .

The paper was back with an editorial on the subject on 6 March; it regretted a parliamentary vote, on 16 March, against recognition; made a commentary in favour on 17 March; and again on 18 March; and later in the year reported meetings of merchants favourable to recognition which took place in Liverpool, Manchester and Leeds, finally to report, on 6 July, on the meeting between Rivadavia and Parish, in Buenos Aires, when the formalities of diplomatic recognition were carried out.

Parish travelled to Buenos Aires with instructions from George Canning, the Foreign Secretary, to collect as much information as possible about the new country. It was Canning's stated policy that Britain should 'bring the New World into being in order to redress the balance of the Old'. The minister's task was, apart from representing the government in all matters concerning Britain, to supply British merchants with the best possible picture of the people and the land they were to deal with. However, the posting also afforded Parish an excellent opportunity to pursue his interests in natural history as soon as he had settled down with his wife and three children. A fourth child, Frank, was born to the

Parish family in Buenos Aires.[11]

The consul's correspondents for much of his studies were Dr Redhead, in Salta, and Dr Gillies, in Mendoza, both long-time British residents. Joseph Thomas Redhead, born in Antigua in 1767, and a medical graduate at Edinburgh was, according to his own report to Buenos Aires authorities in October 1804, born in Connecticut, United States. This, however, may have been to avoid an eviction order against Britons; Spanish colonial authorities announced from time to time that they had received orders barring the subjects of one nation or another, according to which was in conflict with the Spanish Crown; foreigners therefore registered different places of origin. Redhead settled in the northern province of Salta in 1809 after a career which had included imprisonment in France and scientific research in Peru. He was later chased out of Salta by the Spaniards, who suspected him of being in touch with anti-Spanish revolutionaries. He thus sought refuge with the man who was organizing a revolutionary army in the north against the Spanish, General Manuel Belgrano. Redhead followed Belgrano through his victories at Tucumán, in September 1812, and Salta, in February 1813, and defeats at Vilcapugio, in October, and Ayohuma, in November 1813, and attended Belgrano at his deathbed. After independence Redhead settled down to his medical career again, acting as consultant to locally prominent families. He is quoted frequently in Parish's book, *Buenos Aires and the provinces of the Rio de la Plata* (1838), for supplying geological and archaeological notes on northern Argentina. Redhead died in June 1847.[12]

Parish's other correspondent, Dr John Gillies, lived in Mendoza from 1823 until 1828. He was a Scot who had sought the benign Andean climate for a severe pulmonary infection and spent his years there studying the region and sending botanical collections and rock and metal samples to Edinburgh.[13]

While his arrival was a welcome event, there is evidence that Parish was autocratic in his relations with the British community. He was convinced that all he did for British residents was in their own best interest and would accept no argument. His wish to arbitrate in all the community's affairs – using his authority to take the chair at all meetings – once led him to court, after he had antagonized a resident Irish physician, Dr John Oughan, one of several Irish doctors of some renown in Buenos Aires.[14]

However, apart from these minor domestic setbacks it was a time of rapid advances in contacts between Britain and the River Plate and communication soon began to improve. The first British packet, *The Countess of Chichester*, had arrived in Buenos Aires, from Falmouth, in April 1824, and the packets were soon to achieve a near weekly frequency. Yet, while this held promise for trade in the future, colonization hardly grew at the time. The newly founded River Plate Mining Association and the River Plate Agricultural Association, which had been started by British residents for the promotion of immigration and colonization for mining and farming, failed to attract any large number of colonists from Britain. The leading personality was a Briton named John A. Barber Beaumont, who had first tried colonizing the banks of the Parana river in 1819.

A sign of a large community is having its own newspaper, in this case *The British Packet and Argentine News*, founded by Thomas George Love in 1826. He was born in England, in 1793, and is thought to have travelled to Buenos Aires some time between 1815 and 1819. Love appears to have been a versatile writer, with a good education. He apparently had a somewhat strange appearance, as he had no hair on his head, not even eyebrows.

Rivadavia became the first president of a semi-united Argentina – so named by a constitutional draft in the early 1820s – in February 1826; but from the start was sabotaged from all sides. The Emperor of Brazil had just declared war and blockaded the River Plate. The blockade cut eighty per cent of Buenos Aires' revenue, and the government dipped into the Baring Brothers loan and into the bank; it also ordered the printing of banknotes to finance the war, bringing about financial crisis. Meanwhile, the provincial political chieftains, known as *caudillos*, became hostile to the Buenos Aires administration, accusing Rivadavia of wanting to assume dictatorial authority over the whole country instead of limiting his rule to representation in foreign affairs and aid in budgetary planning. He was also accused of ignoring proposals for a future federal system of government. The Buenos Aires congress was divided in the consideration of policy towards Brazil's blockade; 'moderates' seeking appeasement and negotiation over possession of Uruguay, the 'hawks' calling for immediate military occupation of the disputed province. In a gesture aimed at winning support, Rivadavia offered his resignation in June 1827 and was shocked to see it accepted. His successor, Colonel Manuel Dorrego, made peace with Brazil, reached through the mediation of a British envoy, Lord Ponsonby, whose proposal hinged on the creation of the buffer state of Uruguay. Ponsonby, an experienced diplomat, had little regard for Dorrego's nationalist views and no respect for his ideas that Buenos Aires should share the revenue from the port with the provinces in a federal system.[15] But Ponsonby's disatisfaction may have also been due to his dislike for his posting to South America. An exceptionally handsome man, who thought that his place was in the centres of civilization and not in its outposts, he had been sent by George Canning – who eagerly sought an end to the war between what were to Britain two important trading capitals – apparently to please George IV who was envious of the attention paid Ponsonby by Lady Elizabeth Conyngham, who had great influence in the English court.

Rivadavia's failure, and with him the idea that Argentina could be directed from Buenos Aires – and the equal failure of attempts to create a federalized nation because of the rivalry between provincial chieftains – unleashed a power struggle in which Dorrego was removed from office and executed, in December 1828. But his executioners, led by General Juan Lavalle, a widely respected officer who had won fame and fortune during the battles for independence from Spain, failed to take over government. Power was seized by General Juan Manuel de Rosas. A tough *caudillo*, whose authority in Buenos Aires province had been built on the bloodiest discipline as a ranch owner and as a military leader, Rosas became Governor of Buenos Aires in December 1829, at the end of one year of civil war.[16]

British interests had been seriously affected by the time Lord Ponsonby was sent to find a settlement to the war between Buenos Aires and Brazil. At the beginning of the war, British interests were estimated at £1·5 million in export goods and cash, plus the

£700,000 in government bonds from the Barings issue. At the end of 1827, Parish estimated that British holdings had fallen to £492,000, of which part was in land and about half in hides. However, there was no question of British interests being wound up. There was still a large number of Britons resident in Buenos Aires and their business and institutions would soon continue to expand.

With Parish's encouragement, a group of British doctors and other residents in Buenos Aires started the British Philanthropic Institution, in 1827, with the aim of affording 'temporary relief to British subjects unable to support themselves or their families, in consequence of sickness, accident or other unavoidable causes; to assist widows and orphan children left destitute; and to provide medical assistance and funeral expenses in special cases', according to a pamphlet distributed by the organizers. A notice in *The British Packet and Argentine News* on 15 and 22 December 1827 announced that the British Philanthropic Institution advised subscribers to meet at Faunch's Hotel on Christmas Eve to organize further the community's medical services. The Institution became known as the British Friendly Society the following year; and changed its name once more to the British Medical Dispensary in 1840.

Parish stayed in Buenos Aires until 1832, when he took away with him a collection of notes and boxes full of his archaeological and botanical finds. A first edition of his notes was published in 1835, after which he received additional material and with that he published *Buenos Ayres and the provinces of the Rio de la Plata* (1838). He died aged eighty-six in August 1882, at St Leonards, England.

Britons in Buenos Aires during Parish's term were a mixed crowd with many difficulties and settling problems. José Antonio Wilde, in his book *Buenos Aires desde setenta años atrás* (1880), describes Britons as having a comfortable income but being troubled with many problems of adaptation. These problems ranged from the serious, such as coming to terms with the legal system and widespread corruption, to the everyday nuisance: Wilde said that 'English women, particularly, suffered when walking in the streets, owing to the insolence of the urchins who made fun of their bonnets.' The author said that in the eyes of the 'lower classes, every foreigner was an *inglés*, and every *inglés* was called Don Guillermo'. Wilde did not give the reason.

Life in Buenos Aires was a succession of work-filled days, with little entertainment – until the time when an amusement park opened. This was the *Parque Argentino*, in what is today almost the city's centre. British residents called the at that time almost inaccessible swamp the 'Vauxhall Gardens', probably as a result of a notice in *The British Packet and Argentine News*, on 26 July 1828: 'Vauxhall – it is with much satisfaction that we can assure our readers that a plan is in considerable forwardness to establish an imitation of that delightful place of recreation, in one of the suburbs of Buenos Ayres . . .'

The park was also known as Wilde's Gardens because the land, owned by James Wilde, was his share in the £20,000 initial investment. It suffered permanently from poor access roads; but eventually progressed and reached a peak of success in 1850, when Wilde bought most of the shares to secure continued ownership of the land. The park had a theatre, an open air concert stand, a ballroom, a restaurant and tea room, and a circus with a capacity for 1200 people.

The Vauxhall was essentially a business proposition. Several of its shareholders were Britons and members of the Commercial Rooms. This latter organization founded in 1810 and reorganized in 1829, grew rapidly attracting local members and, inevitably also government suspicion that merchants meeting at the Rooms' premises were doing so to plot against authorities by the manipulation of the price of gold. However, no official action was taken until 1840. A decree ordered the confiscation of the property held by native enemies of the government who were marked as such either by personal statements or by official identification. This did not affect most foreign residents; but it upset commerce with their native partners. To counter this, a group of British and North American businessmen met at Beech's Hotel in May 1841, with United States Consul Amory Edwards presiding, to form the Society of Foreign Residents, which also was to be used as a stock exchange. *The British Packet and Argentine News* of 12 June 1841 announced that the foreign residents had launched their

Society 'on Monday last at Beech's Hotel'. The government allowed the club to function, but forbade merchants born in the River Plate provinces to become members. They did, however, use the premises, for an hour a day, as a stock exchange. In the 1850s native-born members were readmitted. Belgians, Swiss, French, Germans and North Americans, as well as British residents, were on the earliest members' lists. Among the British founding members were James Barton – one of the founders of the Bank of Buenos Ayres – and Thomas Armstrong, a member of the bank's board and at one time holding up to forty-five per cent of the bank's shares. Armstrong was one of the town's wealthiest merchants. The British were the strongest national group among the Society's members. And by carefully planned marriages, into North American and German families that owned the biggest trading houses in their own communities, this strength was extended.

The Society was the forerunner of today's Strangers' Club, the oldest social club in South America, renowned for many years for having the town's most influential merchants among its members. With the Society, the life and business, social calendar and sporting fixtures of Buenos Aires were all decided by members who used their marriages, churches, masonic lodges, clubs and European trading houses to compete for an ever increasing share of Argentina. Out of the Society grew a business organization: a fraternity of stockbrokers formed early in the 1850s. So proud of their power were they that they called the group *El Camoatí*, which is a South American wasp with a fierce sting. The sporting world was an extension of the Society and members started the Foreign Amateurs Race Sporting Society – which had its earliest meetings in 1849 – that became the predecessor of Argentina's élite Jockey Club.[17]

7

Preachers, Churches and Schools

A growing community could be expected to require its own institutions, such as hospitals, libraries, schools and a church. While most of these were in their early stages of organization, the outlook for the practice of their religion was bleak for Protestants. Non-Catholics were still considered pagans by many people in Buenos Aires.

Before 1820 non-Catholics could not be buried in Holy Ground. They had to accept conversion or simply try not to die in Buenos Aires. Otherwise, friends or relatives had to dispose of bodies on the shores of the River Plate or seek an understanding or bribable priest. As far as Protestants – which included members of the Church of England, known as Episcopalians or Anglicans, North American Presbyterians, Scottish Presbyterians and North American Methodists – were concerned, a funeral was a privilege. During the days of Spanish rule, the authorities occasionally ordered the burning of a body of a 'pagan' as part of the affirmation of the faith. The practice had been abandoned in the early nineteenth century; but for many years after it was not uncommon for native Catholics to pass unconcerned by the crudest funeral where a body of a foreigner was interred by men hired by family or government to dispose of the dead. Sometimes these carelessly buried bodies were visible on the surface after a heavy rain.

Tolerance proved to be somewhat limited on occasions. An often-cited incident occurred early in the 1820s when an Englishman did not kneel as the procession of the *Santo Viático* – taken to private homes as part of the administration of the last rites – passed and as a result was beaten with a stick by one of the soldiers in the procession's escort. Foreigners usually fled when the effigy of this saint, or of any saint, was paraded, to avoid kneeling in the muddy streets; but a magistrate later ruled that non-Catholics did not have to kneel.

As a group the British residents needed a church not only for worship, but as a point at which to gather. Church building had to wait, however, until after the 1825 Treaty of Friendship, which included a clause permitting freedom of worship. This did not mean that services were not held, but that they were restricted to private homes. Travelling preachers – Anglicans, Presbyterians or Methodists – were all the resident Britons had and their success depended on the devotion of the head of each family. Missionary work and preaching outside Buenos Aires did not start until after 1830.

James Thomson, assisted by a Mr Tate, held some of the first religious services in private homes for small groups of people. The first such service recorded by him was held on 19 November 1820. Thomson, travelling under the auspices of the Royal Lancasterian Society (or British and Foreign Bible Society), was responsible for trying to introduce teaching methods along the lines of the Joseph Lancaster system. Thomson became well known to most of South America's liberation leaders – who, in many cases, wanted to see the liberal methods of education of Europe introduced in their countries – as he travelled, spreading the Protestant gospel, through Chile, Peru, Ecuador, Colombia, Mexico and Cuba. The *Gaceta de Buenos Aires* of 30 May 1821 announced that he had been made an Argentine citizen by special government decree.

At that time several members of the British community formed a committee to establish a 'Protestant Burial Ground', a name which the cemetery administration used for some years. At a public meeting of British subjects on 15 December 1820 it had been decided to send a memorial to the government asking for permission to create such a service for foreigners. The committee was given government permission, in February 1821, to buy a small plot of land outside the city in the Socorro district, on what is now the elegant Juncal street. Between then and July 1824 seventy-one Englishmen were officially interred. This number, however, included Germans, Swiss, French, North Americans and other aliens: as the government licence for the ground specified that burial was limited to Britons, for a non-British, non-Catholic to have a funeral, relatives had to have the nationality of the deceased changed.

While this advance was made, Anglicans and Presbyterians were taking the first steps into one of the fields in which the British would become strong in Argentina: education. There have been always many English-language schools in the country and their history starts in the early years after independence. James Thomson's earliest efforts to start British education in Buenos Aires were followed by those of a Mrs Margaret Hyne, who established the first British school for girls at her home in Buenos Aires in 1823. The school was attended by about seventy children. The end-of-term tea parties for children and parents, which became dances after the children had been sent home, were a regular attraction in Buenos Aires. The school closed in 1842, when Mrs Hyne returned to Britain.

Parish wrote to Canning in May 1824 advising of 'the very great want felt here of the presence of an English clergyman', largely because 'the number of British subjects in Buenos Aires and its neighbourhood is estimated at two to three thousand persons', [Buenos Aires had a population of 50,000.][1] With few exceptions they were 'all Protestants, and as such have no place of public worship to resort to in this country. Their marriages, christenings and burials are performed in the most irregular manner. It is only very recently they have been allowed any Christian burial, and that the Government has been induced to permit Protestants to bury their own dead in a small enclosure which has been purchased by a subscription for that purpose.' Canning replied in August that the proposed Treaty would cover such religious requirements.

After Thomson the next church ministers to arrive in Buenos Aires were North American Presbyterians; but it was the Reverend John Armstrong who, following his arrival in Buenos Aires in August 1825, gave Britons in the town their first regular services. Armstrong had been bound for La Guayra, in Venezuela, after some time in Honduras; but he was ordered by the Society for the

Promotion of Christian Knowledge to go to Buenos Aires, Chile and Peru, then to Colombia – eventually to go from there to La Guayra – on an expedition of religious exploration. The Buenos Aires church register records that he officiated at the first marriage on 27 August and at a first baptism on 30 August 1825, while the first burial in the British cemetery at which Armstrong officiated is dated 23 October.

Armstrong became the first minister of a Protestant church officially established in Buenos Aires. He gathered the community with the assistance of Consul Parish and rented a chapel, which had been built by the Jesuits in about 1750. The new British Episcopal Church of Saint John the Baptist – the Anglican church in Buenos Aires – was consecrated on 25 September 1825.

The following month Parish reported to Canning that

> by the 12th article of the Treaty with this country, I have the satisfaction of acquainting you that on the 25th. ult. the British Protestant service was publicly performed in Buenos Ayres before a numerous congregation of His Majesty's subjects. The opening of a Protestant Church for the first time in South America naturally excites much attention and observation on the part of the natives of the country, and it is of proportionate importance that our service should be respectably performed.

The next step would be the construction of their own church.

The British Packet and Argentine News of 26 August 1826 carried a 'Notice to British subjects' which said that a consular chaplaincy act had been passed in July 1825 'enabling His Majesty to grant assistance towards the building of Churches and Hospitals, the maintenance of Burial Grounds in Foreign Ports and the furtherance of charitable objects where any considerable number of His Majesty's subjects may be residing ...' Readers were invited to a meeting to be presided by Parish.

The consular chaplaincy act was, apart from a generous gesture by the British Government to make life more comfortable for expatriates, a master stroke for the support of trade expansion. The encouragement of building of community institutions such as churches gave British expatriates a greater sense of security and of protection by their own government and hence a reason to remain in distant ports where Britain had growing trade interests. Canning had decided that the best way to avoid the trauma of the loss of colonies – such as the loss of the North American territories – was to strengthen Britain's presence in the independent countries.

The British church in Buenos Aires was recognized as a consular chaplaincy and the British government defrayed half of the chaplain's expenses; the remainder was raised by subscription, at first, and later by the rental of the sittings in the chapel.[2]

A notice in the *British Packet and Argentine News* on 30 September 1826, signed by the Reverend John Armstrong as chairman of a committee of fourteen British residents, said that it had been decided to investigate the state of education in the community. Members of the committee visited private homes to interview parents and then drew up a register of all children between the ages of three and twelve years. As a result of the committee's report, recommending the earliest possible creation of more schools for English-speaking children, a kindergarten school for children under the age of seven years was started by a Mrs María Thompson, with the assistance of merchants and landowners John Parish Robertson and Thomas Fair.

A school for boys was opened that same year by Henry Thomas Bradish. This was the Foreign Commercial Academy and achieved the status of a highly regarded educational establishment for all foreigners in the town. Many boys of the British community, including Admiral Brown's sons – among other locally prominent names – went to this school. Bradish was a retired English army officer with a love for parades – he was also described as a little insane by contemporary writers; but this may have been no more than a small quota of eccentricity. One of Bradish's seasonal problems was the theft of fruit from the school's orchard and he naturally suspected his students. He therefore combined his – and their – fondness for military drill and his desire for discipline and organized the boys into uniformed, rifle-carrying patrols, and made them march up and down the uneven lanes between the trees, guarding the ripening fruit.

One of the features of those and later years was the roving master, who played an important part in the lives of English and Scots living outside Buenos Aires. There are many references to this brand of teacher and they are often shown as being highly educated, in certain cases the products of Edinburgh, Oxford,

Cambridge and London universities. This kind of educator lived on farms or at farming colonies, always as a guest of the parents of the children to be taught. He shared the table, the fireside and the best horses in the stable; but apparently he never stayed for long. Occasionally these teachers settled and started schools of their own. This was common among the Irish, whose teachers started several schools in provincial cities.

Towards the end of 1828 the Scots in the congregation decided that they did not want to continue sharing the English church. They found a minister, Dr William Brown, then at a Scottish colony in the town of Monte Grande, and asked him to head their own church in 1829.[3] This might have gone smoothly if the Scots had not publicized the rift and also sought the subsidy due to a consular chaplaincy. This was resisted by Parish who immediately found himself in conflict with Dr Brown. In Parish's view the British community was divided into the traders and store owners of Buenos Aires, an altogether better class of people, and the Scottish labourers of Monte Grande, a group considerably lower in the social scale. Dr Brown was angry at Parish's refusal and threatened to cause a minor scandal by appealing to the British Parliament for a consular subsidy. In addition to his desire to keep the community under one church roof, Parish feared, quite reasonably, that the Buenos Aires Government would not tolerate more than one British church in the town. The Scots fought their case and were finally given permission to have their own church, though only after Parish's successor, Henry Stephen Fox, applied for such authorization from the local authorities a few years later.[4]

Plans for the construction of a church for the Episcopalians of St John the Baptist started to materialize in 1829. One local builder, Thomas Whitfield, offered to erect such a building for 60,000 pesos (the exchange rate was roughly one peso to a shilling). The government authorized the transfer of a piece of land, which had been the burial ground of the Merced Convent, at 25 de Mayo street number 270, in reply to a request for such a plot, made by the British consul.

Meanwhile, space problems at the Protestant Burial Ground were becoming severe and in March 1829 permission to extend the cemetery was sought. The British Government granted a subsidy to help finance the expansion; but when the consul, Charles Griffiths, applied for a permit to remove the cemetery, this was refused. The plans for construction of the church had caused resentment among Catholics and the government was not prepared to start a second controversy over the expansion of the burial ground approximately one and a half miles from the church. So the cemetery committee decided to buy a plot outside the town. However, because of fear of incurring public criticism for assisting the foreign heathens, it was not easy to find an owner who was prepared to sell his land to the British community, the difficulty being that it was to be used as a cemetery.

Nevertheless, progress was being made in another area. Several mixed schools were opened in 1829. There was a Buenos Aires Foreign School Society which took girls and boys and introduced a grant system to cover education fees for a number of children. Gilbert Ramsay, who had worked at the Parish Robertsons' Scottish colony in Monte Grande as a teacher, started his own college, later the Buenos Aires Boys' School.

The cost of the new Episcopalian Church building, designed on neo-classical lines, the first of its kind in Buenos Aires, reached £3832. The plans were by Richard Adams, an architect who travelled to Buenos Aires to work in the Scottish colony at Monte Grande. The inauguration service was held in the church on Sunday, 6 March 1831, followed by noisy and self-congratulatory celebration.

> The early years of St John's were passed amongst much tribulation to the inhabitants of Buenos Aires. Indeed even when it was still under construction, there were not wanting superstitious and bigoted people who held the opinion that a long-continued drought and its consequences were sent as chastisement on the Government for having granted a site for the Protestant Church, which site had formerly been part of the burying ground of the Merced Church and Convent ... Shortly after the Church was built, the long years of the tyranny of the celebrated Rosas began and although the British residents were not directly affected or molested, the work of the Church was necessarily limited and could not extend beyond the city.[5]

There were two reasons for the limitation of the church's activity to the town's borders. One was a government ruling which forbade the recruitment of native-born people into an alien religion. The other was that even without such a ruling travel or work outside of the town were extremely dangerous, the land being the domain of bands of troops and militia supporting rival political groups; no lone wanderer was safe from attack.

According to *The British Packet and Argentine News* of 30 April 1831, 'the first marriage solemnized at the chapel' took place 'on 27th inst., at the British Episcopal Chapel, by the Rev. J. Armstrong, Captain J. Presley, late of the Argentine schooner brig *Fama*, to Cecilia, daughter of Mr John Tweedie, of this city. All the British merchant vessels in this port hoisted their colours and signal flags in compliment to the happy pair and the brig *Elizabeth* fired a salute'. Tweedie, a gardener and botanist, was a Scot and a member of the Monte Grande Scots' colony.

Life in the community was centered on the church and Britons tried to avoid involvement in local politics by concentrating on their business activities and showing interest in the fate of fellow-Britons in the city. Charles Darwin, the naturalist, wrote in his diary that he was reminded of England when he took tea with Mr and Mrs Lumb, a British family name that would be prominent in Buenos Aires business during the next forty years. Darwin found a number of well-stocked English stores in town and in them he was supplied with clothes, riding gear, toiletry, tobacco, books and every personal item he required. As for life in the British community, the writings of Darwin and other travellers leave a dominant impression of the British as living in an atmosphere of class-conscious conviviality. The rich were under the moral obligation to make money, take care of the poor or less fortunate expatriates, and ignore inasmuch as possible the life and politics of the native population.

However, this atmosphere of insular peace was upset by one of the community's greatest scandals. It all started when William Torrey, a North American Presbyterian minister who had arrived in Buenos Aires in 1827, performed the marriage ceremony to wed Samuel Fischer Lafone, a successful Anglican businessman, to María Quevedo y Alsina, a Roman Catholic, in 1832. Lafone was born in Liverpool, in 1805, and had reached Argentina in 1825.

Before 1832 marriages between Protestants and Roman

Catholics had taken place, with or without the required Papal dispensation, according to the strength of the convictions of the families involved. Marriages were generally held under the theoretical protection of the 1825 Treaty between Great Britain and Argentina, by which it was established that there would be tolerance for denominations other than the official Roman Catholic religion. When those involved were not concerned with the religious formalities, these were overcome rapidly in private arrangements with the curate. But the dispute within the Quevedo family, of comfortable and established merchant stock, over María's marriage, brought the practice into the open because her father disapproved of a wedding with a 'heathen'.

In June 1832 Bishop Mariano Medrano publicly repudiated the Lafone–Quevedo marriage. He accused Protestants of being bigamists who left their families in Europe to go to Buenos Aires, and once in South America inveigling the local maids. It was obvious that the Bishop had been informed of María's marriage by her father and even if the repudiation sounded exaggerated, it was accepted by a prejudiced society in a small city. Lafone, when approached after the wedding and as publicity grew, flatly refused to be converted in order to marry and, as a staunch member of the Church of England, saw no need for dispensation. On 2 July a criminal court judge passed sentence on María Quevedo and her mother, Manuela Alsina, and ordered them to spend a month in a convent, the *Casa Pública de Ejercicios*, for their transgression.

The sentence appeared to be particularly severe for the newlyweds; but punishment did not stop there. Lafone and Torrey were each fined one thousand pesos. The witnesses to the marriage, mother-in-law Manuela Alsina, North American merchant Charles Ridgely Horne, the bridegroom's brother, Alexander Lafone, and a French journalist, Alfred Bellemare, were each fined five hundred pesos. Furthermore, Lafone, his brother, Bellemare, Horne and Torrey were ordered to leave the country, under a ruling dated 20 August. The five men were kept under arrest until such time as their expulsion could take place. The court's decision had annulled the marriage and ruled that the groom must renegue his religion if he wanted to stay in the country and marry the woman.

The British and North American communities were beside themselves with indignation and the British consul, Henry Stephen Fox, was asked to intervene. He approached the Buenos Aires Government to ask for leniency; but apparently gave up all efforts to mediate when the British residents insisted that their demands be given special treatment. Fox, angered at being given orders, rejected the residents' proposal that they 'are to be considered a separate community exempt as British subjects from the operation of the law of the land and enjoying rights distinct from those of the citizens of the Republic'. Fox told the residents that they had a good deal under the Treaty of Friendship and in many cases the local government went out of its way to be accommodating. But Fox must have used his office privately on the appeal for mediation by Lafone and Horne. Lafone was a well-known and liked businessman and Horne was a successful adventurer much admired in the town. Dispensation to marry, without conversion, was applied for and, in the meantime, Bellemare also pressed the French representative, Washington de Mendeville, to help put an end to his predicament. The Governor, Juan Manuel de Rosas, issued a pardon and ordered the freedom of all concerned on 18 September 1832. The Church's dispensation took some time to come, so much so that the couple sought and won the support of the government in their demand for speed from the Church.

Finally, on 17 June 1833, the Reverend John Armstrong was able to report that, 'After having been first married according to the rites of this country [the couple] were married at the British Episcopal Church according to the rites of the United Church of England and Ireland.'[6] The witnesses were Manuela Alsina de Quevedo and Charles Ridgely Horne,[7] Alexander Lafone having returned to Montevideo and Bellemare also having travelled away from Buenos Aires.[8]

While the Lafone–Quevedo marriage occupied public attention the Protestant Burial Ground committee managed to secure the purchase of a suburban *quinta* or residence with a large plot of land, owned by a Manuel de la Serna, west of the town, for which £131 were paid. The government authorized use of the land as a cemetery early in 1833, nearly two years after the inauguration of St John's Church, and burials at the Socorro cemetery stopped.[9] The first man to be buried in the new grounds on 31 January 1833, was William Hudson Priestley, a British merchant and landowner who had been killed by a stray bullet, fired by members of one of several political gangs. The cemetery committee was given legal status in that year under the name of British Cemetery Corporation. Apart from Anglicans and Presbyterians, North American Methodists and German Evangelists were subscribed to the cemetery. Architect Richard Adams was in charge of the project of the perimeter wall, the layout of internal paths and the chapel; the foundation stone of the latter was laid in November 1833.

During that decade what is now the oldest English-language school in Buenos Aires, St Andrew's Scots School, was started. It began as part of the Scots' church in 1838. Courses for boys opened in April of that year and for girls in September. St Andrew's school was among the most affected by a ruling which barred Catholics from attending schools where their religion was not taught. The number of native-born Catholic pupils whose parents wanted them to have an English education at the school was high; hence the damage caused by the discriminatory legislation was considerable.[10]

While the 1820s were the years of consolidation of the community churches and institutions, the next decade brought the impulse to spread the gospel further afield. The pioneering Reverend Armstrong, though his work was concentrated in Buenos Aires, encouraged missionary work in the rest of the country thoughout his stay in the River Plate.[11] Armstrong worked on this right through the decade until *The British Packet and Argentine News* of 30 April 1842 reported that

> The Reverend Armstrong preached his farewell sermon at the British Episcopal Church on the morning of Sunday, 17th inst. And on Sunday morning last the Reverend Barton Lodge delivered his first discourse at the same church. The congregation on both occasions was very numerous. The Reverend John Armstrong has quitted Buenos Aires for ever. He embarked on Monday last, on board H.M. packet *Cockatrice* which sailed the same evening.

The first to have any measure of success in religious work in the

Patagonian region was Captain Robert Fitzroy, of HMS *Beagle* – which would later sail with Charles Darwin aboard – in 1830. During his passage round Cape Horn that year, he took aboard four natives, whom he transported to Britain in order to see how they adapted to European education and surroundings and in the firm belief that Western civilization and religious instruction would be good for them. He named them York Minster, Boat Memory, James Button and, a woman, Fueguia Basket. Boat Memory died of smallpox; but the other three were put in the care of William Wilson, a preacher in Walthamstow. York Minster was put through the ceremony of marriage to Fueguia Basket. The experience was to last a little over a year. The *Beagle* sailed out of Plymouth on 7 December 1831, with the three Patagonian natives, the Reverend Richard Matthews – who had asked to be taken on the journey so that he could learn about Patagonia – and Charles Robert Darwin, a young naturalist, as passengers aboard. Matthews and the three Patagonians were put ashore in January 1833. The natives went back to their people and told them about their experiences, but only Jemmy Button kept up a pretence of maintaining some European habits, and before long even he returned to his former style of life. Fitzroy took the ship into shelter, to explore the area and to keep watch on Matthews who was in his first weeks ashore. The captain's wariness helped to save the young missionary from physical injury and abuse.

On 6 February 1833, the crew of the *Beagle* saw Matthews, almost naked, run to the shore followed by a crowd of screaming, laughing natives who had stolen all of his clothes and property. This first effort to convert the Yaganes tribe thus ended in failure.

One of the most famous of all Protestant missionaries in Argentina was Allen Francis Gardiner, sometimes referred to as Captain Gardiner – and indeed his fame probably derives more from his persistence in his travels than from his success in his evangelization work. Born in June 1794, in Berkshire, he was educated at the Portsmouth Naval College. He left the navy for missionary work following the death of his first wife in 1834. He then decided 'to become a pioneer in the Christian mission of converting abandoned souls', according to his own letters. He went to Natal, as governor of the South African province, and later went to Australia and New Guinea. Neither area had the people or the atmosphere he sought, so he returned to Britain where, in 1836, he married a parson's daughter. In 1838 he set out for Buenos Aires.

Gardiner went to Patagonia, but failed to get permission from Patagonian chiefs Corvalán and Wykepang to settle there. He moved to Valparaiso, in Chile, and from there, in November 1841, to the Falkland Islands, where he built his own home. Shortly afterwards he moved on to Tierra del Fuego, again failing to reach agreement with the native Indian chiefs on the establishment of a mission with their co-operation. He crossed to the Bay of San Gregorio and there, at last, found a nomad chief, Wissale, who would allow him to preach in the region. With this assurance, Gardiner returned to England and put his case to the Church Missionary Society, which rejected his plans. This rebuff had only a limited effect. In Brighton, on 4 July 1844, he founded the Patagonian Missionary Society. In December Gardiner boarded the *Rosalie* and sailed to Patagonia, accompanied by one assistant. They were back in the Bay of San Gregorio on 2 February. Their first look at the hostile and barren coast was discouraging and Gardiner preferred to wait aboard until he sighted Wissale. Captain Boyes, the ship's master, waited with them for a month, but eventually had to put them ashore, leaving them with a barrel of salted beef. They wandered about the country in search of Chief Wissale and found him in mid-March: thin and weary, he and his tribe were half-starved from their continued failure to find food. Wissale was hostile and demanded provisions; Gardiner had none to offer.

Gardiner and his assistant waited for a ship; when the *Commodore*, bound for Valparaiso, entered the bay, they asked for help from the captain and crew. They secured some food for Wissale and also a warning from the captain to the chief to treat the Englishmen well. After the *Commodore* had sailed, Wissale became belligerent again in his demand for food. When a Chilean merchant ship sailed by Gardiner again secured some privisions for the natives, but this time he decided that to stay there would be a useless risk. He returned to Britain.

He was in Montevideo, aboard the *Plata*, in November 1845.

He tried to go up the Paraná river in search of a mission site north of Buenos Aires; but the local government had closed the river in a dispute with Paraguay and with Uruguay, so the missionary was refused permission to travel north. Gardiner took the long way round. He sailed around the Cape to Valparaiso, where he arrived at the end of January 1846. From there he sailed to Cobija and rode across the Atacama desert to Tarija and, in March, swam across the River Pilcomayo to enter the Mataco and Chiriguano tribal territories. His first sight of southern Bolivia gave him new ideas for a mission site and with his new plan he returned to England.

At this stage it might be easily assumed that Gardiner's religious wanderings were those of a lunatic. But his fervour and his courage to travel in far-off lands moved many people in Britain to admire and support him. And he fitted in with a strong current of opinion in Britain that held that the Church's teachings had to be taken to otherwise doomed peoples.

In Southampton, in February 1847, he sought greater support from the Church Missionary Society for a mission in Bolivia. It was not to be; a revolution in Bolivia prevented him from going to work there. Once again he decided to try Tierra del Fuego and talk to the Yagán indians. But they were hostile and he was forced to keep his distance from them from the day he arrived in April 1848. He returned to Britain in August, where financial difficulties forced him to send to auction what little property he owned. He was about to give up his quest when a friend came forward with a gift of one thousand pounds. So in September 1850 he started out again, in Patagonia, with six followers – Dr Richard Williams, John Maidment, Joseph Erwin, John Bryant, John Pearce and John Badcock – and settled, successfully at last, among the natives at Bahía Aguirre (Banner Cove), on Picton Island.[12]

On 22 October Samuel Lafone, then resident in Montevideo and the local representative of the Patagonian Missionary Society, ordered a ship to sail to Picton Island to seek news of the missionaries. The ship's crew found the bodies of Badcock, Pearce and Williams on a beach. Another ship found the bodies of Gardiner and Maidment, about one mile from the other three. The remaining two men were never found. The last entry in Gardiner's diary was dated 5 September: 'How great and wonderful and loving is my God's benevolence. He has maintained me four whole days in spite of no food, without feeling hunger or thirst.'

Gardiner's failures were balanced by the success of his society. A children's home and school was named after him, in Córdoba province, and the society itself – now the South American Missionary Society – is still in existence, based in Tunbridge Wells, England.

As the century progressed, and once the churches were firmly established, community efforts concentrated on starting schools – often consisting of no more than one mud and straw classroom and an outhouse – all over the country, wherever Britons gathered. In Buenos Aires what was for many years the city's best-known English school, the Buenos Aires English High School, opened in 1884. The founder was a Scot, Alexander Watson Hutton, who had arrived in Argentina two years before with the appointment of headmaster at St Andrew's Scots School. Watson Hutton's entry to British education in Argentina was revolutionary because he brought with him school customs and teaching methods used in Britain. Not least of these was the introduction of sport into the curriculum. This was to be one of the most important aspects of his own High School, which opened with a gymnasium and a tennis court. The school formed the *Alumni* soccer club, which dominated the association football championships for several years. It is still referred to as a model in Argentine soccer history.[13]

8

Governor Rosas and the British Doctors

General Juan Manuel de Rosas, Governor of Buenos Aires between 1829 and 1852, classed equally as national hero and dictatorial villain, is still a subject of controvesy in Argentina. Some, political conservatives and economic liberals, describe him as a near-feudal leader who concentrated too much power and became a despot. Another trend among historians argues that even the excesses were committed, at times, in the name of a better nation and not purely to safeguard personal pre-eminence. Those who champion him call him a father of Federalism in Argentina; his enemies claim that he weakened the provinces and, as a cattleman, he secured benefits for the big landowners alone.

Rosas, born in 1793, in Buenos Aires, was thirty-five when he began to gain influence in the politics of the River Plate. He was a cattle rancher who administered his property – inherited and expanded by his family, established in Buenos Aires for more than a century – with the toughest discipline. He was known to mete out severe physical punishment to his *gaucho* farmhands or *peons* when they fell out of favour; though he was also famed for generous rewards when business went well, a custom that won him a large and devoted workforce which became his own private army. His men were tough *gauchos* armed with knives and lances, who made cutting throats an art and rode in gangs that terrified all those they approached. With this force Rosas joined the opponents of the centralization of government in Buenos Aires and the presidential regime led by Rivadavia. On the resignation of Rivadavia, in 1827, Rosas announced his support for Colonel Dorrego, who promised to introduce measures towards a future federal administration of Argentina. Dorrego's plans were truncated when he was removed from office and executed by a rival officer, General Juan Lavalle, representing the Buenos Aires centralist forces gathered in the *Unitario* party. Dorrego's death precipitated a civil war that lasted almost one year. At the end of the fighting, Rosas, who had sworn to avenge Dorrego, was the victor and with him the *Federal* party. The Assembly of Representatives, sympathetic to Dorrego's cause, offered Rosas the government of Buenos Aires 'investing him under the existing circumstances and state of the country with such extraordinary powers as might be considered necessary for the public peace', the British minister wrote on 12 December 1828.[1]

Resident Britons' attitude towards Rosas was favourable, as the British generally favoured strong-arm rule as a guarantee of order. The British minister, Woodbine Parish, in his correspondence to the Foreign Office, complimented the new governor

> after his extraordinary and successful exertions for the reestablishment of the legitimate institutions of his country he has justly deserved such a mark of public gratitude ... I have the satisfaction of having been long and well acquainted personally with all the individuals who compose the new Government and I believe I may confidently say that they are all honest and well-disposed men ... [2]

William Hudson, the novelist and naturalist, said in his book *Far away and long ago* (1922), that

> the portrait, in colours, of the great man occupied the post of honour above the mantelpiece in our *sala* or drawing room – the picture of a man with fine clear-cut regular features, light reddish-brown hair and side-whiskers, and blue eyes; he was sometimes called 'Englishman' on account of his regular features and blond complexion. That picture of a stern handsome face, with flags and cannon and olive-branch – the arms of the republic – in its heavy gold frame, was one of the principal ornaments of the room, and my father was proud of it, since he was a great admirer of Rosas ... He was abhorred by many, perhaps by most; others were on his side ... and among these were most of the English residents of the country ...

Under stable government Buenos Aires started to pull itself out of the economic mess caused by the cost of war with Brazil and, after that, by the interruption of much normal business during one year in which gun battles in the streets of Buenos Aires and field battles outside the town were a recurring event. The British residents were able to return to trading with the return of security.

British consul Henry Stephen Fox reached an agreement with Rosas in July 1830 for payment of adequate compensation to British subjects for losses sustained during the war with Brazil. Claims totalled £21,000 for the seizure of the cargo of seven ships.

However, an undercurrent of lawlessness was still in evidence. Gangs of Rosas' supporters – who included some of the *gaucho* cavalry who had assisted him to reach power and the lower-class element of the town, most of which came from the slaughter houses south-west of Buenos Aires – were much in evidence. They took upon themselves *vigilante* duties that were welcomed by many people, because they offered some safety in the muddy ill-lit streets. But they were also a political body which brutally suppressed any opposition to the government, terrorizing the non-partisan population as well as the opposition.

The three-year term to which Rosas was appointed came to an end in 1832. He requested that the assembly invest him again with extraordinary powers, which were refused, although he was asked to stay in office for a further term with the Assembly assuming its full legislative powers. He refused, and resigned in December.

Rosas, in appearance a proud and courteous man, was out of office for twenty-eight months. During that time strife in the town grew again. Rosas' supporters were bent on the overthrow of the weak administration that had succeeded their chief in Buenos Aires, by then a town of 60,000 population. Bullets flew everywhere and the streets were dangerous to walk in while government troops, as much as the rival gangs, used the opportunity to loot stores and homes and rob any civilian who ventured out alone. The city's leaders, the political élite in the *Unitario* party did little to keep order. Charles Darwin, the naturalist, in Buenos Aires between September and November 1833, disliked the wealthy local male: 'He is a profligate sensualist who laughs at all religion; he is open to the grossest corruption; his want of principle is entire.'

Rosas himself had set out in that year on a campaign to rid Buenos Aires province of indians – not many by then, but gathered in their *tolderias* or villages of about one hundred natives each; but their men slaughtered white men's cattle in reprisal for the loss of the right to roam freely about the wide open land of the Pampas. The campaign was a massacre of the tribesmen and of their old people, while the young women were auctioned off by the officers for the pleasure of the soldiers. The children were enslaved. The campaign ended when Rosas had rid the province of indians as far south as the Colorado River, which encouraged white population to establish southern towns. The general himself ordered the transportation of prostitutes from the streets of Buenos Aires to Tandil, so that they could make a contribution towards increasing the population.

Rosas returned to Buenos Aires in October 1833 as his supporters staged a revolt to reinstate him. It was known as the 'Revolution of the Restorers' – and 'Restorer' of the law was the name Rosas would use for himself later. He was offered government and again he rejected it, because the terms were not right. Finally the Assembly of Representatives agreed to his conditions and in April 1835 he took office with full powers. Almost immediately Rosas set about consolidating his authority in the provinces outside Buenos Aires, by military action or alliances. He accepted the principle of Federalism; but those *caudillos* who opposed him he attacked. By an existing agreement Buenos Aires represented the rest of the country in all matters concerning foreign affairs. Within three years Rosas' stubborness in all his foreign contacts and his reluctance to submit to bullying – while he considered himself the leader of a full-fledged country up to any European standard – took him into conflict with France and the French blockaded Buenos Aires.[3] He liked the British and thought that their criticism of his methods was unfair and for this reason felt it was a personal rebuff when a Mr Dickson wrote to him from London to say that he could not be present as Buenos Aires representative at the Coronation of Queen Victoria – because Dickson was a British subject and therefore could not be accredited among foreign representatives even though he held the right credentials.[4]

Rosas blamed his enemies for such incidents. His suspicion of the existence of conspiracies against him – suspicions which were often well-founded – prompted a ruthless persecution of opponents. His weapon against his political enemies was the *Mazorca*, a semi-secret society of Rosas' supporters who employed thugs, known as *Mazorqueros*, to destroy the opposition. The reward for the gangs was permission to loot their victims' property. Hundreds of known opponents fled to Uruguay to escape torture and death by the thugs who attacked any man, woman or child who was not wearing the red emblem of the Federal party. The slogans of the gangs and of the party ranged from the simple *Viva Rosas* and *Long live the Restorer* to the more ambitious *Long live the holy confederation* (of Argentina) and the chilling *Death to the savage, disgusting Unitarians*. The slogans were printed on red ribbons, headbands, scarves, sashes and lapel badges. The excess reached such an extreme that Rosas had to order a cessation to the terror, decreeing the execution of *Mazorqueros* who acted without his orders.

By 1842 the terror declined. The British survived the horror because they were subjects of a nation Rosas respected and wanted to be respected by. As long as Britons were seen to be out of local politics they were not personally disturbed.

The Buenos Aires governor laid siege to Montevideo in 1843 to support General Manuel Oribe in his battle to impose a *Rosista* or federalist style of government in Uruguay, ruled by General Fructuoso Rivera, allied to the Unitarian party of Bueno Aires. The siege, followed by a deficient blockade which was to last nine years and become known as the *Guerra Grande*, brought a protest from Britian and France, prompted by Rosas' enemies in exile in Montevideo and by British merchants who were prevented from using the rivers Paraná and Uruguay. The closure of the rivers isolated Paraguay, a country which merchants claimed a right of access to. Paraguay declared war against Rosas; Britain and France demanded a settlement; but the Governor of Buenos Aires refused to reach an agreement and as a result Britain broke relations in July 1845. A combined British and French fleet blockaded Buenos Aires in the following year. The Anglo-French fleet captured Admiral William Brown's ships, which were trying to blockade Montevideo, took Colonia and the island of Martín García and eventually forced a passage up the River Paraná.

The resistance to Oribe, and to Rosas, in Montevideo, was

organized principally by foreign residents, who formed brigades according to their nationalities and bought guns and horses for use in battle. One of the more famous of those brigades was that led by the Italian Giuseppe Garibaldi. Peace was signed by British consul Henry Southern, with Foreign Minister Tomás Arána, in November 1849 in Buenos Aires.[5]

The blockade's biggest single action was at Obligado, on the River Paraná just north of Buenos Aires, on 20 November 1845, when shore batteries put up a day-long battle against the combined naval forces to stop them from going up the Paraná. Of this *The Times* of 21 January 1846 wrote: 'The allied squadrons, we hear, had destroyed the batteries erected by Rosas at the entrance of the river; and the large fleet of trading vessels assembled at Martín García were expecting immediate orders to proceed to their destinations ...' (133 merchantment were in Montevideo harbour). On 29 January *The Times* commented:

> No attack would in all probability have been directed against the forces or the positions of Rosas upon the right bank of the stream, if he had not endeavoured to convert the authority he undoubtedly exercises in Buenos Aires into a sovereign right over one of the principal rivers of the world, for the purpose of excluding foreigners from access to the interior of the country.

There was some local animosity against the British community in Buenos Aires during the Anglo-French blockade of the port of Buenos Aires; but the effects may be considered modest bearing in mind that it was Britain that was cutting revenue from Buenos Aires. A May 1846 decree authorized any person who captured a member of the British or French fleets to kill him. One such victim was a Mr Wardlaw, mate of the *Racer*, who was driven ashore by a storm while cruising near Ensenada, Buenos Aires. He was murdered 'with most refined cruelty, being cut, scored and mutilated in a most dreadful manner', said *The Times* of 17 August 1846. An instance of atrocities against foreigners by soldiers of General Oribe – Rosas' ally – had been given in *The Times* of 10 October 1846: 'An Italian, taken wounded at Tres Cruces [near Montevideo], by Don Jorge Carreras, was trailed at the heels of the latter's horse, his throat cut, his legs and hands severed, he was castrated and flayed, his heart torn out roasted and eaten.'

Robert Bruce, a Scot, had been contracted by the Rosas government to build small craft to beat the blockade. When the government was notified that they were ready, Bruce was told his boats would not be required because negotiations to end the blockade of Buenos Aires were expected to be successful. He protested that he had built the boats at great cost and under contract. Before he could fetch the papers from his boatyard in Retiro, a band of thugs had reached his house, wrecked the property, burned books and papers in the garden and stolen all they could carry. In a brief memoir, Bruce appeared to regret most that the thieves had stolen a box desk with brass clasps; he had kept his copy of his contract with the government in that desk. However, there was even worse according to *The Times* of 29 December 1846, which reported: 'The wholesale murder of Kidd's family, near Buenos Ayres, at the commencement of Mr Ouseley's negotiation [to end the closure of the rivers by Rosas] in July 1845, exceeds only in extent the atrocity of that which was perpetrated by Oribe's soldiers [in Uruguay].'

The British communities were seen to be supporting the warring regimes on both sides of the River Plate yet without openly accusing fellow-Britons on the opposite side of the river, with the exception of the tirades addressed at each other by the newspapers *British Packet and Argentine News* in Buenos Aires and *Britannia* in Montevideo. Apart from the *Packet*'s criticism of *Britannia*'s publishers, without naming them, and of some of the British leaders of the foreign brigades in Montevideo – as well as of the Uruguayan commanders, of course – attacks were not personalized. But *Britannia* spared no adjectives in its references to Thomas George Love, the *Packet*'s owner, for supporting Rosas. Behind this partisan writing must have been the knowledge that Britons were not really part of the local disputes and sooner or later the British on both sides of the River Plate would have to work and trade together again, independently of local events.

British officers trying to open the River Paraná to British and French trade found themselves discovering a new world. Several wrote entertaining accounts of their travels and impressions. One was Lieutenant Lachlan Bellingham Mackinnon, a Southampton officer and heir to a military and writing career, who gave an excellent, even beautiful, description of the river he was then travelling on in his book *Steam warfare in the Paraná.* [6] His travels in Corrientes led him to the home of a Scot, Thomas Paul, whom he believed to have been a member of General Whitelocke's 1807 invading force. The old expatriate asked Mackinnon for two things: a piece of anthracite to show his servants that 'stone' was burned in Britain and a newspaper. Mackinnon gave the old man a copy of *The Times* of 10 November 1845 – it was then the end of February 1846 – and the piece of coal from the steamship's stock. Paul was given supper aboard the steamship, a craft seen there for the first time, an event which raised his social standing among the local population.

The situation of Britons in Buenos Aires and the provinces during the blockade was described in very favourable terms by a wealthy merchant and traveller, William MacCann, who went to Buenos Aires in search of new business and to inspect personally the state of the welfare of the British immigrants who, according to some reports reaching England, were often persecuted by the regime. MacCann was impressed by General Rosas and assured his English friends that there was no persecution. How much business came out of the journey he does not say; but he did leave a good account of his travels in a book, *Two thousand miles ride through the Argentine provinces* (1853). In a letter published by *The British Packet and Argentine News* on 12 June 1847, MacCann announced his intention to write a book and said that he had found that British subjects in Argentina were living a comfortable existence. The letter was translated and reproduced in *La Gaceta Mercantil*, on 15 June 1847, and later in the periodical *Archivo Americano* on 11 September, a sign that Rosas' press was pleased with such favour at a time when the Anglo-French blockade had already run almost half its course. But the letter was also published in *El Comercio del Plata*, of Montevideo, on 21 June, when it was severely criticized by exiles from Buenos Aires.

It is interesting to extract some details from MacCann's book to show what a wide tour could be made using British hospitality and that while Buenos Aires was being blockaded by the British and French, the tour could still be made in comfort. MacCann set out with his friend Joseph Mears on a beautiful 'morning in spring', which was autumn in Buenos Aires, and first called at the *estancia* of Mr Clark, in Quilmes, where he was given all the welcome of an English home. Most of Mr Clark's farmhands were Irish. MacCann later stopped at the home of Mr Bell, a Scot, probably one George Bell who later formed the company known as Jorge Bell e Hijos, a large general trading enterprise with powerful interests in wool exports; Bell's *Estancia Grande*, thirty-five miles south of the city of Buenos Aires, spanned a vast area which included what is now the town of Villa Elisa and a large suburban zone known as City Bell. From the Bell's he went to the Taylor's and then on to one Richard Newton's, near the River Samborombón, the southern limit of the River Plate. Newton is credited with being the first man in Argentina to fence his land, in 1844. MacCann then visited the brick cottage farmhouse of Mr Thwaites, five miles from Chascomús, as well as the homes of Irish immigrants living there – most of them from County Westmeath – and stayed at the house of prosperous, sixty-year-old Mr Murray. He travelled through Dolores and south of that town spent two days with a Scottish family named Methvin. In Tandil, his southernmost point on the journey, he stayed at the home of Mr Swasey, a North American. Tandil was then a sparsely populated town, continually harassed by native indians. Touring the 'frontier' with indian territory, MacCann visited the *estancia* of Dr Dick, a Scot, and the sheep farm of an Irishman named Handy.[7]

MacCann's book includes two letters, dated in February 1848, one from the Reverend William Brown, the Scottish minister, and the other from the Roman Catholic chaplain of the Irish community, Father Anthony D. Fahy. Both assured that British emigrants lived very well in Argentina. Brown said that no Briton had suffered discrimination when he sought employment, a majority had jobs and very little charity was required for the members of his congregation. Father Fahy, who had been in Buenos Aires for four years (against Brown's twenty years), said that he had never met a British subject who was not grateful to the local government for the protection that he had received. He said that there were 3500 Irish residents at the time of the start of the Anglo-French blockade.

The English traveller started on a second journey in November 1847 which took him north of Buenos Aires for two months – at an overall expense of sixty pounds. On one occasion MacCann spent a night at the home of Mr Alexander, who had six thousand acres of land; and in Gualeguay he visited the Brittain family, originally from Sheffield, who had two hundred square leagues of land, a good port on the River Uruguay, and one-quarter of a million head of cattle valued at fifty thousand pounds. However, at least half the stock had been allowed to wander and sometimes die, because of a long drought.

While the blockade was Buenos Aires' main daily news fare a domestic scandal rocked the Rosas regime. It was the love affair of Camila O'Gorman and the runaway priest Uladislao Gutierrez. The incident was used seventy years later by John Masefield for his narrative poem *Rosas* (1913).

Camila was a member of an established Irish Catholic family in Buenos Aires, closely linked with both the local merchant class and British trading houses in the town by long-standing acquaintance: Camila was a descendant of the physician Michael O'Gorman, founder of the Buenos Aires medical school and first hospital service at the end of the eighteenth century. A daguerreotype of her, taken by one of the two specialists in the town – the Britons James Helsby or Thomas Bennet – shows her in the autumn of 1847, just before her romance, as a fairly attractive eighteen-year-old. Into the Socorro parish where the O'Gormans lived went the nineteen-year-old Father Gutierrez, just ordained and given a good posting because he was the nephew of the governor of Tucumán province, who was a friend of Governor Rosas. Very soon the visits of Father Gutierrez to the home of the O'Gormans became more frequent than to the homes of other parishioners. The gossip started; but the influence of the families was borne in mind by any who might have spoken in anything but a whisper. That was until 11 December 1847. That night, Father Gutierrez advised his superiors that he was going to Quilmes, south of Buenos Aires, for a special service. Instead, he met the girl and together they rode north to San Fernando, fourteen miles north of Buenos Aires, and boarded a ketch that was sailing immediately for Goya, Corrientes, four days up the River Paraná. There they opened a small school, introducing themselves under assumed names.

'Wanted' posters went up all over the city of Buenos Aires – except in the neighbourhood of the O'Gorman home, to avoid further pain to Camila's parents. In Montevideo the news-sheets published by Rosas' enemies called for exemplary punishment and declared the incident an indicator of the decadence into which Buenos Aires had fallen under Rosas. The English-language *Britannia*, of Montevideo, exploited the British link to denounce persecution of the girl by Rosas. The lovers' peace lasted only until the middle of 1848. On 14 June they were recognized by an Irish priest, Father Michael Gannon Chitty, nephew of Elizabeth Chitty, Admiral William Brown's wife. Rosas ordered that the couple be transported in chains to Buenos Aires. Camila, pregnant, and Uladislao were executed outside the city, at Santos Lugares, on 18 August. The executions unleashed indignation even among those who had demanded severe punishment.

One Dr James William Eborall, personal physician to Rosas, was also the victim of one of the more brutal methods of the regime's disciplinarians. Dr Eborall – Irish father-in-law of Irishman Edward Mulhall who would leave his mark on Argentine history as the founder of the newspaper *The Standard* – had a large estate on the outskirts of Buenos Aires and enjoyed a profitable practice. Once when General Rosas' personal physician was not available, Eborall was called to assist the Governor, who suffered from a very painful urinary ailment.

After that first visit, Eborall remained among the group of doctors who called on Rosas. But the doctor, probably suspected of having contact with Rosas' opponents, fell out of grace with the Governor and his aides. One morning when Eborall rose and called for his servants he found that nobody came. He walked through his house and found it empty and eerily silent, without any of the usual morning bustle. He reached the front porch and the sight that met his eyes as he looked out into the garden must have frozen him. There he saw all his servants, on the ground, their throats cut and the lawn covered with blood. The regime had chosen this way to caution the doctor against having further contacts with members of the opposition.

Rosas had several British doctors who attended him at different times and all were to be found at the British Medical Dispensary, the organization that succeeded the 1827 British Friendly Society. *The British Packet and Argentine News* of 13 June 1840 had announced a meeting of friends of the British Medical Dispensary at which the British consul, Charles Griffiths, proposed the rental of a suitable building to be used as a hospital, and to 'solicit the countenance and support of HBM's Government'. In 1843 the Reverend Barton Lodge had taken the organization of a medical service a little further when he had asked two subscribers to try to get separate rooms in local hospitals for sick British subjects or otherwise find the best way to protect the community's infirm. As a result of this inquiry the Dispensary had issued a circular in December 1844 which recommended that a hospital for British subjects should be created.

The most important physicians of British stock with a practice in Buenos Aires were Andrew Dick, James Lepper, John Oughan, John Sullivan, Morris Morrison, Alexander Brown – formerly chief surgeon to Admiral Brown – and John Mackenna. The one of most renown was Lepper, for his part in the British Dispensary, as the personal doctor of Rosas, and as one of the founders of the Argentine Academy of Medicine in 1822, when he had arrived in the country.[8] Lepper and Dick worked for a long time at the British hospital; and Lepper would also help Father Fahy at the infirmary which later became the Irish hospital.

Lepper was also frequently called to treat Rosas for his urinary ailment. This led to a close relationship and Lepper was to listen to many of Rosas' long, often angry monologues when he discussed his policies, his enemies and his friends. In recognition of such medical services and comforts, the Governor gave Lepper a house in the centre of the city of Buenos Aires. While a doctor, Lepper took a job at the British consulate, in an administrative capacity. The British minister, John Henry Mandeville, found the doctor an extremely useful colleague because of his links with the Governor. Mandeville had first met Rosas in May 1836 and with Vice-Consul Griffiths had managed to keep a generally friendly, though at times stormy, relationship. Mandeville was repeatedly caught flirting with Manuelita Rosas, the general's daughter, though both the flirtation and the discovery of such behaviour by others was said to be encouraged by Rosas to embarrass the diplomat. Lord Aberdeen, the Foreign Secretary, recalled Mandeville when this awkward relationship with Rosas was reported to be causing the British community great discomfort and when the imminence of the blockade of Buenos Aires required a new and stronger envoy.

The doctors who had organized the Dispensary had announced in the circular issued in 1844 that

> a profound debt of gratitude is owed to the managements of Argentine hospitals for the goodwill which they have shown in receiving our compatriots, but it cannot be thought equitable nor right of us, as Christians and British subjects, to continue to constitute a charge on the generosity of others. Under these circumstances an appeal has been made to all British subjects in Buenos Aires for their assistance in establishing, in conjunction with the Medical Dispensary, an infirmary or hospital with all the necessary equipment for successfully achieving this purpose.

The following June, the British hospital had opened at its own premises, a large rented house. It was the first effort by a foreign community in Buenos Aires to care for its own sick members.

Mrs Nesbit, 'a respectable widow who for many years has been a nurse at a dispensary in Newcastle', was employed as the hospital supervisor, according to a statement published in *The British Packet and Argentine News*. She occupied the drawing-room of the house as office and bedroom. The *patio* was partitioned through the middle. On one side was the hospital and on the other side lived the owner of the building, Mrs Wilson, and her family. The landlady told members of the British community that she was often disturbed by the groans and complaints of patients, but, out of a sense of charity, did not report her objection. The hospital had five rooms for male patients, with a maximum capacity of twenty people. In its first year the hospital admitted one hundred and twenty-seven patients (fifty-two of them seamen) and two hundred and thirty-one were visited at their homes by the medical attendants. In 1847 the hospital moved to a 'highly salubrious' section of town, near the 'Vauxhall Garden'. In the new premises about thirty patients could be accommodated at fees of ten pesos per week. Mrs Nesbit took on an assistant, a sailor named Wilkinson, who had first been her patient and later became her husband. Gastric fever and rheumatism were recurrent causes of death; but registers also showed cases of scurvy and senile decay, while some seventy per cent of the deaths were caused by alcoholism.

In 1848 anaesthesia was used for the first time. Dr Mackenna reported:

> The first successful use of ether in surgery in this city was effected in our hospital. In this way we were able to verify the extraordinary fact that the inhaling of this delicate vapour by mouth and nose produces a state of lack of sensitiveness in which the most severe surgical operations can be carried out without pain.

The hospital grew unhindered by the government, Rosas being aware that it was, after all, to the city's benefit to have such an institution – a view he did not have of either the Anglican Church or of the British-run stock exchange.

Rosas' downfall was near, although he remained a strong man to the last. The British minister in Buenos Aires, Henry Southern, wrote to Lord Palmerston on 10 January 1851:

> It is not wise to judge lightly the motives of a man who has discovered the means of governing one of the most turbulent and restless people in the world, and with such success that, though there is much cause for complaint, and not a little discontent, still the death of General Rosas would be considered by every man in the country as the direct misfortune. It certainly would be the signal of disorder and of intestine quarrels which could reduce the country to misery.

The end of Rosas' regime came with the defeat of his forces at the battle of Caseros, west of Buenos Aires, in February 1852. General Juan José de Urquiza, Rosas' most trusted officer and undisputed leader of the province of Entre Rios, led a rebel army, reinforced by Brazilian and Uruguayan troops, against the dictator – Brazil enthusiastically contributing to the Governor's defeat in the hope of a solution to the long dispute over relations with Uruguay and over use of the rivers Uruguay and Paraná.

Rosas returned to Buenos Aires disguised in an aide's *poncho* or cloak and rode straight to the British Legation where he asked the minister, Robert Gore, for refuge. The diplomat assisted him to reach a British ship in the River Plate which took Rosas to England. Soon after such charitable intervention Gore was to write to the Foreign Office to ask for leave of between six months and one year, or a posting elsewhere, in view of the animosity against him which he encountered in the streets or wherever he went.

Rosas reached England in April to a quite hostile reception. *The Times* of 26 April 1852 said:

> The tolerant hospitality of England has seldom been put to stronger proof than it is at this moment by the arrival in an Irish port, and probably ere long in the metropolis, of the late Dictator of Buenos Ayres. If further demonstration were needed that the soil of Britain is alike open to refugees of every clime, and is not even shut against the representatives of the most atrocious forms of despotism, imbued with bloodshed and expelled by just retribution, it would now be manifest to all the world that the liberty of refuge is absolute in a land that consents to receive General Rosas.

From landowner on the Pampas he was reduced to small holder. He bought Burgess Farm, near Southampton, and lived there for the next twenty-five years until his death. Buenos Aires received the news of his death on 17 March 1877, three days after he had expired. One month later, three days before Rosas' supporters were to hold a mass in his memory, the government forbade all public expressions in his favour.[9]

The fall of Rosas was followed by a decade of turmoil, as the British minister, Henry Southern, had feared; but it was also followed by a new attempt to give Argentina a constitutional system and political stability and introduce new ideas within a liberal economic framework.

The British became a more prosperous community as from 1854, a year in which donations totalling one thousand pounds – double those of the previous year – were collected, according to *The British Packet and Argentine News* of 14 July 1855. And the hospital moved again, to larger premises, in Mr Jacobs' house. The committee paid three thousand pounds for this new hospital, half of which was contributed by the British Government, while another one thousand pounds were raised for equipment with a bazaar held in the foyer of the Colón Theatre (later to become a world-famous opera house).

The building was first described as good because of 'its health, location and interesting view of the river'. But it soon turned out to be in poor structural condition and expensive to repair. The problems caused by the cost of upkeep were partly overcome by a charity performance by Spalding and Rodgers' 'Rodgers' Ocean Circus Company' in 1861. The following year attitudes and accommodation had changed, and the rule banning female in-patients was repealed. However, the hospital's report for 1864 said: 'It is found that there exists a very strong prejudice against going into a hospital, among the working class of our countrymen, but more particularly among those recently arrived from England, who generally spend all their means in seeking a cure outside the Hospital before applying for admission.' In contrast, there was some concern at the large number of Irish who did use the hospital facilities. 'Fully sixty per cent of the gratis patients were Irishmen, who have been admitted readily as any other British subjects; although our countrymen we regret to say that with very few exceptions the Irish residents in Buenos Ayres have declined to subscribe, alleging that they have to support the hospital managed by the Sisters of Mercy.'

The hospital was saved from near bankruptcy at one point by a bazaar at which £2800 were raised and of which *The Standard* wrote in June 1865: 'At two in the morning the bazaar terminated, amid the greatest good humour, and the assembly dispersed with pleasurable recollections of the fancy-fair, and almost regretful that years are likely to elapse ere we all meet again in such harmony and good fellowship. It has been quite a Carnival for our British and foreign public ...' There was yet another move to come for the hospital. *The Standard* announced in March 1887: 'Our English-speaking readers will learn with satisfaction that the new British Hospital in Calle Solís is ready for occupation.' It had the services of Dr Cecilia Grierson, a grand-daughter of one of the early Scottish settlers and one of the first women to graduate from the medical school of the University of Buenos Aires. The hospital stands on this same site today.

9

The Islands Issue

A pause must be made here to tell the long story of disputes over the Falklands (Malvinas) Islands, occupied by Britain and claimed by Argentina. The British in Argentina always had a direct interest in the islands as settlers and colonizers.[1]

British history attributes discovery of the Falkland (Malvinas) Islands to mariner John Davies, sailing in the *Desire* in 1592; Sir Richard Hawkins reported sailing off their northern shores in 1594. In 1598 Dutchman Sebald van Weerdt reported visiting them, but it was John Strong, in the English ship *Welfare*, who sighted, charted and named them Falklands, after the First Lord of the Admiralty, one century later. The French claimed to have known of their existence since long before, from mariners who sailed out of St Malo; hence they called them Les Isles Malouines, from which the Spanish took the name Malvinas.

In 1764 Louis Anton de Bougainville established a colony there with twenty-nine settlers, including five women and three children. He took possession of the islands in the name of the King of France and promptly left, to return in January 1765, when the colony numbered eighty people. Soon after, by an agreement between France and Spain, the colony was transferred to Spain.[2] At the same time, ignoring this deal, Captain John Byron, grandfather of the poet, took possession of the islands in the name of George III. An artist, T. Boutflower, travelling with Captain Byron, made several maps of the islands with illustrations of buildings at a south-eastern settlement named Port Egmont, and with heavily clothed people among penguins and other Antarctic fauna. The assumption from such illustrations is that there were a number of people living on the islands. The pictures of the islands give the impression of a Shetlands or Hebridean landscape.

Spain protested against the British claim, basing its protest on the fact that the mainland was its colony and therefore the off-shore islands were Spanish Crown property. While diplomatic exchanges between Britain and Spain went their bureaucratic way, nationals of several countries appear to have lived on the islands without much contact but in harmony. Spain, not being prepared for war over so little territory and not having the support of France in such a possible conflict, abandoned the dispute, though not the claim to sovereignty.

The argument between both countries was at the point of reaching a solution in June 1770 as the crowned heads of England and Spain agreed that the islands might be Spanish. But then Captain Juan Madariaga, ordered in the previous year to carry out the eviction of British settlers, attacked Port Egmont. When news of the Spanish raid and the threat of eviction reached Britain, anger in political circles forced the dying issue back into the open and settlement with Spain was rejected. However, because of the precarious situation of the colonists the *Endeavour* evacuated all Britons in May 1774. On departure they left a plaque reading: 'Be it known all nations that Falkland's Ysland with this fort are the sole right and property of his most Sacred Majesty George the Third, King of Great Britain.'[3] It was at this time that Dr Johnson, in one of his pamphlets, warned British politicians against heeding the hawkish element in their ranks who were calling for war with Spain for possession of the islands. War over so little was not worthwhile, the writer warned.

The islands returned to being the domain of sealers and a staging post for mariners. Spain appointed a succession of governors, most of whom spent much of their time in Buenos Aires. This occurred until the revolutionary movement took over the government of Buenos Aires in May 1810, when Spanish settlers on the islands were evacuated to Montevideo for fear of a raid by the rebels.

The Buenos Aires Government moved to take possession of the islands in 1820. The actual occupation was made by a North American, David Jewett, who had been awarded the rank of 'army colonel in the navy' in January 1820 and put in command of the ship *Heroina*. He arrived at the islands on 27 October and on 6 November took possession of them with the formality of a twenty-one-gun salute.[4]

On arrival at the archipelago, Jewett found fifty foreign ships, including ones from Liverpool, Leith, London, New York and Stonington. Jewett notified the masters of all vessels that he had been 'commissioned by the Supreme Government of the United Provinces of South America to take possession of the islands', a statement that met with general ridicule and rejection. Unable to cope with this situation he left the islands in April 1821.

Buenos Aires' politics and war with Brazil postponed official interest in the islands. However, their existence appeared to be remembered in June 1828 by a decree that announced the decision to appoint a 'political and military commander' as governor. The islands were a former Spanish colony and so the territory was considered automatically to be part of the newly independent territories. As the government could not find a civil servant to instal as governor, a man named Jorge Pacheco, a former officer in the Buenos Aires army who was owed a sum of money by the government, was offered the concession of part of the islands in lieu of the State's debt. Pacheco accepted and paid one of his own creditors, Luis Vernet, by offering him a partnership in the colonization of the area around Port Louis, in the north of the East Falkland.

Luis Vernet, said to have been born in Hamburg of French parents in 1791, had arrived in Buenos Aires in 1817. He agreed to go to the islands, hoping to make a fortune there in whale oil and seal-skins. Pacheco remained in Buenos Aires as his representative. Vernet's concession from the government which included appointment as governor, stipulated that he had to organize a settlement within three years. In 1829 Vernet's band included ten men from Buenos Aires, ten English or North American seamen, Vernet's brother and brother-in-law, eighteen blacks – former slaves – hired under contracts for ten years, twelve black women, seven Germans, eight families of unspecified nationality, four English families and six English bachelors.

The British consul in Buenos Aires, Woodbine Parish, and later his successors, Henry Fox and Philip Gore, warned the Buenos Aires authorities that Britain regarded appointment of Vernet, or of any authority on the islands, as an unfriendly act, because the United Kingdom had a claim to their possession.

At the time of their arrival on the islands, Vernet's settlers were seen to be no more than another group of colonists moving in. Although they had to do some building they found shelters and houses – mostly quite derelict, but which were nevertheless usable for immediate protection – which had been built in several parts of the islands and were used frequently by seal hunters and seamen.

In his capacity as commander of a section of the islands, Vernet was given the 'right' to demand duties from all foreign ships. When the British and North American seal hunters, who knew no law in the region, were shown a scrap of paper which established taxes on their catches, it was considered a laughing matter. The islands were a prosperous colony with up to 20,000 head of cattle, most of them roaming wild, and a population of seventy people in the north of the East Falkland, around Port Louis. The law of the islands had been, for years, that imposed by ships' masters who had registered births, as well as deaths, since before 1810. Births were generally registered as British. Relations between the existing settlers and the newcomers were cordial. There was enough space for all on the islands, where people were welcomed by the local inhabitants because they represented a new link with civilized lands far away. However, when Vernet went about establishing his authority, it jarred, even though he did do so peacefully. The British and other seamen who called at the islands scoffed at the idea of somebody other than themselves establishing a government in Port Louis. Vernet set a scale of duties on catches which some ships did pay; but more often masters promised to pay while they enjoyed Vernet's facilities and hospitality, including care for sick crew members; then disappeared without ever settling their debts. Vernet accused North Americans of killing thousands of seal, including pregnant females and young, until the animal was extinct in many parts of the archipelago.

To enforce conservation, without which he foresaw his own commercial destruction, Vernet hired Captain Matthew Brisbane, of the British schooner *Elbe*, to patrol the Falkland shores. He also published and distributed a warning to ship's masters about the introduction of the patrol. Brisbane, who knew that part of the South Atlantic well, was soon to become not merely a coastguard, but Vernet's partner as well. Brisbane's first action was to capture three North American schooners, which would cause Vernet serious trouble. The ships were the *Harriet* and *Breakwater*, of Stonington, Connecticut, and the *Superior*, of New York. The captain of the *Superior* reached agreement with Vernet and left one thousand skins as payment for the duty; but then lodged a complaint of piracy against Vernet with the United States consul in Buenos Aires. As regards the *Breakwater*, Vernet confiscated all the ship's documents and put a five-man guard aboard. But the ship's pilot and crew overpowered the guards at night and sailed straight to its home port in North America with the news of Vernet's outrage. The *Harriet* had less luck; but its captain was to become the direct cause of Vernet's troubles and, indirectly accelerated British occupation of the islands. Vernet reached agreement with the *Harriet's* captain that they should go to Buenos Aires where the dispute would be settled by the courts. The captain agreed to take Vernet and his family to Buenos Aires on the condition that the *Superior*, which belonged to the same owner as the *Harriet*, suffered no further delays when it called at the islands.

The captain, on arrival in Buenos Aires, accused Vernet before the United States consul, George W. Slacum, of piracy. The arrival of the *Harriet* in Buenos Aires was reported by *La Gaceta Mercantil* on 22 November 1831 as being evidence of Buenos Aires' authority over the islands. The escape of the *Breakwater*, as told in North America was reproduced by *The British Packet and Argentine News* on 3 December; but the report in this case expressed concern that the incident was far from concluded. Consul Slacum, a minor official looking for a career, was not averse to the prospects of a row and the ensuing publicity and lodged a protest with the Minister for Foreign Affairs, Tomás de Anchorena.

While this small legal and diplomatic issue began to grow in importance in Buenos Aires, the commander of the United States fleet in the South Atlantic at Rio de Janeiro received reports of the publications about the *Superior* and *Breakwater* and ordered Captain Silas Duncan, of the United States Navy ship *Lexington*, to sail to the River Plate, investigate the extent of the dispute and give protection to North American property in the area if necessary. Duncan decided that the issue demanded a visit to the islands, according to a letter to Slacum who transmitted the message in rather abrupt terms to the Foreign Affairs ministry. The ministry reminded the consul that he was a junior official and that his letter was an infringement of accepted codes of conduct.

On 8 February 1832, *La Gaceta Mercantil* reported that the *Lexington* was back in Buenos Aires, with a group of islanders held as hostages in reprisal for the *Harriet* incident. Duncan's log did not record this; but contemporary reports accused him of untempered destruction and unjustified imprisonment. When Duncan released them, his forced passengers reported his rampage. Public indignation only accentuated official frustration. Captain Duncan took refuge in the allegation that there was no reason for him to recognize the sovereignty of Buenos Aires over the islands while Britain had a claim to them: he justified the damage caused as merely being practised against intruders. He also questioned Vernet's moral authority, and there seems to have been some ground for this: Woodbine Parish had earlier reported Vernet's contacts with the British Legation to suggest that he would not mind a take-over of the islands as long as he could recover something of his original concession. The Buenos Aires authorities dismissed these arguments and confiscated the *Harriet*, later selling it by auction.

In an attempt to settle the quarrel, the State Department named Francis Baylies, a lawyer, to head the United States mission in Buenos Aires, in June 1832. Baylies' insistence that Vernet should be tried for piracy won him an invitation to leave the country and relations between the two countries were all but interrupted during the next eleven years.

Duncan's action started a long series of claims. Vernet demanded compensation, which he did not get. The Buenos Aires Government sought material reparation for its damaged pride. Britain lodged a complaint against the appointment of Vernet as governor while possession of the islands was disputed. Buenos

Aires insisted on the need for an apology from the United States and recognition of the act of aggression, neither of which they got. Argentine correspondence with the United States continued through fifty years until, in March 1886, the State Department would advise Argentina's representative in Washington that the case was to be discussed no further while the islands' possession was disputed with Britain.

Immediately after the *Lexington* raid, Buenos Aires appointed Sergeant José Francisco Mestivier as governor of the Falkland (Malvinas) Islands. He travelled there on a schooner commanded by José Maria Pinedo, the new coastguard. Mestivier's administration started on 10 October 1832, and almost from that day the settlers disobeyed his orders. The troops he had taken – criminals, tramps and deported felons – mutinied and killed him. Pinedo took over, at which point the British ship HMS *Clio* called at Port Egmont, on 20 December. Pinedo welcomed the *Clio*'s captain but at their first meeting, instead of offering the expected assistance in restoring order on the islands, the British officer advised his host that he was there to claim the islands for the British Crown. Pinedo returned to his ship and the next day the Argentine flag came down for the last time on the Falkland Islands. In its place the Union Jack was raised.

The evicted Argentine agent arrived in Buenos Aires on 15 January. With him were seven soldiers who were summarily executed for the murder of Governor Mestivier. Again public anger was aroused, but briefly; civil disorder, political upheaval and a renewed threat of civil war were more important. Thus, in a report dated in Buenos Aires on 28 March, *The Times* could inform its readers on 1 June that, 'little is now said of the Falkland Islands' affair, but all are anxiously waiting news from England on the subject. The Americans here are delighted that they have got out of this scrape, and that the odium now rests on John Bull'.

Manuel Moreno, the Argentine minister in London, filed the first formal protest against the British occupation in June 1833. His efforts were ignored as much by the British Government as by Buenos Aires. On the islands there was an attempted rebellion against British rule by a group of settlers led by Antonio Rivero on 26 August 1833; but this was rapidly crushed. Rivero and his small gang of followers were responsible for the murder of Vernet's partner, Matthew Brisbane, and of one of the islands' suppliers, W. Dickson. HMS *Challenger* arrived at the islands in January 1834 and put a party ashore to hunt the rebels. They were caught and Rivero was transported to Britain where he was put on trial.[5] The court ruled that it had no jurisdiction over the islands and Rivero was freed to return to Buenos Aires and to obscurity.

In January 1838 the British minister in Buenos Aires, Mandeville, wrote to the Foreign Secretary, Lord Palmerston on the opening of the new session of the House of Representatives:

> It [the inaugural speech by Rosas] then adverts to the worn out question of the Falkland Islands and declaims as usual upon the injustice of its occupation by Great Britain – without, I believe, receiving much sympathy or support from the public, except the very few persons who have speculated on an establishment there. It will make an annual paragraph in the message until the subject dies of exhaustion ...

In that same January Britain rejected a suggestion by representatives of Rosas that the British claim to sovereignty over the islands might be accepted in exchange for cancellation of the Baring loan. After that, diplomatic reclamation became subdued.

A town, mostly of Scottish settlers and seamen who brought their womenfolk from Britain or from Buenos Aires, grew on a bay south of Port Louis – on the north-eastern corner of East Falkland – eventually to become the capital, Port Stanley. Some of the settlers became landowners on the mainland, in southern Patagonia, and travelled unhindered between the two points. Whale oil, seal hides, cattle farming and fishing made Stanley a prosperous trading town as well as a useful port for refuelling and taking on provisions for shipping to the Pacific.

In 1851, the Falkland Islands Company was incorporated by royal charter. The idea behind the Company, a merchant group that would be concerned with the commercial exploitation of the colony as well as keeping order among the population and safeguarding the territory's security for the Crown, had some of the marks of the great trading organizations of the eighteenth century. And it remains the main commercial concern in the islands to the present time.[6]

10

The Irish

Jesuit records in Buenos Aires show that the first Irishman in Argentina was a priest, Thomas Fehily (or Field), of Limerick, who died in Asunción, Paraguay, in 1625. Between that date and the establishment of the Viceroyalty of the River Plate in 1776, many Irish went to Buenos Aires to open trading houses or to seek employment with merchants. Some were religious refugees who had opened commercial houses in Spain, then went to Buenos Aires to open branches; those were the wealthier emigrants. The others – the drifters, adventurers and colonists – arrived by the ways that the poor are forced to use. The list of prominent immigrants might start with Dr Michael O'Gorman, who founded the town's medical school in September 1779. There were some Irish in the town at that time, though the population census ordered by Viceroy Vertiz in 1778 did not mention them.[1] There were many Irish soldiers in the British invasions of 1806 and 1807, which left behind several hundred deserters.

Admiral William Brown is the hero of the Irish in Argentina, besides being one of Argentina's great naval officers. In the army, General John Thomond O'Brien is the most famous of British names among those who accompanied General San Martín. In the early days of San Martín's campaigns General O'Brien is mentioned as a good bullfighter. On a more serious note, it was O'Brien who made the first effort to organize Irish residents in Buenos Aires for the support of their own charities, issuing a circular to this effect dated in April 1829. O'Brien had taken over this role as organizer as a result of the death, in 1828, of a Dominican priest, Father Burke, who had started a loose association for mutual assistance within the community.

In the 1840s Irish immigration increased sharply because of the famine at home, and especially after 1843 when another of the community's most prominent figures started life in Buenos Aires, at the age of thirty-three. Father Anthony Fahy became a leader of his countrymen and encouraged emigration to Argentina during and after the 1845–7 famine. It was Fahy who, in a letter dated in November 1849, staunchly refuted an article in the *Dublin Review* which said that Irish settlers were being abused by Rosas during the Anglo-French blockade. The letter gave rise to enquiries and, eventually, to further emigration to Argentina.

A poem, *The Kilrane Boys*, written by a schoolmaster, tells the story of twelve men and a woman who left County Wexford for Buenos Aires in April 1844. Some of the names mentioned there are carried today by families long established in Argentina.[2] Family stories handed down said that later the men and women of Wexford in Buenos Aires province had a feud with those of Westmeath. In one place, the town of Salto Argentino, the parish priest held separate mass services each Sunday to avoid a fight. Throughout the century, the church services a family attended were not referred to by their times but by the county of origin of the worshippers attending. However, they did mix at the 'native' mass and ushers made sure that seating arrangements were such that rival families were kept apart.

The Irish community in Buenos Aires, and in the provinces, numbered several hundreds by the mid-1840s. *The British Packet and Argentine News* of 22 May 1847 published a long list of subscribers to the Irish Relief Committee in Dublin. The list is an original genealogical guide to trace the history of the Irish in Argentina. Another list of names, the subscribers to the Buenos Aires Irish hospital, which started in 1848, constitutes a second important source for Argentine–Irish history. During its first year, the hospital admitted 158 patients – 116 men, twenty-six women and sixteen children. Fahy presided at meetings of the hospital committee.

Father Fahy had many roles among the Irish. One of them was that of forceful matchmaker. He found the young lasses – who often came out from Ireland at a tender age and who might have been led into trouble or undesirable company – adequate lodgings with good, religious and Irish families as a first step. When the Irish lads came to town, from cattle-droving, agriculture or ditch digging – well paid while there were few fences – Fahy unlocked the girls. He organized dances at the homes of landladies or acceptable boarding houses and there decided the appropriate introductions and matches. In this activity Fahy had to work very hard and fast. He had to catch the men as they arrived in town at the end of each month, before they had a chance to spend all their wages on prostitutes and on getting drunk. The urgency of engagements was also determined by the men's need to get back to their jobs on the farms. The girls who could not be matched were found employment as maids or cooks or governesses.

Fahy's task of saving the Irish community's money was a difficult one. There was not much money. A novel, *You'll never go back* (1946), by Kathleen Nevin, states that an Irish cook employed by a family in Buenos Aires could earn £20 while a private teacher or nanny earned £35, a year, at about mid-century.

The cities did not have as strong an Irish presence as did the countryside and the villages. Irish immigrants were, in a great number of cases, farming folk and peasant stock. Many of the Irish lived in poverty, often with no more than an old blanket or heavy cloth for a front door to their wattle and mud *rancho.* The first hint of prosperity was demonstrated with an improvement in the door, from cloth to wood and later maybe a small window cut in the wood, then paint, etc. . . . After a good harvest, an improvement in status might be shown by adding a top storey to the *rancho*, built directly on the existing walls, with reinforced corners and beams, but with no eye for a straight line. This at times made the finished construction look like the crooked house in the rhyme, with ground-floor walls rising in one direction and the top-floor walls slanting in another.

Often in the 1850s and 1860s a Union Jack flew above these homes, more as a matter of safety than of allegiance. The habit had been introduced during the Rosas regime, because the dictator had once ordered his *gaucho* cavalry not to attack any place bearing that flag. There had been some confusion during the

Anglo-French blockade; but the habit returned and was kept for many years after Rosas had been overthrown.

Attacks by native indians in the south and west of Buenos Aires province were not an uncommon hazard for outlying homes. The Irish opted for burial of their stocks of alcoholic spirits and money savings except for a small quantity of each kept in the house. The result of this was that during attacks, and after the occupants of a *rancho* had fled or been killed, the indians went about digging up the floor of the house and the yard in search of the 'booty'.

In 1855 the Irish hospital moved to buildings bought and furnished to house a convent. The nuns to occupy it were the Sisters of Mercy, a group of whom arrived from Ireland in 1856. The nuns managed the hospital as well as a welfare service for the Irish in Argentina. In March 1873 a committee took over the management of the hospital from the nuns; but with such bad results that the hospital closed four years later.

Fahy died a victim of a yellow fever epidemic in 1871. *The Standard* of 21 February wrote: 'On Monday morning at three o'clock he rose from his chair, proceeded to shut the doors and windows and desired his servant-man "to go to bed as he felt better". The servant-man got up an hour later and found him dying; he expired about 4.30 a.m. in the 67th year of his age.' His executors were Michael Duggan and Thomas Saint George Armstrong. The latter, mentioned already, was a prominent member of the Irish community. He was their success story. He was one of the city's wealthiest merchants and remained a very powerful man all his life. He had been taken to the River Plate by his parents in 1817 and in Buenos Aires in 1829 he married into a wealthy Spanish family. He became a senior partner in an insurance business, owned a beef-salting plant, and was a shareholder in the Western Railway, which ran from Floresta to Luján. He owned prime land in Santa Fé, by which ran the Central Argentine Railway; was the largest single shareholder in the Buenos Aires Bank; held stock in the Buenos Aires–Ensenada railway and was among the founders of the stock exchange.

Duggan, a wool and hides broker, had convinced his Irish–Argentine customers to subscribe to a fund to start a newspaper for the community. The paper was *The Standard*, a four-page weekly. It was published by Michael George Mulhall until 1 May 1861, when, with his sheep-farmer brother, Edward Thomas Mulhall, they launched the daily, printed in English and French. Thus started the newspaper that for nearly one century was to be the doyen of the Argentine Press. It was the first newspaper in South America to instal Linotype machines and it enjoyed a full share of Argentina's growing prosperity. Edward Thomas Mulhall was born in Dublin in 1832 and married Eliza Sarah, daughter of Dr James Eborall, in 1856, when she was only fifteen. So young was the bride that she was sent back to school while her husband was occupied with his own work. Michael George Mulhall, also born in Dublin, in 1836, was later the author of *The English in South America* (1878).

The two brothers also published *The Handbook of the River Plate*, a guide to the area which appeared between 1861 and 1885 in annual editions, in English and Spanish. Although their newspaper was often disliked by fellow-Irish who condemned them for being too favourable towards the English – the paper's columns referred to 'our Gracious Queen' Victoria, and all British were 'English' – the Mulhall brothers were personalities in Buenos Aires. In 1869 a decree ordered two hundred copies of the daily *The Standard* for reference in government offices. President Sarmiento commissioned the Spanish edition of *The Handbook of the River Plate*, which spread their reputation throughout Spanish America. By 1875 the Mulhalls claimed that they were shipping abroad 20,000 copies of *The Weekly Standard*, published every Wednesday.

Edward died at his home in Buenos Aires in 1899 and Michael died the following year in Ireland.

In 1875 the Irish community got its own paper – dedicated more to Irish affairs than *The Standard*. This was *The Southern Cross*, a weekly started by Dean Patrick J. Dillon who, as Monsignor Dillon, became a provincial legislator after the 1880 elections. This 'Catholic newspaper in the English language' was preceded by another Irish paper, the weekly *Western Telegraph*, which was published for two years after 1870.

The 1870s again saw the influx of Irish immigrants, in contrast with the decision of the Sisters of Mercy to leave at the end of the decade. *The Standard* announced their departure in its 28 September 1879 issue, where it said that the reasons for such a decision included the sacking of the Jesuit College in February 1875, criticism of the nuns' work – both factors reflecting the attitudes in Argentina in a period of strong anti-clericalism as part of an imitation of European-style economic liberalism – and the failure of the Irish hospital. The nuns returned to Buenos Aires in the 1890s. In their absence a new Irish order, the Passionist Fathers, started work in Argentina in 1879.

Emigration from Ireland was actively encouraged and financed from Buenos Aires, both privately and by the government. During the next twenty years it was not uncommon to see news items such as this one in *The Times* of 11 August 1881: 'The Argentine government are anxious to arrange with the English government about Irish immigration on a large scale. Congress voted £40,000 to assist immigrant passages.' Or on 29 August: 'General Roca, the President of the Argentine Confederation, is preparing accommodation for a large number of Irish emigrant families to arrive here next month.'

A notice of the St Patrick Society in *The Standard* in May 1873 notified readers that 'arrangements are being made for the bringing out of Irish emigrants to the River Plate at reduced rates . . . a reduction of £3 per adult passenger has been offered and by return mail the Society hopes to be able to conclude arrangements on the basis of £10 per adult passenger.' The offer appeared to be reasonable by contemporary standards. A Royal Mail Lines advertisement in *The Times* on 22 February 1870 said a first-class fare to Buenos Aires and Montevideo cost £35, a second-class ticket was priced at £20 and a third-class fare cost £15.

Publication of the notice in *The Standard* was part of the St Patrick Society's efforts to increase Irish emigration to Argentina, one of the main reasons for the Society's existence at that time. Irish emigrants were good and cheap labour. Argentina owes much to the Irish. However, while there were the poor there were also those who thrived rapidly. British Consul Henry Cowper reported to the Foreign Office in the 1870s: 'The progress of Buenos Aires is mainly due to the industrious Irish sheep-farmers.' The Irish did indeed gain a large share of this business. Mulhall, in

Right: William Carr
resford, commander of the
)6 landing at Buenos Aires
ıoto: National Portrait
llery)

Below: General Whitelock's
pitulation at Buenos Aires in
y 1807 unleashed a wave of
ger in Britain at the loss of the
ver Plate colony. Cartoons
liculing him were frequent in
e months before his court
ırtial in 1808 (Photo:
ıtional Army Museum)

Have you taken the flint out

Now fellow if thou hast a spark of courage left take this

WINGING a SHY COCK.

3. *Above left:* The church of Santo Domingo painted by English artist Emeric Essex Vidal. One of the oldest churches of Buenos Aires, it patio was a popular meeting place. The watercolour by Vidal dates from 1820. The church shows the damage caused by shells fired by nat gunners against British troc who took refuge there in 18 The white spots on the remaining tower represent cannon shells, which are stil stuck there today (Photo: British Library)

4. *Above right:* General Juan Manuel de Rosas, dictator o Buenos Aires between 1829 1852 (Photo: National Histc Museum, Buenos Aires)

THE

British Packet,

AND

ARGENTINE NEWS.

PRO BONO PUBLICO.

☞ This Paper will be published every SATURDAY, with the exception of an occasional irregularity which may arise from the arrival of the British packets. The Subscription for three months, $8. All communications to be addressed to the Editors, and left at the Printing-Office, No. 17, Calle del Peru, where Subscriptions are received.

No. 1.) BUENOS AYRES, FRIDAY, AUGUST 4, 1826. (Vol. 1.

TO OUR READERS.

No Prospectus of this Paper having hitherto been printed, we think it proper to explain the views and expectations which have induced us to publish it.

We have calculated on receiving encouragement in the establishment of an English Newspaper from three classes of persons.

1.—From British residents in Buenos Ayres, and perhaps hereafter on the coasts of the Pacific.

2.—From Natives of Buenos Ayres, and foreigners acquainted with, or desirous of attaining our language.

3.—From persons in Great Britain connected with Buenos Ayres.

We have imagined that it may be acceptable to British residents in Buenos Ayres, by furnishing them with a general summary of English news, and that it may be read by natives of Buenos Ayres, and sought for by persons in England, for the intelligence it may contain relative to this country, its institutions and progress. To meet these objects, it will be divided under two heads;—the one dedicated to extracts from English papers as they may be received by the packets, or other opportunities;—the other, to events passing in the United Provinces, or neighbouring Republics, worthy of attention, especially such as the enactments of Congress,—the general progress of the country,—information which may be interesting to the Commercial Body, and to Emigrants,—fluctuations of the public Funds,—prices of the articles of consumption, &c. &c.

The summary of our news from Europe will seldom require comment from us; but that respecting this country being partly intended for persons at a distance, will lead to occasional remarks and observations, for the better elucidation of such articles as we may give under that head.

With respect to our political opinions, we shall say but little. The chief standard by which we estimate the merits or demerits of any political measures, is their propriety and policy, independently of systems or theories, which we feel no anxiety to defend or oppose, more than the experience of the past, or present circumstances recommend. Our main object is to convey political information, and to explain it, when necessary, to the best of our abilities. With this view we solicit, and shall receive with thanks, any communications from our friends tending to the promotion of our purpose; but party spirit, personality, and religious controversy, will be carefully excluded from our pages. We shall not omit opportunities for the introduction of occasional varieties which may be agreeable to some of our readers. The present size of our paper is not such as we could wish; but, should it meet with sufficient patronage, as soon as circumstances will allow, [illegible] sheet, and thereby to extend the range of our articles, and afford room for the insertion of English Advertisements.

GREAT BRITAIN.

IMPERIAL PARLIAMENT.

The Earl of Aberdeen presented a petition from a person in the county of Essex in favour of the Greeks. This was the first petition which had been presented on this subject of very universal interest. He did not know what were the intentions of His Majesty's Ministers respecting the Greek cause, and did not mean to inquire; but it would be a mistake to suppose that the people of this country did not feel a deep interest in it. If the public had hitherto [illegible]tained from petitioning on this subject, it was probably for the same reason which induced him and others to leave the question entirely in the hands of His Majesty's Government, whose sincerity and zeal there was no reason to doubt.

Mr. Hobhouse, on a subsequent petition, did not despair of the Greek cause, though Missolonghi had fallen. If Napoli di Romania defended itself with half the courage, it could hold out a long time. The French government had played an unfair part: they had encouraged the Turks against the Greeks. He had a list of French officers on half-pay now serving the Pacha of Egypt, and of Austrian vessels that regularly aided the Turks.

A Bill has been brought into the House of Commons for remedying the delays and inconveniencies of the Court of Chancery, the result of a report of the Commissioners appointed for this purpose.

The Corn Laws are to receive important modifications. The reason for these concessions to the demands of the manufacturing interests, may be found in the depression which the latter have recently suffered.

There is but one object of importance which principally occupies the public mind, and that is the dissolution of Parliament, which, at the departure of the packet, was expected to take place about the 1st of June.

Electioneering is likely to receive a vigorous impulse, from the peculiar situation of the Empire at the present time; more particularly on the part of those who are ever ready to attribute those partial evils which are inseparable from the fluctuations of a great commercial and manufacturing nation, to the operation of legislative enactments; and we have no doubt there will be considerable changes in the members of the lower House.

"Preparations for the general election are making in every part of the kingdom: and we never remember any occasion on which there were more spirit and activity in all the populous towns and boroughs. In Preston the business has begun merrily, and it is [illegible]

5. *Left: The British Packet an Argentine News* was Buenos Aires's first English-langua weekly (Photo: National Library, Buenos Aires)

Right: William Henry Hudson, writer naturalist. His memoirs ianticized the wide open country for British reader

Below: Front page of the first issue of *Herald,* later the *Buenos Aires Herald,* h hard facts and politics for the British eller and merchant

THE HERALD.

No. 1. BUENOS AYRES, FRIDAY, SEPTEMBER 15, 1876.

ebster, Prince & Kimball,
orth American Dentists.

enos Aires—347 Cangallo 347
(corner of the Mercado del Plata).

ontevideo—141 Camaras 141
(corner of Buenos Aires).

Gebbie & Dodds,
apers, Clothiers & Tailors,
53—Defensa—53.
ays Goods on hand suitable for the Camp.

John Grant,
ookseller and Stationer,
CANGALLO 69.
—
Single Copies of the *Herald* for Sale.

Coquet, Brito & Small,
American Dentists,

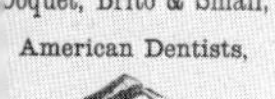

no connection with any other house in ity, and no partners except the under-

ecayed Teeth saved and made useful ings of Gold, Silver and other materials.

rtificial Teeth inserted by the latest d, so that the closest inspection cannot them from the natural ones, being per- useful in eating, talking, &c.

itrous Oxid Gas for extracting teeth ut pain, guaranteed to be chemically and acknowledged by all surgeons of e and America to be the safest anes- known.

are using Morison's Dental Engine for ating Decayed Teeth and Cleansing the and are constantly receiving every- new for the benefit of dentistry.

onsultation costs nothing.

Office open at all hours.

uet, Brito & Small,

M. S. Bagley & Co.,
Biscuit Manfacturers.

Our Biscuits embrace a great variety of styles and flavors, and bear favorable comparison with any imported. The Tins in which they are packed (our patent) are unequalled in any part of the world. Another, and perhaps the greatest advantage our Biscuits possess, is their being "perfectly fresh," whereas those imported have to undergo a long sea voyage, and other delays, which must be patent to all does not improve their flavor.

Our Biscuits are warranted to be free from all adulteration, and made from the best and purest materials. Our care in this respect has been rewarded by a continually increasing demand throughout the country, a decided and incontrovertible proof of their excellence.

Wherever our Biscuits have been exhibited they have been awarded the highest premiums. We are the only manufacturers of Fancy Biscuits in this country. Our list comprises 35 varities.

For children we recommend our justly celebrated **Hesperidina Biscuit.**

Ask your Grocer for

Bagley's Biscuits

Retailed in all first-class Groceries in the Argentine and Oriental Republics.

When you ask for **Hesperidina** be sure you get it, as some dealers sell the counterfeit for the sake of extra profit.

M. S. Bagley.

F. Schwarz y Hermano,
Ingenieros,

Constructores de Buques, Máquinas y Calderas.
Fundicion de Fierro y Bronce.
Molinos, Aserraderos, Motores á Vapor é Hidráulicos, Máquinas Agrícolas y de Picar Tabaco.
Especialidad en Norias y Máquinas de Sacar Agua.
San Luis 6 (cerca de la Casa Amarilla).

Amateur Photography.

Gentlemen who wish to have an interesting and at the same time instructive amusement, could not find a better way of passing the leisure hours of Spring and Summer than by learning Photography. It is easily learned, costs very little, and is an endless fund of Amusement.

At the **Photographic Warehouse, 165 Cangallo,** books of instruction and all the requisites can be had of the best quality and at moderate prices.

Solutions made up and verbal instructions given.

Frames.—The neatest and cheapest Frame of the day (just the thing for the times) is the Rustic Oxford in Walnut, to be had of all sizes and prices at the Warehouse. Rich Gilt Frames, oval and square, for portraits, from life-size downward.

Miscellaneous Articles.

To English Travellers.

Englishmen and others visiting Buenos Ayres will find every home comfort at the

Hotel de la Paix,

(corner of Cangallo and Reconquista),

which is the largest and best in this city. Charges are most moderate.

Wines Superb.

Table d'Hote on European style, with Room, Gas Lights and Attendance.

Hotel Provence,
(Established 1850),
33—Cangallo—33.

Fine suits of Rooms for Families. Cleanliness, Attendance, and Cuisine of first order.

Visitors of short stay in town, Board and Lodging at $50 per day.

Families and Regular Visitors at conventional rates.

Orders for Breakfasts, Dinners, Suppers, Lunches and Pic-Nics despatched al primer cartelo.

N.B.—Night Porter.

Joseph Perez & Co., Proprietors.

Agencia de la Singer Manufacturing Co.

Gran Rebaja de Precios.

Unicos Agentes para el Imperio de Brasil y Rio de la Plata para las

Legitimas Maquinas de Coser "SINGER,"

Milford y Lidgerwood.

Hilo, Seda, Agujas y demas útiles, hecho espresamente para las máquinas.

Depósito—CHACABUCO 65.

R. A. Osborne, Agente.

Kramer & Co.,
Relojeria y Joyeria por Mayor y Menor,
69—Florida—69.

We beg to invite the public to inspect our stock of Jewellery, at our newly-opened establishment Florida 69.

Newland Brothers,
American Dentists,
18—Suipacha—18
(Between Rivadavia and Piedad).

We have just received a large consignment of the newest Dental Goods from the United States, and are thus enabled to offer the latest inventions of the professions; amongst them may be mentioned

White's Prize Medal Engine

(the first introduced in this country), for excavating and cleaning the teeth; novelties both in Operative and Mechanical Dentistry; all of which we shall have much pleasure in exhibiting to those persons who may do us the honor to call.

We have practised dentistry for fifteen years in Philadelphia, Montevideo and this city, and can guarantee work of the highest order in every branch.

Painless extraction of Teeth by Nitrous Oxide Gas.

Offices always open.

James Pollard's

Carpentry, Cabinet, and Ship Joinery Workshops are now at

135—Piedad—135.

Conservatories and Greenhouses at the shortest notice.

All kinds of Office and Bank Fittings. Workmanship always guaranteed.

The Largest Stock of
Watches and Jewellery
in the Country.
Birthday Presents.
Christmas & New Year Presents.
Wedding Presents.
Fabre Bros. & Co.,
Victoria 109.

Steamboat Agency
52 Cangallo 54

For Rosario, Paraná, Santa Fé and intermediate ports, in combination with the Northern and Campana Railways.

Sundays for Rosario and intermediate ports, the Provenzor.

Tuesdays for Rosario, Santa Fé and intermediate ports, the Provenzor.

Thursdays for Rosario and intermediate ports, the Provenzor.

Saturdays for Rosario, Santa Fé and intermediate ports, the Capitan.

Books! Books!

Parsons on Marine Insurance.
Sheep Husbandry.
The Irish Rebellion.
Unity in Variety.
History of Ireland.
Grecian Stories.
Present Day Papers.
The Huguenot Family.
Wealth and Welfare.
Sacristan's Household.
The Highland Parish.
A Life for a Life.
The Resurrection.
The Starling.
Gathered Leaves.
Truth in Tales.
A Tale of Eternity.
Lord Gratham's Speeches.
Wind Wafted Seed.
Occupations of a Retired Life.
St. Julian's Wife.
Against Wind and Tide.
Seward's Travels.
A. Haggart's Humboldt.
Gutlaff's History of China.
De Profundis.
Histories of Greece, Russia, Turkey and Poland.
Human Sadness.
Elements of Agriculture.

Poetry.

Milton, Byron, Pope, Moore, Scott, Cowper, Longfellow, Thomson, Wordsworth.

Libreria Anglo-Argentina,
69 Cangallo.

Exchange Office.
Ramon Vinas & Co.,
87—San Martin—87,
(Opposite the Bolsa),

Buy and Sell National Bonds, Certificates of the Argentine and Hypothecary Banks, Bolivian Paper and Silver, Paper of the banks of Montevideo, Brazil, England, France and Italy.

National Bank Notes bought.

Short Ounces bought.

Bills on Montevideo granted.

CASARES.
ELINA:
IN SHEEP.
all classes of Insects in Sheep, Horses, way, and without any danger to the person
ND GIVES IT A GOOD COLOR.
of Calles Rivadavia and Rioja.
EDWARD CASEY, 160 Calle San Martin.

CHUBUT INTERMEDIATE SCHOOL
AUGUST 1908

8 and 9. The Welsh in Patagonia. Into the empty valley they brought their customs and language, colonizing much of northern Patagonia. The pictures show a meeting hall and a classroom in Gaiman, Chubut (Photos: Gaiman Regional Museum)

MEDI 10.1911.
YSGOL GANOLRADD
Y WLADFA.

ıe railways were the mark of ·itish expansion in Argentina, d their nationalization in 1948 ıs the mark of the end of British ıfluence

. *Above:* The Buenos Aires ıstoms House, built by a British chitect, and the terminal of the ıenos Aires to Ensenada railway ctured in 1889

. *Right:* A station on a closed anch of the once grand Central gentine Railway. Built in itish style, the station is now ed by squatters

FERRO-CARRIL DEL SUD

The land conquered: British engineers built the railways in Argentina to bring produce to the port of Buenos Aires. And Britons bought large sections of land alongside the tracks to secure cheaper movement to market

12. An early view of the Great Southern Railway with *carretas* crowding the loading park

13. The harvesters that fed the railways – an almost picture-postcard view of the Pampas

14. Some British customs never caught on: such as the English style of horse riding, which was held in contempt except in elegant society. The cartoon by the late Luis J. Medrano, titled *Riding*, reflects the rejection by the native of the riding school product

15. Britons were responsible for introducing most sports in Argentina, from cricket early in the nineteenth century to hockey early in the twentieth. Tennis arrived late in the nineteenth. This family snapshot shows a group of founding members of the Quilmes Lawn Tennis Club, started in 1893

the 1885 edition of *The Handbook of the River Plate*, said:

The Irish and Scotch sheep-farmers hold from twenty-two to twenty-four millions of sheep, for the most part in the province of Buenos Ayres; the clip of their flocks never falling below one hundred million lbs. of wool. They possess likewise 1,600 square leagues of land [eleven million acres] in Buenos Ayres, Santa Fé, Entre Rios and Córdoba, which, with the houses and fences, represent a value of ninety-three million dollars. The aggregate of pastoral wealth in the hands of Irish and Scotch (including as such the children born in the country) amounts to 162 million dollars (£33 million).

In the *Handbook* chapter on Buenos Aires province Mulhall said:

There are in the province fifty-eight million sheep, of which number it is estimated that thirty-two millions belong to Argentines, eighteen millions to Irish and Scotch and eight millions to other nationalities ... An ordinary Irish or Scotch sheep-farm of a square league counts 20,000 sheep, as our countrymen prefer to have the best lands, which bear heavier stocking than the rest.

Such land went for thirty-six shillings an acre. Of course, it was only the wealthy Irish and Scots who had all that; it was not so much when divided up in the community. In *The English in South America* Mulhall said that there were 25,000 in the Irish community in 1878, with an overall capital of about £2 million.

The Irish in Buenos Aires always made a mark on Argentine life and in the last part of the nineteenth century it was as town-founders. Venado Tuerto, an area of English-speaking and German farmers and where the polo club became a famous centre of the sport, was founded by Edward Casey, whose links with British and European banking groups were strong. Casey bought a piece of land seventy kilometres square in 1879 and started the town with a couple of buildings. The first settler was a Scot. Casey also founded the town of Pigüé in 1884, which he populated with French families. He was first-generation Argentine, born in 1847 of Irish parents. Near Venado Tuerto there is a town named Murphy, started by John Murphy, born in County Wexford. Another town, north-west of Venado Tuerto, is Cavanagh, the founder being Thomas Cavanagh – a family name that is well known in Argentina in polo and business – born in Arrecifes of

Irish parents, possibly one of *The Kilrane Boys.* There are towns called Dennehy, Duggan, Roberts, Santa Lucía – named after one Lucía Culligan – Gahan and Kenny, Diego Gaynor, Maguire and Ham.

There was a proliferation of Irish names both in Buenos Aires and outside the city in the 1880s. There were 2500 of them in Father Curran's parish, which included the towns of Navarro, Lobos, Guardia del Monte, Las Flores, Tapalqué and Saladillo, in Buenos Aires province. They were rough folk, obedient to their God, whom they shared with the 'natives' – although that was about all they would share. Most hands on an Irishman's farm were Irish, and 'native' help was only hired at shearing time. In San Pedro there were one thousand Irish; at Cármen de Areco there were also one thousand; seven hundred Irish sheep-farmers lived near San Antonio de Areco; there were one thousand at Capilla del Señor, three hundred at Pilar and five hundred at Chacabuco. A register of cattle brands compiled by one Estevan Parle, published in Liverpool in 1885, showed a majority of Irish names among the brand-owners.

Their names, even the famous, are too numerous to list. They went into every branch of industry, the arts, science, commerce and politics.[3] By the end of the century they had their own élite, a landowning minority that had married into Patrician society, which had left behind the insularity of the early immigrants. For all of them 'home' was a place of the mind, a distant memory, which they had left never to go back.

11

The Scottish Settlers

The history of the Scots community in Argentina begins in 1825 with the arrival aboard the *Symmetry* of a group of people who were to form a settlement at Monte Grande. Scottish colonists and merchants had been resident in Buenos Aires long before that and, in fact, before the Spanish rule had ended in 1810, but not as a community of any significance. The first record of an expression of Scottish nationalism in the River Plate was the celebration of St Andrew's Day with a dinner at Faunch's Hotel, on 30 November 1824, but more than a strictly Scots meeting it was an international event. It was presided over by John Miller – whose local fame derived from being the importer of the first Shorthorn bull to Argentina – and was the occasion on which the British Consul, Mr Parish, announced the signing of a Treaty of Friendship for the establishment of diplomatic relations between Britain and Buenos Aires. For this reason the banquet went down in history. The organization of such reunions was eventually to be the preserve of the St Andrew's Society.[1]

The creation of a Scottish farming settlement in Buenos Aires had been the idea of a Scot, Daniel Mackinlay, founding partner in the *estancia*, or ranch, *El Espartillar* with Thomas Fair. Mackinlay is believed to have been banished to Buenos Aires by his family in 1801 because of a forbidden marriage to a Caribbean beauty, Jamaican-born Ana Lindo. He became a man of wealth and among his many properties was a large house on the hill on the south edge of the city of Buenos Aires, which is today the national history museum. But before he could give shape to his idea of a Scottish colony he became ill, eventually to die in 1826, near bankrupt.[2]

The Scottish colony at Monte Grande was therefore started by John and William Parish Robertson who proposed its creation to the Buenos Aires Immigration Commission at the end of 1824. Mackinlay was to have been the partner of the Robertson brothers in their colonization venture; but the decline of his health and fortune precluded this. The brothers planned to bring to Buenos Aires no fewer than 200 Scottish families, with at least 600 people. The Robertsons asked the government to make available land which the immigrants could farm as tenants. The government agreed to the principle in March 1825; but the fiscal land was not made over. The Robertsons overcame this problem by buying 6475 hectares (four leagues) south of Buenos Aires. The land had had many owners; there is a deed dated in 1740 which gives it the name of farm or *chacra* of Monte Grande, because of a large peach orchard (the *monte*). Although the settlement's official name was *Colonia de Santa Catalina*, that being the name of the Robertsons' neighbouring farm, it became known as Monte Grande.[3]

The *Symmetry*, commanded by Captain Smith, sailed from Leith on 22 May 1825 and arrived at Buenos Aires on 8 August with the Scots aboard. They were the first group of European immigrants that had been carefully organized. Liberals such as Bernardino Rivadavia, the foreign affairs secretary and later President of Argentina, hoped it would be the vanguard of legions of hard-working northern Europeans who might help to build the country. The Treaty of Friendship, signed in 1825, was the most solid guarantee the immigrants had, because it assured them of certain civil rights in a country with an alien culture. At the time of the signing of the Treaty a government commission had been formed to promote immigration. Its business was to lure Europeans to Buenos Aires and it advertised in many cities that there was much work and profit to be gained. Foreigners were also assured that they could practise their religions, even though there was a widespread reluctance in Argentina to accept such a situation, and in some provinces intolerance was vehemently expressed.

Aboard the *Symmetry* were 220 passengers for the River Plate:

forty-three married couples, forty-two single men, fourteen single women and seventy-eight children. There was John Tweedie, aged fifty, previously a foreman at the Royal Botanical Gardens in Edinburgh; and physician William Wilson, aged twenty-five; there were two land surveyors, John Christian, aged thirty-nine, and James Cathcart, twenty-three; first-class carpenter William Speed, twenty-six; builder James Brown, twenty-five; architect Richard Adams, thirty-two; nine masons, a smith and four carpenter's apprentices. The Scottish papers did not notice their departure.[4]

The colonists' stories are told in a compilation of articles by James Dodds, originally published in the church magazine *Life and Work.* Copies of the book are collectors' items today, because many were destroyed soon after publication.[5] The reason for the destruction of the book was that many descendants of colonists who had prospered in Argentina did not like the sight of their forbears being recorded as maids, servants and peasants who had arrived in the River Plate in 1825.

The colony was a long-term investment, the idea being that colonization of land improved its quality for farming, and this would attract more colonists. A sufficiently large number of colonists would eventually force the government to establish transport facilities between the colony and the city. This would increase the value of the neighbouring land owned by the original investors.

Each tenant farmer had been equipped with selected implements, from spades to saddles imported from Scotland; and the total investment for each able worker – including transport for his family and goods – averaged £165. This expense was covered by the Robertsons. In addition each family head or single man received a rent-free plot of land which had to be worked for a minimum of five years. After that the land reverted to the Robertsons or the tenants could buy their plot at preferential terms.

The group of colonists included uneducated farmhands attracted by the idea of owning their own land and the more educated individuals – already mentioned – who had set out with a spirit of adventure. The times were, after all, the early years of an age of adventure in Britain. They were tough men and women who had to sleep under the stars at first, in winter weather, while they built their homes. By the end of 1825 the settlement was established and temporary shelters were being replaced with more permanent buildings. The colony became the supplier of salted butter to Buenos Aires, which had until then done without. By 1828, besides the main residence of the Robertsons, architect Richard Adams and his crew had built thirty brick buildings and about forty-seven *ranchos* – mud-and-wattle huts. They had also built a church, the Presbyterians' first in Argentina, from which Reverend William Brown took care of the colony's religious instruction.[6]

The Monte Grande colony prospered and was the government's planned showcase for the future attraction of immigrants to the country. In August 1828, *The British Packet and Argentine News* published a long report on the progress of the colony's 326 Scots and 188 native-born inhabitants. The newspaper praised Mr Tweedie for the invention of an implement with which to uproot thistles and said that the colonists had made their own bricks to build their homes.

In December of that year General Lavalle overthrew the Government of Buenos Aires and early in the next year a civil war began. In May 1829 the Scottish colony found itself at the mid-point between the camps of rival generals Lavalle and Rosas, and the settlers fled to Buenos Aires. It must be assumed that few were prepared to stay to defend what was in fact other men's property, however hard they had worked on it. The failure of the colony made the Robertsons nearly bankrupt, as they had put most of their capital into the venture. By 1832 there were only three Scots on the land: Thomas Graham, near the site of what was to be the town of Monte Grande in 1889; Turnbull Clark, at the Chacra Santa Catalina; and William Grierson at the farm named Paraísos.[7]

Many of the settlers stayed in the city; others moved south to form what eventually became fairly large Scottish colonies in Quilmes, San Vicente and Chascomús. Some achieved wealth, and a few might even be ranked as 'cattle barons'. The Scots, like many Irish, became pioneers in places all over the country, particularly in Patagonia, a land that owes most of its colonization to them.

Men of the two [Scots and Irish] nationalities in Argentina, as everywhere else abroad, are more ready [than the English] to adapt themselves to their environment and assume the habits and manners of the people among whom they have cast their lot. The Englishman in Buenos Aires does not even associate freely with his own countrymen either in business or pleasure. The various sections of the English colony prefer to live alone.[8]

The Scots who went to the city of Buenos Aires became rapidly assimilated into the resident British community, which had the tendency to consider them socially inferior. But Thomas Young, a farmer, died a very strong landowner, and James and William White set up the biggest cart transport company at the time. Thomas Fair became a substantial landowner; his sixty-square-mile *Estancia El Espartillar*, near Chascomús, bought in partnership with the Mackinlays in the 1820s and later wholly owned by Fair, remained in the family until just before the Second World War. John Tweedie, the botanist, travelled widely in the Argentine provinces and explored the Brazilian coast up to Rio de Janeiro. He corresponded with naturalists throughout South America and is credited with introducing bougainvillaea to many British gardens, as well as the Bigonia Tweediana (Tweedy Trumpet Flower), the Verbena of the Pampas and other species.

While the Scottish community was concentrated at Monte Grande, Scots living in Buenos Aires had gone to the settlement to attend services given by the Reverend Brown. But when the settlers were dispersed and Brown and many others went to Buenos Aires, it was decided that a church should be started in the city. Brown advised Consul Parish that the Presbyterians would require their own premises.

As already mentioned in an earlier chapter, the Scots' church in Buenos Aires had its beginnings, like so many other British community institutions, at Faunch's Hotel, at a meeting on 22 December 1828. Gilbert Ramsay was appointed the founding committee's secretary. On 6 February a meeting at Jeffries' Hotel approved the committee's recommendation that Scots in Buenos Aires should form the 'Scotch Presbyterian Chapel' and break away from the Episcopalians. Two rooms at the home of the Reverend Brown were filled to overflowing by more than 100 people on 15 March for the chapel's first service. An appeal for funds for a building was made; but this was a difficult task, as most British residents had already contributed to the British Episcopalian Church. In January 1830 the Presbyterian church committee decided that consular chaplaincy status should be sought for the Scots.[9]

Reverend Brown and his assistant, Gilbert Ramsay, proposed that their application should be formalized at a meeting of the Episcopalian Church. But the idea of a split in the church antagonized many members who rejected the proposal. Parish, in a letter to the Earl of Aberdeen, the British Foreign Secretary, on 13 March 1830, described Brown's entry as 'not in the most decorous manner'. Parish was satisfied that 'every merchant of respectability who attends Church at all supports that established with the sanction of His Majesty's government'; but Brown's congregation was formed 'by the lower orders of his countrymen ... chiefly mechanics and agricultural emigrants to whom may be added a very few of the clerks of the mercantile houses'. Parish ruled that Brown and Ramsay were out of order 'unless they chose to subscribe to the real objects of the meeting', which were to discuss matters concerning the Anglican Church. Brown protested and threatened to take the issue to the local government. Parish headed off the protest by going to the Foreign Ministry first and there asking officials to warn Brown against making the community dispute a public scandal – a thing which would have been quite easy to provoke given the generally hostile attitude of a Catholic city towards foreign religions – and the Scot was duly cautioned. However, the government later allowed the building of a new church after the mediation of Parish's successor, Consul Fox.

The foundation stone of the Scots' church was laid on 25 February 1833. The site and the building, designed by Richard Adams,[10] cost a total of £4000 and the congregation was free of debt by 1837. The minister's allowance was raised by the church's subscribers until 1838, when he was made a consular chaplain.[11]

Presbyterian services were taken into the provinces as from 1849, when the Reverend James Smith, a licenciate of the Presbytery of

Glasgow, took over from Brown. As Smith had not been ordained by the time Brown left, an arrangement was made with Herr Siegel, the pastor of the German Evangelical Church, 'to take over such duties [christenings, weddings], thus reciprocating services which had been frequently rendered by Dr Brown to the German community in Buenos Aires', according to the church records.

The Scots' second church, at Florencio Varela, was inaugurated in February 1855. It was built by British architect Edward Taylor, who had settled in Buenos Aires in 1823. His most important work included the lavish *Progreso* Club (1856), the Customs House or *Aduana Nueva* (1858), the German church and several other public and private buildings.[12]

In 1857 another church was opened, at Adela, near Chascomús, eighty miles south-west of Buenos Aires. Chascomús was in the early stages of becoming a large and booming town and for a few years after December 1865 was the terminal of the Great Southern Railway, before the lines were extended. The origins of the Chascomús chapel lay in a meeting in May 1857 at the 'Adela' farm, owned by James Dodds, James Burnet and George Bell since about 1853. The meeting, presided over by Thomas Bruce, decided that a *Rancho Kirk* – an amusing denomination which combined coming to terms with the land they were in and their Scottish roots – would be built near Lake La Yalca, on the farm where Bruce lived. Dr Smith had held services in private homes at the 'Adela' farm since 1854; but the local community had grown big enough to support its own church. Subscriptions to be paid by farmers who owned sheep were set at the value of ten sheep for every one thousand owned and the value of each sheep was established at thirty pesos. The farmhands, who did not own sheep, were not asked to make any contribution while the few Scottish clerical workers and teachers in the neighbourhood were invited to help with the organization of the social activities of the church and with its administration. Smith inaugurated the *Rancho Kirk* in mid-November 1857. It was a mud-and-wattle building which, nevertheless, had its own minister, whom the wealthier Scottish farmers in the area agreed to provide with a horse and a servant.

The next step for the Scots of Chascomús was to mark off a

Presbyterian cemetery, which was opened in January 1868 and was immediately filled to capacity by victims of all denominations killed by an outbreak of cholera. In 1872 the cemetery was moved alongside a new church nearer to the town of Chascomús. The deaths register of the early days of the cemetery shows that the majority of male deaths was caused by alcoholism. Because of the frequency of this cause of death, the church officers soon decided that it would no longer be entered in the register to avoid embarrassment to the next of kin.

As a Scottish community in Chascomús began to prosper, a brick church became an increasingly desirable attribute. Such a church was duly built, and was opened in November 1872, a large building with neo-classical front, standing on its own in the middle of open fields.[13] After that the Scots in Chascomús decided it was time to create a school that would be independent of tuition at the church and for the children of many parents who were restricted to imparting elementary education at home as the only supplement to church classes and Sunday school. So in 1889 Chascomús got an 'English High School', which was quickly followed within a year by a competing 'Real English High School', both of them staffed by local Scots, each with a teacher employed under contract from Buenos Aires.

These schools were, of course, for Scots families who were unable to send their children to the St Andrew's Scots School in Buenos Aires. The school had been started in 1838 and had at first been run by the Reverend Brown and his wife, with the assistance of a Miss Dick, before a committee found sufficient funds to engage an experienced master from Scotland. The first name given to this institution was that of 'Scotch National Schools'. Among the school's earliest rules was one that said parents could only visit their children on Tuesdays, which discouraged attendance by native Argentines who were not acquainted with the principle of boarding schools. Parents were asked to pay for tuition, but if that was not possible a school committee could decide, in a few cases, that children should be boarded and taught without charge. The Reverend Fleming, who arrived in Argentina in 1879, reorganized St Andrew's Scots School, for several years in a financially precarious state and catering for very few children, by taking on new staff, introducing higher standards and attracting greater support from the community. Alexander Watson Hutton, an honours graduate of Edinburgh, was appointed headmaster in 1882 and by the time he left a few years later, to start his own English High School, he had raised the standard of education at St Andrew's and given the school an air of efficiency. The school stands today in the Buenos Aires suburb of Olivos and is among Argentina's better-known private educational establishments.

Scots institutions today are the church and St Andrew's Society of the River Plate – one of the most active by far within the British community in Argentina. The school still carries its Scots name but has exceeded the boundaries of a community. The Society's annual events, such as the Caledonian Ball, in July, and the Gathering of the Clans, in the spring, are two magnets not only for Scots but for the wider British and Anglo-Argentine communities into which the Scots have merged.

12

The Welsh Settlers and Other Colonists

The landing of a group of 153 Welsh emigrants on the Patagonian coast on 28 July 1865 marked the renewal of Argentine attempts to attract what were described as 'hard-working' north European immigrants. The government in Buenos Aires was delighted at the prospect of a Welsh settlement in Chubut. A message sent to the national congress with a description of the potential colony in Patagonia, written by the Argentine Interior Minister, William Rawson (see chapter 4), contained much praise for such a plan and for the possibility of populating the region. The contract was signed for the Welsh settlers by D. G. Whalley, MP; David Williams, Sheriff of Merioneth; and Sir Love Jones Parry, of Madryn Castle. The 153 colonists were to be the advance party in a contract to ship 300 to 500 families from Wales to Patagonia each year for ten years. They would receive fifty square miles of land for every 200 families; they would be free of taxes; and when the region reached a population of 20,000 it would be made a province of the republic. The first group of colonists was given four pieces of cannon with which to defend themselves and were promised 3000 sheep, 200 horses and fifty cows. The initial inspection and approval of the land they were to occupy south of the River Negro had been the responsibility of one Lewis Jones, later the first governor of the colony.[1]

The colonization of the country's empty south as a way to improve trade with the native Patagonians and to confirm claims of sovereignty over a territory whose possession was in dispute with Chile was the Argentine Government's clear aim. The settlers had an equally clear desire for the preservation of their own national identity, with commercial gain and service to the Argentine authorities as very secondary targets. The Reverend Abraham Matthews, in his chronicle of the early days of the Welsh in Patagonia, said that the colonists were generally educated men and women, interested in the arts and concerned with protecting the Welsh language and traditions from the ravages of the English industrial invasion. According to him they sought an uninhabited country where they could establish their own government, keep their national customs, be a constructive element, not be assimilated by the adopted land, form Welsh congregations and Welsh schools, and achieve such a domination over the land as to avoid disappearing under the influence of neighbouring inhabitants. The writings of Captain Fitzroy of the *Beagle* had been the first to influence to draw them to Chubut. The attractions of the territory were said to be so great that emigration agents who had lobbied in favour of the United States had to admit their defeat. A Mr Michael Jones had been inspired some years before by the idea of a colony in Patagonia, far away from all other places which drew immigrants. Born in 1822 in North Wales, Michael Jones was approaching middle age when the Patagonia settlement started. He had been the headmaster of Bala Congregational College, at Bala, Carmarthen, from which post he said he could see the deterioration of the Welsh language and customs under the effects of the encroaching English. His wife had a small private income and this they used to get their plan under way. Apart from his own travel expenses, he paid the expenses of the mission that travelled to Buenos Aires to sign the colonization contract. He also covered the expense of chartering the *Mimosa* which sailed from Liverpool on 25 April 1865 with the first Welsh emigrants aboard.

The venture began with the inevitable hardships of such a journey. Disembarkation took place on the beach of what is today called Puerto Madryn and shelter was found in several large caves on the coast. The diary of the Reverend Lewis Humphreys records the death of Elizabeth, daughter of William Jones, aboard ship before the landing on 28 July. The following day, one Dafydd Williams, of Aberystwyth, was lost when out on a search for water. The remains of his body were found some time later. On

5 August, Margaret, the fifteen-month-old daughter of Evan and Ann Davies, died, and the next day saw the death of the eighteen-month-old son of John and Elizabeth Hughes.

But according to his report to the Welsh Colonizing and General Trading Company Ltd, reproduced in *The Standard* of Buenos Aires in February 1867, the Reverend Humphreys thought that he had every good reason to be optimistic about the future. He complained that

> On my return from the Welsh colony I was astonished and grieved to learn that many false accounts have been published throughout Great Britain, to our detriment. New Bay [Golfo Nuevo], the place where we landed, extends twenty-two miles inland and is seven miles across the entrance. It forms a splendid port, perfectly sheltered from all except the east wind, which, however, very seldom blows; and it is spacious and deep enough to accommodate the whole navy of Great Britain at anchor. Mr Downes, the mate of the *Mimosa*, assured me that New Bay is the best port in South America for vessels to enter and remain in perfect security.
>
> The River Chupat [Chubut] flows through at least three distinct valleys, divided from each other by chains of hills. The settlement is at present confined to the lower valley, which is about forty-five miles long and about five miles broad on an average. On the whole the land is dry, though there are a few swampy parts ... The unanimous verdict of every one is that the climate is delightful and very healthy. A few were ill some weeks after landing, owing partly to the fatigue of carrying and arranging heavy goods and partly to their frequently getting wet through and allowing their saturated clothing to dry upon their persons ... Indigestion, headache, toothache, colds and consumption are unknown here although I and many others have frequently slept in the open air night after night in the depth of winter, which is so genial that no evil effects followed an amount of exposure which would certainly have proved fatal in any part of Great Britain. I believe every person in the colony ate double what sufficed him at home. With such an excellent climate it is not surprising that the land should be extremely fertile.

The Reverend Humphreys' picture of a great future included some warnings that 'none of us chose to kill cattle for food, owing to the paucity of their numbers', but to counter this the 'territory literally swarms with *guanacos*, armadilloes, ducks, geese, partridges and ostriches and the river and bay furnish an ample supply of fish. The hares are very large and commonly weigh from eighteen to twenty lbs ... In the proper season seal-fishery is carried on to a great extent along the coast of Patagonia, principally by English and North American sailors.' On 15 September 1865 the commander of the district of Patagones, with government officials from Buenos Aires, 'performed the ceremony of formally giving us possession of the territory and naming our first town Rawson, in honour of Dr William Rawson, the minister of the interior, who has manifested a deep and true interest in the establishment of the colony'.

Immediate financial difficulties were overcome in part when the colony sent a representative, William Davies, to Buenos Aires at the end of 1865 and he obtained a monthly grant of £145 from the government, to be awarded until such time as the colony could be self-supporting. It was a substantial investment, reflecting the government's desire to colonize Patagonia as soon as possible.

In addition to the official help, there was 'valuable assistance afforded by the indians'. Good relations were established with the nomadic natives, most of them of the Tehuelche tribe, but also Araucanos and Peuelches, who soon began to adapt some words of the Welsh language to make up for the deficiencies in their own vocabulary and to facilitate communications with the settlers. One such word was *bara* (bread), and many in Chubut still remember indians in winter begging for *poco bara* (a little bread). The indians' demand for alcohol caused the first big crisis in the lives of the near teetotal colonists. Reluctantly the Welsh soon included this in their trade with the natives in order to reach a better deal and to be able to compete with other traders who had no qualms about supplying alcoholic beverages to the natives.

There were a few deserters and more were to follow; but in those early stages Humphreys could say that they were an exception.

In March 1866 a sealer entered New Bay and two of the settlers availed themselves of the opportunity to migrate to the Falkland Islands, praying to be removed from the Welsh settlement. The memorial they drew up misrepresented the true state of affairs and was dispatched without the knowledge of the general body of settlers. In consequence of that memorial Her Britannic Majesty's ship *Triton* visited the colony in June last to remove the people in a body if necessary. This offer caused the greatest astonishment in the settlement ... We at once declined to leave the colony and the *Triton*, having assisted us to repair our little schooner and presented us with a cask of lime juice, left us where we chose to remain.

However, in January 1867 the colony's president, Davies, and the Reverend Matthews went to Buenos Aires to ask the government to transfer the colony to some other part of the country. Despite Humphreys' optimism, drought had caused the failure of the wheat crop in November 1866 and only about six families harvested small amounts early in 1867. In addition, local traders who thought that their commerce was threatened by the Welsh colony's improvement of relations with the indians – which included more humanitarian treatment of servants than that seen during General Rosas' campaign in southern Buenos Aires and fewer attempts at defrauding the natives – were spreading malicious rumours about the Chubut settlement to damage the Welsh image among indian leaders and to try to make the settlers move away.

Opposition to moving came from the former governor of the colony, Lewis Jones, who had resigned in October 1865 when blamed for mismanagement, and was now working at *The Standard* printing plant in Buenos Aires. A newly formed Chubut colonization company in Buenos Aires – in which shareholders included several British residents in Buenos Aires who contributed towards purchase of large plots of land neighbouring the Welsh colony – also opposed the move, hoping to profit from an eventual rise in land values. However, a small number of families decided to try their luck elsewhere, principally in Rio Negro, only a few hundred miles north, where they were not too far from the colony. Another few travelled to Santa Fé, over one thousand miles north, which had become the most favoured province for colonization because of the fertile soil and good communications. A majority of the Welsh remained in Chubut after the national government promised increased support against bad traders. Such assistance never came.

By August 1867 there were 124 people in the colony. Of the 153 who had arrived in 1865, forty-four had left and sixteen had died, while twenty-one had been born and ten other people had joined the settlers. The original plan to bring three hundred to five hundred families every year from Wales had failed because instead of the early success which had been hoped for, there had been too many failures and these made it difficult to attract recruits for emigration to Patagonia.

The colony was administered by a council, which passed laws and was responsible for public works. There were two courts, one of justice – with a judge and twelve-man jury – and the other of arbitration. Each male colonist had to serve as a policeman for three months out of each year, under threat of losing his voting right if he refused. The colony's wood and stone chapel was also the grain depot and worshippers used the sacks of wheat for pews. The chapel was used as the seat of the council, the site of a stock exchange and sheltered a small office where a council member heard complaints or handled matters relating to financial hardship or 'welfare' of members of the community. Every event of public interest was debated or celebrated in the chapel.

The colony subscribed to payment of one bed at the British Hospital in Buenos Aires, a custom which was abandoned when public health services and communications improved in the district. The colony's ministers, Humphreys and later Matthews, had no privileges or income and worked on their own farms.

The colony's first years were a time of extreme hardship. Drought and flooding alternated to damage crops year after year. This problem was partly overcome when one Aaron Jenkins started a system of irrigation ditches in November 1867, an experiment which immediately attracted more financial assistance from Buenos Aires, authorized by Interior Minister Rawson.

In January 1868 the colony made further progress by producing its own periodical, *Y Brut*. Its first news was disaster, as the colony's schooner *Denby* sank on its return from the port of Patagones, where it had gone for provisions. All six aboard were lost. The boat was replaced by the national government, which presented the colony with the schooner *Mary Ann* in 1869; but this had to be sold the same year because there was no money to repair damage caused on its maiden voyage. The disaster news seemed unending: the wheat harvest was wiped out by heavy rains and flooding in 1870, the government subsidy was stopped in

June of that year and there was a poor crop again in 1871. By April 1871 a Royal Navy ship called to know what had become of the settlers, of whom nothing had been heard for over a year. The *Myfanwy*, owned by Mr Michael Jones, among whose earliest plans for the colony had been the hope to establish a trading link between Wales and Chubut, was the only other ship to call that year.

In addition to the problem caused by the climate, the Welsh had to depend for trade and tolerance on the unpredictable, if usually peaceful, indians. On one occasion the indians stole sixty-five horses, leaving many colonists without any way to plough the land.

However, in 1873, after some good harvesting, Chubut Valley wheat went on the Buenos Aires market for the first time, attracting high prices. The most immediate effect of this success was the statement by the government that far more would have to be done for the colonists, to attract immigrants. Towards the end of 1875 and in 1876 about 500 joined the colony from Wales and the United States. In 1878 the colony started publication of its second paper, *Ein Breiniad.*

Ever since the beginning of the colony, which opened the country to peaceful settlement, the Welsh explored the land and rivers to the south and west, reaching the Andes foothills in October 1885, immediately starting new settlements there.

Although the history of the colony reads in its greater part as an uninterrupted chain of disasters, the tenacity of the settlers, who had uprooted in Wales and put all they possessed into making the colony work, had made some impression in Britain. Their idealism and the publicized government support that they were given aroused interest and fund-raising for the colonists in the United Kingdom. Encouraged by this concern and although the colonization terms of the original contract were unlikely to be achieved, the Argentine Government declared the territory of the Chubut river, a barren north Patagonian stretch with a rich valley running its length and spanning the country from the Atlantic Ocean to the Andes, a province of the republic in 1884. Most of the new province's authorities were Welsh. The demarcation of the provincial boundaries was based in part on the arbitration by a United

States officer, General Osborne, who in 1881 had made Patagonia east of the Andes Argentina's and west Chile's. The persistence of the colonists, and of the government, encouraged another 400 settlers to emigrate from Wales in 1886. Ten years later a form of British political recognition of the colony took place, when David Lloyd George, temporarily out of Parliament, spent several months on a visit to what he called the 'little Wales across the sea'.

The visit amounted to an enormous moral encouragement for the settlers – who felt their position strengthened by the presence of a British political personality. However, losses from severe floods in 1899, bad markets and the call-up of young men to serve in the Argentine army precipitated the departure of 300 settlers in 1902, an exodus which was reported in great detail in *The Standard* of Buenos Aires in July of that year. The paper reproduced columns of interviews from the *Western Mail*, whose Liverpool correspondent covered the arrival of the Chubut emigrants returning to Britain and preparing, in some cases, to re-emigrate to Canada. (The *Mail* at one time was closely linked to the agents of the colonists and had always shown concern for Welsh Patagonian interests.)

The need for more immigrants, the fear of failure in the Welsh settlement, a fear born with the colony, as well as the desire for a greater colonization effort had prompted the Argentine Government to send immigration agents to Europe. They went to Britain and Germany, principally, to find more families to put on the land and populate the frontier territories. While disenchantment and euphoria alternated in Chubut, immigration agents managed to attract settlers to other parts of the country.

The agents' job was not an easy one and they often ran into trouble. In Germany they had been harassed repeatedly as it was not considered desirable that men fit for the army should be lured away. In Britain emigration had been successfully organized by the government but there were objections voiced from certain quarters over letting members of the working class go to places outside the Empire, where they were thought to be of better use to British interests. Reports from Argentine consuls in Liverpool, Glasgow and London published in *La Tribuna* as from January 1864 showed that efforts to promote Argentina as a land which offered the best prospects were facing the problem of unfavourable comparison with the opportunities offered by Canada and Australia. Furthermore, British officials advised prospective emigrants that they should go to the colonies. The British emigration commission had issued a warning in February 1870 against going to Argentina where, it said, several Britons as well as other foreigners had been murdered.

The warning brought a reply from the Argentine minister in Paris, in March 1870, refuting the accusation and claiming that such statements were morally damaging to Argentina. The minister declared that there had been 40,000 immigrants in 1869 who had entered the country voluntarily and were working there in peace. The minister's letter was carried in full, with remarks of approval, in *La Tribuna* and the paper later reported that the British Government had ordered an end to publication of the warning notice, 'which put the Argentine Republic on a level with the semi-barbarian peoples of the interior of Africa'.

The newspaper *El Nacional*, far from taking such an accommodating line, reported on 12 April 1870, under a headline that read '125 murders', that the British Press was concerned about the fate of Britons travelling to Argentina. *El Nacional* argued that 'instead of being offended [by the murders] they should be grateful if they [the Press specifically, but the public in general] knew the motives'. The victims were apparently drunken sailors, ruffians and vagrants caught in riverside brawls, a burden to society, which was best rid of them.

The difficulties for the regular and comfortable flow of immigrants arose not only from government attitudes and press coverage, but also from the promoters and operators of the emigration business, who aroused suspicion and fear in prospective emigrants. The business had several stages of profit. There was, in the first instance, the arrangement for the transport of a number of people for a fee; there was the sale of a colonization plan, charged for as a fee for the promotion of the area to be colonized and the recruitment of colonists; and there was a land deal, where promoters acquired land cheaply or by government grant, the land was populated with immigrants as tenants and the organizers waited for the time when the sale of the land could be made at a profit. This latter method also included the purchase by the promoters of land surrounding the colony as the neighbouring area also rose in value.

A society named the Emigrant and Colonists Aid Corporation Ltd wrote to Argentina's President Sarmiento in April 1870 offering to send thousands of Britons to Argentina. The first offer was for one thousand families at a cover charge of £175,000. To get the immigrants, the government had to allocate a plot of fiscal or expropriated land, preferably near the rich eastern flank on Paraná river, put it in the Corporation's trust for the first year while the immigrants were settled, and then float a bond issue to cover the total estimated cost of the colonization. But it never came off. On 24 May, *La Tribuna* carried a reader's letter which stated that the proposal had been made to several British colonies and had been rejected because it was too expensive and the people to be installed as colonists were undesirable.

Soon after, on 3 June, *La Tribuna*, which took a keen interest in immigrant promotion as a patriotic campaign, reported that eighty immigrants, including a minister and a physician, had sailed from Southampton to set up a colony in Santa Fé. The group was to settle on a piece of land of 27,000 acres and the venture was supported by 'some officers of the English army'. Each colonist had subscribed £150.

On 22 January 1873 a report in *La Nación* said that there were 486 Britons, among several other nationalities, in colonies in Entre Rios, Santa Fé and Córdoba.

In many colonies, the Justice of the Peace was a foreigner, of the nationality predominating in the colony, which could lead to favouritism and squabbles in their local population. Assimilation was not easy. Disputes that led to battles and looting at times brought diplomatic representatives to the defence of the colonists and, on some occasions, even the gunboats were sent. In 1876, Santa Fé saw an Italian gunboat sail up the Paraná because of an uprising of Italian colonists who were protesting over the unfair treatment and arrest of one of their number. British gunboats were also seen off Santa Fé during another dispute in 1876, between the

Bank of London and the River Plate, and the Santa Fé Government, which had fallen behind with its repayment of a loan from the bank. As a result of these two interventions, antagonism between locally born people and foreigners grew. For example, when a policeman once threatened a British consul with a pistol, the officer was publicly congratulated by his senior.

Not all immigrants arrived with adequate financing and the promise of work on the land. A report from the officer in charge of immigration in Rosario advised the Central Immigration Commission in December 1873 that 107 Britons and Germans had arrived from Paraguay and all were so impoverished that a public subscription had to be raised to help them. Some Britons arrived from Paraguay – where one colonization programme had failed owing to extremely unsettled political circumstances and war – in better conditions: between 21 June and 4 December 1873 there arrived in Rosario 370 Britons with money in their pockets and, many of the men being skilled workers, they found work immediately.

The luck of immigrant colonists varied. *La Nación*, on 18 January 1874, carried a translation from the French-language *Courrier de La Plata* which reported severe ill-treatment and rotten accommodation for 1000 passengers who arrived in the ship *La France.* Thirty people died within twenty-four hours of disembarkation.

But immigration promotion was in fashion. In November 1875, R. Stephens & Co., of Glasgow, proposed the emigration of 140 Scottish families in four years to set up a colony at Port Desire, in Patagonia. Scots colonists were recommended on the grounds that all over the world they had proved to be 'the most useful'. Although that plan failed, the Scots went on almost to 'own' Patagonia, just as the Irish spread over Buenos Aires and the Welsh inhabited Chubut, holding vast farming concerns. In Patagonian folklore there is the story of a Scot who took three years to drive a flock of several thousand sheep from Buenos Aires to Patagonia, crossing two big rivers and stopping for the lambing seasons and shearing at the homes of other Scots.

Copies of Mulhall's *Handbook of the River Plate* were distributed in British working men's clubs to attract immigrants.

Ontario, in Canada, however, offered settlers free passages and 200 acres of land free to a family man and 100 acres to any man over the age of eighteen. The only conditions were that three acres should be cleared and sown each year, that a house of at least 20 ft by 10 ft should be built, and that the settler should live there at least six months of the year. By comparison the Argentine Government in 1878 offered meagre concessions to immigrants: 'They are landed at the expense of the Government, boarded and lodged free for five days, assisted to pass the Customs House, afforded every information to enable them to find employment and finally sent free to wherever they elect to settle.' The result of this policy was the opening of 'immigrants' hotels' and cheap fares for immigrants and the performance of the government in the matter fell considerably short of expectations. An official notice said, 'The wages during the harvest, which lasts four months, are from thirty to forty-five hard dollars [£6 to £8] per month, with board and lodging.' European emigrants were advised to arrive between October and January; but those with a capital of between £80 and £120 'may come at any season of the year'. Land sold at 2s 6d per acre, payable over ten years, in many parts of the country.

Although this publicity did not win northern European immigrants in any great number, there was nevertheless an avalanche of easily assimilable Latin nationalities from Southern Europe, and they altered the genetic and cultural character of the *Criollo* population of Argentina, which had been around the one million mark in the mid-nineteenth century. The effects on Argentina of such a large number of immigrants would have been greater had not nearly half of all immigrants left the country again. This arrival and departure was due mainly to the fact that the promise of big land stakes in the provinces proved largely an illusion. During two decades up to 1890 immigrant peasants found that their dream of owning land was blocked by a ruling landed class which was in control of much of the farming and grazing land and was expanding the vast *estancias* to the exclusion of newcomers. Towards the end of the century an economic crisis caused the selling of some land and the opening of the country, in previously unexploited regions, to smallholders.[2]

Britons arriving in Argentina between 1857 and 1915 to make a new life amounted to only one per cent of the approximately six million immigrants in that period. The 1869 census showed that there were 10,637 Britons resident in Argentina, while the census for 1895 saw the figure rise to 21,788. There were 29,772 in 1910 and 27,692 in the 1914 census. In the latter year the total population stood at 7,885,237 and three-quarters of the adult male population in Buenos Aires was foreign-born.

In spite of the difficulties for organized colonization many colonies were successful. One of these, in the district known as the English Colony of Sauce Grande, on the Sauce Grande River, near Bahía Blanca, was established in 1868 by a group of families who, in turn, settled others. At one time the colony totalled 150 people. Frequent attacks by native indians caused losses in cattle, property and lives, which forced several families to leave, thereby further weakening the colony. The settlement, and the fighting against the native indians, produced two famous personalities in the history of southern Buenos Aires colonization. Their renown came from their courage fighting indians and success as trackers. One was John Walker, known as *Facón Chico* (Small Knife), and the other was his cousin, Henry Edwards, called *Facón Grande* (Big Knife) because of their dexterity with knives in both work and battle. The reference to the size in each case was to their physical appearance and not to their blades. The cousins were later to be used as characters in Scottish writer Robert B. Cunninghame Graham's book *Mirages* (1936).[3]

Military censorship stopped information about attacks by native indians from reaching Buenos Aires newspapers, because the government believed that such news would frighten away potential commerce opportunities and immigrants. The correspondence of the colonists at Sauce Grande, to their agent in Bahía Blanca, named Edmund Goodhall, is therefore a valuable witness to the period.[4]

Letters from Walker and Edwards to Goodhall about the attacks by the 'darkies' and the 'brutes', as well as comment on the incompetence of the local army garrisons in protecting colonists eventually were to bring about, not just stronger censorship, but the decimation of the southern Buenos Aires and the Patagonian native indians by the Argentine army. The organized assault, defeat and near annihilation of the native tribes was called the 'Conquest of the Desert' – the desert being the name given to the flat open southern Pampas and northern Patagonia – an event which is still looked upon with pride in Argentina. One study of the Argentine Government's policy at that time says:

The evidence suggests that much of the impetus behind the formulation of the aggressive policy against the native Americans stemmed from the pressure exerted on the Argentine Governments by several European nations. This pressure derived from the complaints received by several of the European embassies and consulates in the Argentine from the numerous European subjects who resided in the various frontier settlements to the effect that their lives and property were threatened by native American raids. The European nations maintained that the protection of these settlements was the responsibility of the Argentine Government. Thus the British Government made several such protests following the raids on the Bahía Blanca settlement and those on the property of the Central Argentine Land Company at the end of 1872.

The 'aggressive policy' referred to was, of course, the Conquest of the Desert, headed by General Julio Roca, later president of Argentina for two six-year terms.[5]

The drive to kill, imprison, humiliate and terrorize was first directed against the men in the indian camps, but later extended to the women and the children. The previously mentioned study also says:

While the Conquest of the Desert was seen by the Argentine authorities as a 'praiseworthy and necessary accomplishment', it caused considerable grief among the Welsh settlers. Several neutral sources attest to the Welsh regrets about what they regarded as an entirely unnecessary tragedy and it did nothing to improve the relationships between Welsh settlers and the Argentine officials.

The decision to pacify the native indians by force took on many aspects. There was the raid and slaughter, mass arrests, enslavement, and also a kind of blood sport in which a prize was paid for every indian killed. In a book called *Twentieth century impressions of Argentina*, published in 1911 to mark Argentina's centenary, a chapter on Patagonian natives says:

In the earlier days of white settlement in Tierra del Fuego the indians gave trouble killing the settlers' live stock – probably impelled by hunger resulting from the growing scarcity of the *guanaco* and other indigenous fauna on which the aboriginal was wont to feed. These depredations naturally gave rise to the organisation of punitive expeditions, in which short shrift was granted the marauders ... With shame it must be confessed that these outrages were committed not by the Latin races – for it is only in recent years that the Chilean and Argentine have come into the country – but by men of British stock and extraction ... After a while the havoc among stock wrought by the indians grew so great that the *estancieros* paid £1 a head for every *macho*, or male indian, killed. At first the bow had to be brought in before the money was paid; but later on an ear had to be cut off and shown ...

There were many adventures as arduous as those of the Welsh in Chubut and the English in Sauce Grande, although there were also many more peaceful. There was a Boer and British South African colony called the *Colonia Escalante*, near Comodoro Rivadavia, in Patagonia, as from December 1902. They were sheep farmers working with very little capital and were plagued by financial difficulties. In 1938 two-thirds of the colony was repatriated. And there were also some Australians. They settled in Rosario and Buenos Aires for a time at the end of the century. Most were deserters from another colony, the *New Australia*, set up in Paraguay in 1893 by two boatloads of bushworkers and tradesmen. The colony was led by a journalist, William Lane, who had set out on the *Royal Tar* in July 1893 to find his own Utopia outside Asunción.[6]

There were still colonies being set up after the First World War, such as that of the San Javier Land and Forest Company, which started colonization at Puerto Rosario, Misiones, populated by English ex-servicemen, who soon became disenchanted and returned to Britain. Another Misiones province colony, at Puerto Victoria, was a fraud. Settlers were lured with photographs of a site that had never existed. The pictures showed women in fur coats entering glittering stores and well-dressed men at dance halls across the floor of which was strung the name of the colony. Only when the potential colonists had paid their contributions and had travelled to Argentina did they learn that they had been cheated.

The failures, though distressing, make no more than anecdotes now. The overwhelming impression is of success. The Welsh in

Chubut, as the Scots on their farms further south, made Patagonia accessible to Argentina. In the rest of the country the small farming colonies provided the foundation for a communications and trade network which was to be built and operated by the British for many years. Many colonies have ceased to exist, of course, as ownership of the land changed hands and succeeding generations emigrated to other parts of the country. But in every corner of Argentina, in buildings, land developments or just in the name of a hamlet, the colonists' influence and work is still there to be seen.

13

The Sporting Life and Entertainments

The British took their sports wherever they went, primarily for their own enjoyment; although they did teach the natives the secrets of their forms of amusement. Some sports were assimilated while others remained specifically British. Cricket remains a British community activity, although with enough interest in Argentina to make two divisions. Soccer is a national sport in Argentina. Rugby has five divisions in Buenos Aires, in addition to a schools division and several provincial leagues. British sports became an important part of national life and the only aspect of the British community that put Britons in close social and cultural contact with Argentines. Nevertheless even in teaching all the sports to Argentines, the Briton kept to himself.

> The Briton, settled in the country and carrying on business there, true to national characteristic devotes himself to his own affairs and does not figure conspicuously in the cosmopolitan social amenities and gaieties of the Metropolis. He has taught the Argentine the science of horse-racing, of rowing and of boxing, also how to play cricket, football and tennis, which sports and games the latter pursues with spasmodic zest so far as they appeal to his instincts for amusement, for the average Argentino of Spanish descent has not the physique for arduous athletics. The Briton also acts as judge at the cattle shows. For all that he has done for the industrial and general development of the country in which he has figured pre-eminently, he is held in the highest regard by the Argentinos, and for his trustworthiness he is everywhere respected. But he has not become Argentinised, assimilated with the life of the country ...[1]

The British started their sports activities, their theatrical performances and other entertainments – such as the already described Vauxhall Gardens – for their own amusements as soon as there were sufficient numbers to gather and organize such pastimes. All these activities would eventually expand after the fall of Governor Rosas, with the growth of commerce and the laying of the railways.

The first British sport to be taken to Argentina was, by a margin of several decades, cricket. The officers who were captured in the British invasion of 1806 played the game for the first time in the neighbourhood of San Antonio de Areco.

With independence in the River Plate and, later, British recognition, there came greater commercial activity and more cricket. About mid-1831 a Buenos Aires Cricket Club was formed by a group of English residents. The club started with twenty-five members and one year later had received challenges from teams formed especially for the four or five matches played that season. Interest appears to have waned and by 1835 there were appeals in *The British Packet and Argentine News* for players to join teams to play against ships' crews. The club survived until 1839 and was replaced by the Anglo-Porteño Cricket Club which, in 1844, had field days and cricket matches organized jointly with another new club, the Albion.

By the early 1850s a pitch of sorts had been established at Palermo de San Benito, on the north side of the city by the river. The surface was bumpy and is said to have aroused complaints from the players. But it was their very own first playing field and the area was to become the cradle of Argentine sport. Cricket legend says that in February 1852 there was a match on at Palermo on the day when Rosas' troops were defeated at Caseros. Some of the soldiers returned to Buenos Aires from the battlefield via Palermo, where Rosas' residence stood.[2] As the troops tramped by, the men on the playing field stopped their game to applaud the dishevelled soldiers and then returned to their play. It is also part of the sport's legend in Argentina that a short time later, during a siege of Buenos Aires, when the city's government decided that the port and surrounding area should secede from the provinces as a result of a Constitution drafted in 1853 in Santa Fé province, the English community was cut off from the cricket field.[3] An application to the commander of the troops besieging

Buenos Aires succeeded in obtaining permission for the players to pass through the lines for their game.

In the late 1850s a new Buenos Aires Cricket Club (today called the Buenos Aires Cricket and Rugby Club) was founded, with a field and clubhouse on what is now the city's fashionable Alvear Avenue. In December 1864 the club inaugurated a new field at Palermo – leased by the Municipality of Buenos Aires – with a match against an eleven formed by the officers of HMS *Bombay*. The club opened its pavilion and stands one year later. By 1866 and during the cricket season, the club organized its own omnibus service between Plaza de Mayo, in front of Government House, and the field, so that enthusiasts could reach the frequently arranged matches between the club and sailors' elevens. In April 1868 the British Consul, Frank Parish, captained the club's first international team to play in Montevideo, where the Argentine side won. It was in 1875 that the club had its first location problems when the city authorities asked the club committee to relinquish possession of the land. The club was offered grounds outside the town but these were rejected. The committee then invited the President of Argentina to become an honorary member of the club and acceptance of the invitation kept the municipality at bay.[4]

Two other early clubs were the Flores Cricket Club and the Buenos Aires Zingari Cricket, Athletic, Sport Club formed in the late 1870s. Later, clubs were organized throughout the provinces, mainly through the efforts of men working in British-owned companies.

Horse-racing on a round or oblong (called in Buenos Aires at the time *à la English*) course was preceded by flat races known as *cuadreras* (measured in *cuadras* of 150 yards). But it did not take long for the English version to win greater acceptance because of its attractions as a spectacle and because of the formalities and drama of the 'Turf'. A first race, organized by a specially formed Racing Society whose members were foreigners and for the most part British and North American, was held on the beach in Barracas, on the south side of Buenos Aires, in November 1826. It was called a 'spring meeting' and ten horses took part. Thus the history of Turf in Argentina had started.

It was not, however, until 1849 that the Foreign Amateurs Race Sporting Society was formed by a group of members of the Strangers' Club.[5] A course twenty-six metres wide and twenty-six *cuadras* long was marked with rope and lime on land belonging to a North American named James White, neighbouring San Isidro, on the north side of Buenos Aires. The society's race committee met at the Strangers' Club and there the Newmarket rules were translated and published for local use. The first thoroughbred imported to Argentina was brought by Strangers' Club member William Thompson, for White. The horse was named *Belgrano*, and won all the races. Thompson, a colourful character who had arrived in Buenos Aires from England at seventeen to join his brother James in a trading company, invited much gossip throughout his life because of his enthusiasm for racing. He was among several Britons who had flirted at some time with Manuelita, Rosas' daughter. She showed a preference for European society, a thing that the Governor's enemies said her father encouraged for obscure political reasons. With his brother's help, William Thompson assisted many people to flee Rosas' police and *Mazorquero* gangs, using the information gained through his flirting with Manuelita to determine how quickly a wanted man or a black-listed family should leave the city. As for his courting, he married Amy Ann Barton, daughter of James Barton – a Scot and co-founder of the Strangers' Club – and they had ten children.

The Racing Society was active between 1849 and 1855. The races it organized usually emptied the city. Among their patrons were Manuelita Rosas and her father who went to the races for the social event. Racing introduced a busier social life to a rather dull Buenos Aires. The sporting events and interest in them provided the British with their principal social link with the native Argentines; however the clubs and their social activities were exclusive to Britons, with a very small membership of sympathetic Europeans and North Americans and few prominent local individuals. While all the population was welcomed as spectators to the races, the cricket and, later, other sporting events, only the British community enjoyed the club life involved. The pattern of a club life, with election of committee members, teas, dances and gatherings, in addition to sport, was established early in the organization of all sporting activities and became a focal point for Britons.

Although the Foreign Amateurs Race Sporting Society closed due to disagreement among its members – over issues such as which persons were eligible for membership – British clubs and societies were spared too much internecine feuding. This was because the British community was, if anything, single-minded in its determination to achieve commercial gain. Differences were aired between individuals, not between factions. There was not the problem suffered by the German and Central European communities, of fierce and regular upheaval, caused by the influx of many who fled to the River Plate after the revolutions of 1848 in Europe.

By the time the Racing Society was dissolved, to make way for several smaller clubs, courses had been marked and were kept carefully in many parts of Buenos Aires province.[6] The Press, after 1860, carried racing reports regularly. One club, a successor to the society, renamed the Foreign Amateur Races, held its first 'spring meeting' in November 1865, with a programme of seven races. *The Standard* announced the meeting in October and said that 'special trains will leave 25 de Mayo and Retiro stations for Belgrano, where omnibuses will be in attendance to conduct passengers to and from the race course'. Catering to punters became a thriving business among the British in and outside Buenos Aires. An advertisement published just before the spring meeting drew attention to *Watson's Hotel, Belgrano*: 'The proprietor of the above hotel begs to advise parties attending the Foreign Amateurs' Races that they can be supplied with hampers made up for any number of persons, containing cold meat of all descriptions, sandwiches, fowls, hams, wines & co. Lunch always ready at the hotel.'

The Standard of 20 January 1874 carried a report on the Azul [Buenos Aires] English Race Meeting, held at *Estancia Buena Suerte* on 8 January, when four races, a steeple chase, consolation stakes and three polo matches were held. This is the first published record of polo matches being played in Argentina, although no doubt it had been played before. In spite of *The Standard* mention of those three matches, the 2 September 1875 issue said that

> the game of polo which has become so fashionable in Great Britain and our Indian Empire has been formally inaugurated in Buenos Ayres by the well-known and popular *estanciero* Mr David Anderson Shennan, of Ranchos, at whose *estancia* [Negrete] the first polo match in South America took place on Monday with all the style and *eclat* becoming so notable an event in the sporting world. Numbers of ladies and gentlemen invited from Buenos Ayres arrived by Saturday morning's train at the Villanueva station, where Mr Shennan had horses and waggonettes in waiting for them, the distance to the *estancia* being two and a half leagues.
>
> Notwithstanding the large number of Mr Shennan's guests he had accommodation for all, the house being one of the finest in the province ... Saturday night brought some more guests from town, two of whom had ridden the whole way, ninety miles, and arrived just in time for supper, not looking at all fatigued.

The polo played at that party at *El Negrete* was quite different from that seen today.[7] Three matches were played on Monday before a late lunch, each lasting about an hour, without stop except for injury. The first two teams had six on one side, named *City*, and five on the *Camp* side. The uneven numbers were decided as a way to balance the better-trained *Camp* team against the less skilful riders on the *City* side. The two teams later mixed to try to find a better balance of forces for the second match, when *City* became *World* and *Camp* became *England*. Fresh players joined for the third match.

After that grand occasion at *Negrete*, polo prospered in all farming districts where English-speakers were influential. The *Buena Suerte* and *Negrete* ranches remained polo centres for many years.

In 1884 polo went to the city. A match was arranged between a visiting team from Bahía Blanca and the Buenos Aires Polo Club, at Flores.[8] The city's second, and smaller, English-language newspaper *The Herald*, said:

> Among the holiday amusements on Saturday was a polo match at Flores, between clubs of Bahía Blanca and Buenos Aires. Our readers in general are aware that this is a game of ball played on horseback or, rather, ponyback, there being five or six riders on each side, each armed with a

long stick curved at the end with which they endeavour to drive a ball to their adversaries' end of the field of contention. It is one of the most manly games ever invented, requiring great courage and dexterity and the finest horsemanship; the ponies also must be well trained, and then there is no doubt that they enter into the spirit of the game as fully as their riders. With two good teams at play, it is a most exciting scene for the onlookers as well as the players, and we are glad to see that this noble game has been introduced into this country by Englishmen. The Buenos Aires club proved victorious. The ponies of the other club had only arrived on the previous night and had been trained on sand and so were at a disadvantage on the turf.[9]

The beginning of soccer was contemporary with that of polo. Every event was reported in *The Standard* and was well attended. Eventually, of course, soccer was to become the most important of commercial spectacles and riding sports were squeezed out by growing cities and shrinking open spaces.

An announcement in *The Standard* in May 1867 said that the Buenos Aires Football Club had been formed and that the first match was set for 25 May, to coincide with celebrations for Argentina's national day. Among the founders of the club were Thomas and James Hogg, who were both prominent in almost every British sport in the country. The Boca Junction railway station field was under water on the day, so the match was postponed until the next public holiday, 20 June, Flag Day. It was played on the Palermo cricket field and not at Boca. Full sides could not be mustered, so it was an eight-a-side. In the next few years numerous teams were formed. A football league was started about 1891; but there is little published record of its existence except for mention of one match. In February 1893 the Argentine Association Football League was formed at a meeting presided over by Alexander Watson Hutton. The League presidents up to 1911 were all of British descent.

The most famous of all the early soccer teams was that of pupils of the English High School, then run by its headmaster Watson Hutton, the 'Father of Argentine soccer'. As the EHS Club it won the 1900 soccer championship, and then changed its name to *Alumni*.[10] Several of the clubs formed by Britons at the turn of the century, such as Quilmes Athletic, Rosario and Banfield, survive today, playing in national soccer championships. Belgrano and

Lomas de Zamora have remained community centres. In September 1905 a second Rosario club entered the soccer championship with the name of Newell's Old Boys. The club had been formed by former pupils of the Anglo-Argentine Commercial School, in Rosario, the headmaster of which was Isaac Newell.

In the meantime, rugby had made its appearance. In June 1873 the first rugby game was played in Argentina, at Palermo, and soon a committee presided over by the British consul, Ronald Bridgett, and including Thomas Hogg, decided that 'the Rugby Union laws be adopted as the laws of the Buenos Ayres Football Club'. The first match played by these rules took place in May the following year. The newspaper reports of the time said that the first games lasted about three hours and if there were no serious accidents this was a cause for relief which had to be recorded. Women formed a large part of the public and their cheers were often heard above those of the men. During the two years after the first match rugby won so many enthusiasts that it put soccer out of favour. However, in 1875, the government decided that the casualties caused by rugby were too frequent and the game was banned; rugby disappeared from the local sports scene for a time.

It came back in June 1886 when the Buenos Aires Football Club reopened. The new club was a successor to the BAFC formed in 1867 for soccer and which organized rugby in 1873. The first match in the new stage of rugby was played on the Flores polo field, with teams of fifteen aside. Matches were played without any kind of governing authority until 1899, when the River Plate Rugby Football Championship Committee was formed and rules drawn up. One of the clubs that has made its mark in rugby championships in the last few decades is the San Isidro Athletic Club (CASI) which started as an all-English railway employees' club, with staff from the Buenos Aires–Rosario line. The club was founded about the turn of the century; it is first mentioned by *The Standard* on 6 July 1902, in a friendly soccer match.

British club organizers made use of Buenos Aires' proximity to the River Plate and to rivers on the southern and northern boundaries of the city to introduce boating. The earliest records of boating – apart from the sailing regattas announced in *The British Packet and Argentine News* in the 1830s – show that sporting events first took place about 1860. Organized rowing regattas were held first by the Boating Society, which had a mooring stage on the city's passengers' dock. This venture came to an end in a storm in August 1861 when boats were smashed, the pier was wrecked and trees uprooted along the town's muddy riverfront. There was then virtually nothing for almost ten years. The events there may have been in that time went unrecorded with the exception of one occasion when *The Standard* reported, in April 1866, that 'on Sunday the Tigre was crowded', for a boat race which, however, had to be postponed because one of the participants was in mourning. In November 1870 the paper reported four Englishmen had rowed a four-oars from the port of Tigre, north of Buenos Aires, to the city's New Port, a distance of forty kilometres, in two hours and fifty minutes. In that same year, there were several news items and references to an English Boat Club, but no details other than dates of meetings are given about its activities.

The official birthday of rowing in Argentina is taken as the date of the first regatta on the River Luján, on 12 February 1871, in Tigre. This was the inaugural race of the River Luján Rowing Club, organized by Britons. All rowers were invited to become members; but they had to wear the club uniform and their boats had to carry the club's eight-inch square flag. Advertised activities included 'duck shooting'.

The next big race on the River Luján was organized by the Buenos Aires Boat Club in December 1873. Spectators included the President, Domingo Sarmiento, an admirer of Britain and keen supporter of community events; the British Minister, Lionel Sackville West, and the British Consul, Ronald Bridgett. *The Standard* two days later described this as the first real rowing regatta in Argentina, because of the prominent personalities who had patronized the event. The Buenos Aires Boat Club had started life as the Buenos Aires Rowing Club, with its clubhouse on the southern boundary of Buenos Aires, the Riachuelo. Sackville West, a rowing enthusiast much praised by an adulatory local Press, became the club's first president and impressed fellow-members by ordering his own, specially built boat from England. The club's captain was the consul, Mr Bridgett. The club's committee ran into organizational difficulties early in its life. This was reflected in *The Standard*'s 28 December issue in which a notice appeared saying that 'the committee of the Boating Club request any Britisher who may have a copy of the rules and regulations of any similar club at home be kind enough to lend it to the committee'. The club was moved from its Riachuelo premises to Tigre in 1883.

The only English rowing club that remains in Tigre now is the Tigre Boat Club, formed at a meeting of enthusiasts at the Scots school in July 1888. For many years the TBC was reputed to have the best-stocked boathouse in Argentina.

The Lomas Cricket and Lawn Tennis Club, formed in June 1881, at the southern suburb home of a Mrs Henry, appears to have been the first to provide for tennis in an organized manner. It was over a decade before the most famous of Argentine tennis clubs, the Buenos Aires Lawn Tennis Club, was founded by Britons. In the year of its foundation this club started the River Plate championship, which would become one of the most important in South America.

The first game of golf organized in Argentina took place, according to the English-language press sportswriters, in March 1892 over a nine-hole course. The first course, however, was inaugurated at Hurlingham Club in June 1892; the Lomas Club course was used for the first time in July 1893. The Rosario Golf Club opened in 1895 but soon closed because, while there were enthusiasts, there was very little equipment available. The first golf equipment used in Rosario had to be imported and was subject to import duties which were, however, successfully avoided. The clubs were brought ashore from several ships over a few months by players who arranged to visit the ships' masters. The visitors left the docks using the clubs as walking sticks, the port guards being unable to tell the difference.

Boxing in its formal style was introduced in Argentina by the athletics clubs. The originator of the regular practice of athletics was said to be Dr Andrew Dick, of the British Hospital, who is also attributed the organization of foot races.

Hockey arrived in Argentina with the twentieth century. The Buenos Aires Hockey Club was founded in May 1911 by

Englishman Herbert Brookhouse, who had introduced the game in 1905. Women's hockey started at St Catherine's School in 1907 and Brookhouse's efforts led the organization of a league championship in 1908.

Even the first angling club was formed by Britons. The Dorado Club, which started in April 1917 with twenty-two members and had 155 by 1925, became as famous for its pink gins as for its members' catches of *dorado* in the muddy waters of the River Paraná Delta.

While sporting clubs grew in number another activity attracted the interest of the British community and filled leisure hours. However, it was exclusive to English-speakers and within the community to a minority regarded as 'intellectual'. It was the amateur theatre, in which enthusiasts reached standards that usually matched local, Spanish-language professional entertainment but which the British public considered to be a means to fund-raising for charity. This noble purpose gave English-language theatre strong audience support as from 1826. The first performance in that year was of *The Mountaineers*, reported in *El Mensajero Argentino*. Repeat performances were held in July and August and proceeds went in aid of the widows and orphans of Admiral Brown's sailors.[11] The success of this experience led to the formation of an amateur company, where Thomas Love, editor of *The British Packet and Argentine News*, distributed the alms that averaged about £100 a year. The company lasted a few years. Although Love was sympathetic to the government of General Rosas and relations between the Governor and the British residents were never too bad there are only a few mentions of English-language performances in Buenos Aires until 1864. *The Standard* of 13 June 1864 announced a meeting at L'Harmonie Hotel to organize an amateur theatre company. What success this meeting had is not reported. On 15 July the newspaper said that a number of recently arrived Britons were going to start a theatre company. The trouble was finding actresses, the writer said, a reflection of the generalized opinion that acting was not a reputable activity. However, the journalist remarked that 'There is no question about the profits to be derived, as it must prove a very paying business.' The paper offered on loan a complete collection of English drama. On 16 August, *The Standard* reported: 'On Tuesday evening, for the first time in Buenos Aires, we had the pleasure of assisting at public English theatricals.' As with polo, rowing and now theatre it will be seen that *The Standard* had its own rule for determining the dates of origin of some activities in Buenos Aires. The performance was in aid of the 'United States Sanatory Committee' which was raising funds for the wounded in Argentina's war with Paraguay.[12] 'The evening's entertainment was a decided and brilliant success; the ladies especially supported their characters with such consumate grace and ease as to merit an ovation. Each of them was presented with a handsome bouquet.' And on 11 September the newspaper said that the English amateur theatricals at the Victoria Theatre were the talk of the town, actors being stopped in the street and congratulated. 'Seldom has the British public in Buenos Aires spent a pleasanter evening'. The shows consisted of one-act plays, skits and musical numbers.

Once again there is a gap, at least in the reporting on amateur theatre, until 1873 when the English Literary Society was started, 'with the object of promoting intellectual recreation and to cultivate public speaking'. The society was principally concerned with regular concerts and recitals; but it also went into such diverse occupation as organizing a British–Argentine Exhibition of Trade and Exchange. One of its more active members was a miniature portraitist, Walter Ferris Biggs, who arrived in Buenos Aires without work. He was a 'multiple man' – a phrase that might have applied equally to his talents as to his large volume – according to *The Standard*. He was part-time singer, artist, occasional entrepreneur and later became Liberian consul in Argentina.

In April 1874 the Buenos Aires Thespians went on stage at the Alergía Theatre with a farce. 'Proceeds will be placed, in equal proportion, in the hands of the four English-speaking clergymen here ...' the Press reported. Advertising promised a 'grand amateur dramatic and musical entertainment in aid of the English-speaking poor'. The group advertised that its principal patrons were President Sarmiento and the British minister,

Sackville West. The main part of the programme was a thirty-minute, one-act farce, *Fish out of Water* – 'an old established favourite with the British public'. *The Standard* reported later: 'The Thespians have made so successful a debut under their accomplished leaders that we are glad to hear some of our leading merchants have come forward and offered one thousand pesos each towards the establishment of a British Theatrical Association under the name of The Thespians, to have regular amateur performances once a month or every two months'. *The Buenos Ayres Daily News and River Plate Advertiser* raved:

> The critic must be a savage of an unreclaimable order who would bestow one word of censure on the performace of an amateur company of dramatists, making their first appearance on stage and devoting themselves to furthering a charitable object; and as we wish to rank in the higher order of civilisation, our readers may have expected, under any circumstances, to read a favourable report of Wednesday night's performances by the British Thespians ...

Theatrical activity increased in 1877, reflecting an expanding British community. Often, the now famous Colón Opera House, built in 1857, was used for English-language shows.

The Buenos Aires Amateur Dramatic Club was founded in 1887 and would last into the twentieth century. It was rapidly followed by the Buenos Aires Choral Union, in May 1889, and a sense of rivalry grew between the groups. When the Union's committee was published, a newspaper comment welcomed the group saying: 'We hope no cliquism will prevent the success of this society.'

In 1891 theatrical activity moved to a new peak; on one occasion a notice in the Press said that the Brunswick Café would be open until midnight to cater to the public attending the Dramatic Club's show, the American church concert and the Anglican church organ recital. It continued to grow. When the Dramatic Club staged a special benefit performace for the British and American Benevolent Society – founded in 1880 – the Choral Union produced *Pirates of Penzance* and *The Mikado*. The Dramatic Club answered with *HMS Pinafore* and staged sixty-two performances of *Charley's Aunt* in one year. Competition increased towards 1910 when the Buenos Aires Social and Dramatic Union was formed and the Amateur Dramatic Club absorbed the Choral Union. The English-language Press reported with great detail the comings and goings in the different groups, the actors poached by directors, the defections caused by undiplomatic casting and personal liaisons or which prominent businessman had been asked to take part in a group, as well as the secret discussions on the choice of plays.[13] What the Press did not, and could not, report on was the back-stage gossip of flirtations, affairs, strained marriages, which theatre work often produced and which provided the British Community with an element of scandal that it delighted in. The community of effort and influence was at work in the theatre too; in spite of the great activity it was as groups that the British impressed with their performances. There were very few individuals who stood out.[14]

Then the war came and the exodus of Britons depleted the city of English-speaking performers. There was a revival, between the wars and even after that, but the British theatre world in Buenos Aires was never quite the same, quite as hectic, as during that first decade of the century.

14

Travellers' Tales and Other Writings

A few of the travellers to the River Plate in the first half of the nineteenth century returned to Britain and wrote about their experiences, thereby creating a considerable proportion of Argentina's early literature. The 'travellers' literature' is in a class of its own in Argentina, not only because it provided the world with accounts of a little-known territory, but also because it was written in a very particular style. This style relied strongly on the personal impressions of the authors as they travelled across the country or stopped in towns and cities or visited farms and outposts. The private opinions were supplemented with immense detail on the geographical, social and political description of the country. Information of commercial interest – such as the number of trading houses and the names of principal merchants; names of landowners, extension of their land and size of their herds – was also included in considerable detail. This was because not a few of the travellers who committed their impressions to paper were merchants, or sought to be granted the representation of British and European trading houses, or hoped for the support of merchants to pay for the publication of the manuscripts.

Such books are an essential source of reference to Argentina's history, for the amount of detail given and for the many interviews with political leaders and prominent personalities that were included in the text. There were very few of these books by native writers, whose production was politically partisan and not concerned with affairs outside of regional issues, hence failing to give a wider view of the country as would be of interest to foreign and later readers.

The British authors had no special class or category. The most read books in Argentina include one by a priest, Thomas Falkner, in the eighteenth century; one by the first British consul to Argentina, Woodbine Parish, in the middle of the nineteenth century; and one by a merchant, George Chaworth Musters, who wrote on Patagonia in the second half of the century. Writers include soldiers and sailors, adventurers, naturalists, physicians and churchmen.

The writings by Britons, in the particular 'travellers' style', came to an end with the improvement of publishing in Argentina, which made general guides and surveys available in Buenos Aires.[1] The expansion of British interests and investment in the country created a greater demand for information on commerce, communications and natural resources. The style of the old-fashioned traveller became too literary and not sufficiently concise for the changing patterns of trade. Buenos Aires supplied the information as its politics stabilized and its economy grew. There is no cut-off date for the age of British 'travellers' literature', but the form declined after the 1860s.[2]

Of all the writers on the River Plate, the best known to the English reader is William Henry Hudson, a naturalist and novelist who abandoned Buenos Aires and settled in England only to long for the land that he had left. His books describing Buenos Aires, Uruguay and Patagonia take those distant lands to the reader in Britain, creating a nostalgia for wide open spaces with a sensitivity that is very English in its concern for the country. *The Times* said he was 'unsurpassed as an English writer on Nature'.[3]

Hudson was born in August 1841, the third of six children. His parents, originally from Devon, had married in Boston and had travelled to Argentina in 1832.

The Hudsons bought the *Estancia Veinticinco Ombúes*, in Quilmes, south of Buenos Aires, a district created with Quilmes tribe indians transported from northern Argentina.[4] Hudson spent his first five years there, which gave him his initial close contact with nature and with the wildlife of the open Pampa which he would write about with a strong attachment many years later.[5]

When Hudson was six his family moved to a place near

Caseros, from where he could hear the battle in 1852 which ended the rule of Governor Rosas. He was educated at home by his mother and by a succession of tutors who visited the farmhouse. His juvenile carefree life came to an end with his mother's death and a decline in his own health, which remained fragile all his life. At the age of eighteen he spent some time assisting his father in the management of the Hudson *estancia*, from where he moved to the management of a near-bankrupt sheep farm for six years. Since the age of sixteen he had kept notes on the wildlife of the Pampas, an interest which, in 1886, won him an introduction to the Smithsonian Institution of Washington, which asked him to collect bird skins for scientific research. He was paid expenses, but received no wages, a thing which forced him to stop collecting three years later. The fact that he had killed birds for collection appears to have remained a lifelong embarrassment to Hudson and a thing to conceal – until shortly before his death – in his later campaigns in Britain for the protection of birds. However, his notes from bird-skin collecting for the Smithsonian were used as correspondence to the Zoological Society in London, which published the letters in its journal, *Proceedings*. These became Hudson's first published work. After that he went to Patagonia, where he spent a year, followed by two more on the Buenos Aires Pampa, at his own home, at which time he continued to write articles for the Zoological Society. One of these articles included a report on his discovery of a new species of bird, the Black Tyrant (*Cnipolegus hudsoni*).

A desire to see England made him decide to leave Buenos Aires in April 1874. His books about the Pampas and Patagonia, published in Britain nearly twenty years later, are nostalgic in extreme for a beautiful land he had left. But on arrival in Southampton he could think of Buenos Aires only in terms of a small dirty town; and of Argentina as a country that foolishly disregarded its natural wealth and its wildlife. Two years later he married his landlady, a former singer fifteen years his senior. They lived on slender means and the shortage of money prevented him from going far from London to carry out the work he liked most, the study of wildlife in the English countryside. He relied on his memories to produce his first book, *The purple land that England lost* (1885). It was a fictional story of a young Englishman in Uruguay (the 'purple land'). Although his principal character is not described as the most agreeable of persons, the book was seen by friends as being in part autobiographical.

His friends, towards the end of the century, included many personalities in the literary circles of London. They liked his writing and his subjects were exotic, which made them that much more attractive. Hudson's poverty, which he seemed unable to rid himself of, prompted some of those friends, among them Joseph Conrad, Edward Garnett, Robert Bontine Cunninghame Graham and John Galsworthy, to ask the British Government for a pension for him. He was put on the civil list with the generous sum of £100. He relinquished the pension when his books gave him enough to live on.

He had twenty-four titles published and wrote up to the time of his death, in August 1922, just after his eighty-first birthday.[6] His latter years he spent yearning for the open spaces he had known as a young man. He had once written to his brother in Córdoba – who had often suggested that he should return to Argentina – that he should never have left the River Plate. His yearning for that past was belatedly poured into one of his best-known books, *Far away and long ago*, which, apart from a memoir, owed much to his instinct for beauty and simplicity reflected in all his writing. Galsworthy said that Hudson 'is, of the writers of our time, the rarest spirit and has the clearest gift of conveying the nature of that spirit. Without apparent effort he takes you with him into a rare, free, natural world, and always you are refreshed, stimulated, enlarged, by going there.'

Hudson was unheard of in Argentina. The intellectual community in Buenos Aires learned of his existence when Rabindranath Tagore visited the city in 1924 and asked to be told more about Hudson.[7]

Other men sang their praises of the land. Robert B. Cunninghame Graham, a man who made the horses of the Pampas a subject for near worship in his writings, was one of them. Known as *Don Roberto*, born in London in May 1852, the son of a Scottish father and a Venezuelan mother, he was a personality in Buenos Aires, welcomed by the local aristocracy and literary circles. This was as much for his being a Briton in love with *gaucho* life and with the Pampas as for his writings. His stories, essays, historical biographies and especially *The Conquest of the River Plate* (1924) and *The Horses of the Conquest* (1930), combined with his colourful personality, won him the admiration of the Buenos Aires literary élite.[8]

Cunninghame Graham first went to Argentina in 1870 on a farming adventure which turned sour. But he learned about the life of the Argentine *gaucho* and shared the native man's love for the horse. In Argentina he was caught in an attempted coup, though his small participation was soon seen as that of an innocent. However, this forced his departure to Paraguay for two years. There his commerical ventures failed; but the experience gave him material for two books on the country. Several commercial ventures followed, and failed, which gave him a lasting dislike for commerce. In 1878, he returned to Britain, where his activities and interests took him through a variety of occupations, including Member of Parliament and president of the Scottish Nationalists. He travelled again to Buenos Aires, to buy horses for the British army – a mission which he described as distasteful – in 1914 and then again in 1936, the year of his death. He never achieved the fame of his friends Hudson and Conrad; but his writings are a valuable late addition to the bibliography of the merchant and gentlemen travellers of the nineteenth century.

The writing of John Masefield, admirer of Hudson and of Cunninghame Graham, about the Pampas is a mystery of inspiration. John Masefield, Britain's poet laureate up to his death in 1967, wrote the 109-stanza poem *Rosas*, which tells the story of the dictator and a sad *samba* about love trampled on by politics: the romance of Camila O'Gorman and the priest, Gutierrez, and their execution in 1848. How Masefield heard about Rosas is not clear, because he appears never to have been in Argentina. He was in Chile in 1894, while serving his apprenticeship on the sailing ship *Gilcruix*. When he was born, in 1878, Rosas had been dead one year. However, accounts of Rosas' rule were published and sold throughout South America, spiced with all kinds of horror and scandal. The story of Camila and the priest could have been one of these romance-and-blood tales. Masefield's poem *Rosas* was first published in New York in 1918 and was later included in his collected poems. Another poem about Argentina, *The daffodil fields*, written in 1912, was included in the North American edition of *Collected Poems*. It is the story of two English friends and their love for a girl and their *gaucho*-style fight for her, a form of battle learned on the Pampas. The narrative poem was inspired by 'a footnote to Sir W. Mackenzie's *Travels in Iceland*. It is there stated that the events described in the tale [Daffodil Fields] happened in Iceland in the eleventh century'.[9] The background of *gaucho* descriptions could have come from Hudson or Cunninghame Graham. After publication of *A Tarpaulin Muster* (1907) Masefield sent a copy to Cunninghame Graham with the comment, 'In these tales I have imitated everybody, just as, in my other books, I have done my best to imitate yourself'.[10]

The British community's few locally produced writers of note included Walter Hubbard Owen, born in Glasgow in July 1884, the son of a merchant father and a schoolteacher. He lived in Montevideo first and later in Buenos Aires, where he worked in commerce throughout his life. His poems, under a pen-name at first – because he feared that literary interests had to be hidden from his business acquaintances – though later he signed his own name to his production, were published regularly by *The Standard*. In Argentina he is best known for his translation into English of Argentina's *gaucho* epic *Martín Fierro*, a nineteenth-century narrative poem on the bad deal given the *gaucho* in Argentina, written by José Hernández. On the death of Owen in Buenos Aires, in September 1953, a society was organized to perpetuate his memory. A contemporary of Owen, a descendant of eighteenth-century Irish immigrants, novelist Benito Lynch, is often associated with the British community by Argentina's writers. But his entire production was in Spanish.

The English-speaking community's current successor to Hudson and Cunninghame Graham is William Shand, a Scots newsagent who arrived in Buenos Aires in 1938, then in his early thirties. He is a prolific poet, playwright and translator, whose theatre has won him several prizes in Argentina and has given him modest recognition.

British writers about Argentina are legion, of course; but few captured the identity and the feeling of the land as did Hudson and Graham in this century, or as the traveller writers did in the last. All the others appear more detached, less involved with their subject and probably more ignorant of it.

Another kind of writer who told the story of the country was the nineteenth-century newspaper publisher. It all started with the *Southern Star* in 1807, during the British invasion. But that was a short-lived venture. Then came *The British Packet and Argentine News*, after which there were many sheets.

The British Packet and Argentine News started on Friday, 4 August 1826, as a four-page sheet which aimed to cater to the growing British community and profit from the expanding trade between Britain and Argentina. After its first issue it was published on Saturdays, 'with the exception of an occasional irregularity which may arise from the arrival of the British Packets'. It was founded by Thomas George Love, a man active in local British merchant houses, in the Commercial Rooms and social events in the community. He remained the weekly's editor until his own death, in December 1845, although during a brief period, about one year, a man named Alexander Brander is mentioned as 'responsible editor', probably in Love's absence.

Love led the paper to support the Rosas government in the firm belief that strong-arm rule was in the best interests of the British community. Love was succeeded as editor by Ayrshire-born teacher, Gilbert Ramsay, who had arrived in Buenos Aires in 1825. Occasional financial misfortunes made the *Packet* suffer several interruptions in its publication.

Contemporary with Love was another Briton, James Spencer Wilde, though his mark was in a bilingual Press. With other members of a club called the Buenos Aires Literary Society, 'Santiago' Wilde started *El Argos*, a general news weekly which first appeared on Saturday, 2 May 1821, and closed thirty-four issues later. It was reissued as *El Argos de Buenos Aires* in January 1822 and lasted for several years. Wilde is remembered for some collections of essays, a few stage plays and his association with intellectual circles.[11]

Love's success with the *Packet* encouraged others to enter the field, in pursuit of advertising from the merchant houses and shippers. The first competitor was *The Anglo-Argentine* which lasted only a few issues in 1827, the year in which a periodical called *Cosmopolite* folded after eighteen issues. The latter's publisher was Stephen Hallet, an Irishman who had arrived in Buenos Aires in 1821. His next effort was *The American* – thirty issues in 1827 – followed by *Prices Current and Statistical Register*, which was simultaneous with his *The North Star*: neither survived much more than twelve months. Hallet found stability in the editor's chair at the government's *La Gaceta Mercantil*, which published its shipping notices in English on the front page to reach a wider commercial audience. In this job he was assisted by another Irishman, James Kiernan.

Next came *The Cosmopolitan*, sold at James Steadman's English Bookstore. It was published every Wednesday between 23 November 1831 and, apparently, 9 January 1833, for no issues are to be found after that. The anonymous editor announced that his paper would not be involved in politics, but rather would be of a 'purely pacific nature'.

There appears to have been a break after that, perhaps due to the unsettled political situation and then to the fact that the *Packet* took a pro-Rosas position, which may have discouraged competition that was not to be in favour of the government. Only one fierce opponent was published, but that was in Montevideo, where *Britannia*, published as from 1845, never missed an opportunity to attack Love and the Rosas regime.

The fall of Rosas saw the return of the adventurous. An American minister, the Reverend Dallas D. Lore, published *The Buenos Ayres Herald* during 1852 and 1853; a retired United States Navy officer, George Whitaker, announced publication of a weekly, *The Observer*, in 1854, but only printed one issue. This was followed by a sheet called *The Weekly*, published by a Mr Yorkney during 1858 and 1859. A Mr Pilling published *The Commercial Times* from 1858 to 1862.

At this time the most famous of all the English-language newspapers in Argentina made its appearance: *The Standard*, published by the Mulhall brothers.[12] It was to become the doyen of the Argentine Press and a publication consulted and quoted by the Spanish-language publications.

By then the *Packet* had folded, on 25 September 1858, and although it survived its founder by thirteen years it had faltered since the time of Love's death.

The River Plate Magazine, published by a Mr Williams, sought to share *The Standard's* rising popularity; but it lasted only two years after 1863 and then closed. A similar fate awaited *The Mail*, published by a Mr Havers of Montevideo, during 1864 and 1865; the *Argentine Citizen* published by the British Consul in Rosario, Thomas Hutchinson, from 1864 to 1866; the *South American Monthly*, edited by a Mr Carter in 1868 and 1869; *The Western Telegraph*, which was owned by a Mr Connolly and appeared in 1870 and 1872; as well as *Square and Compass*, in 1871, and *The River Plate Times*, from 1872 to 1874, both owned by a Mr Goldworthy. A merger of the organizers of several of these failures produced the *Buenos Ayres Daily News and River Plate Advertiser*, under the editorial leadership of a North American philanthropist, Nicholas Lowe; but this lasted only through 1873 and 1874. More successful was the Irish community's weekly, *The Southern Cross*, founded by Canon Dillon in 1875. It lasted over a century.

While *The Standard*'s growth appeared to be unmatchable, it was time for another story of success. It was *The Herald*, which started on 15 September 1876 under the direction of a Scot, William T. Cathcart, descended from a member of the Scottish colony of Monte Grande. The paper was announced as a weekly, although it published six or seven issues each month. Cathcart sold the *Herald* in January 1877 to a North American, D. W. Lowe, and under new management the paper became a daily. It was known as the Americans' paper and, later, as the Anglo-American paper. *The Standard* was considered the British paper.

When the *Herald* started 'all foreign newspapers in Argentina were regarded as guests and consequently it was argued that good taste and propriety demanded abstention from political affairs. The *Herald*, however, repudiated this idea and contended that a foreign paper was entitled to exercise all the rights and duties of native papers so long as it kept out of party politics'. Hence, in 1878, when a North American barque, *Devonshire*, was seized by the Chilean navy and towed into Punta Arenas alleged to have violated Chilean jurisdiction by loading *guano* in Santa Cruz, the *Herald* pointed out that 'the Atlantic coast has long been regarded by the world as belonging to Argentina and that Chile's wisest course would be to deliver the vessel to the United States with which the country had no quarrel and so avoid war with Argentina. As a consequence, the editor was asked to proceed to Chile ... and as the result of his efforts ... obtained the settlement of the dispute between Argentina and Chile.' In 1880, during a period of civil strife, 'when the revolutionists were prepared to surrender the editor of the *Herald* was asked to become the bearer of the offer ...'[13]

It was the first paper in Argentina to establish a European cable service – through the Havas Agency – the first to have a Transandine telegraphic service, the first to abandon the folio form and adopt the eight-page form and the first to modernize its printing.

The early success of the *Herald*, which soon started a *Weekly Herald* for foreign and country subscribers, slowed down due to economic difficulties. This was made worse by new competition, this time from *The Financial Review* which was published weekly as from December 1891 and, almost at the same time, *The Times of Argentina*, published by James J. Rugeroni. In an effort to strengthen the papers and reduce competition, Lowe and Rugeroni merged their two papers, while the *Financial Review* merged in 1903 with another recently started publication, *The River Plate Sports and Pastimes*, which was published three times a month as from Wednesday, 8 July 1891. The merger of the two latter papers was a success that has lasted to date as *The Review of the River Plate*, catering to the English-speaking business community. The association of the *Herald* and the *Times* was a failure, due to disagreement between Lowe and Rugeroni. They parted, *The Times of Argentina* becoming a successful shipping weekly and *The Herald* an independent, if sometimes faltering, daily.

The Herald was taken over in May 1908 by Thomas Bell, a member of one of Argentina's most established British families and son of pioneer George Bell, founder of a large, land, cattle, wool and general trading company. Bell made the paper the *Buenos Aires Herald* into which he had to put money constantly. He renovated much of the paper's equipment in an attempt to cater to a bigger market; but commercially it was never as successful as *The Standard*. Bell made the *Herald* a public company in 1920; but it only once paid a dividend. In 1925 he sold out to two brothers, Junius Julius Rugeroni and Claude Ronald Rugeroni, owners of *The Times of Argentina*, who kept the paper in the family for the next half-century.[14]

The proliferation of English-language papers appears to be overwhelming in what is a Spanish-speaking community. The reason for such profusion was that the audience existed; it was a big, strong British community, cut off from subscriptions to papers in Britain by their high cost and the long delays in the mail. The Spanish-language Press was accessible to a minority of Britons, the majority not being well acquainted with the language or simply not interested in the country's affairs. Hence the English Press gave British readers a résumé of local news, an abundance of British and European information, as well as a selection of extracts from county papers. For aspiring publishers, publication was not too difficult; advertising from British companies was easily obtained and many European and local merchants also wished to advertise their goods in publications read by the generally higher-income British community. This catering to the British was often obvious in the Spanish-language Press: a newspaper called *El Diario*, founded in 1881, published a magazine supplement called *Tit Bits Argentino*, aimed at Britons. This newspaper kept an office, for correspondence, subscriptions and advertising on the Strand, in London.

15

North American Businessmen and Bandits

Buenos Aires set the United States as a model to follow, when politicians charted a course to rid the country of the close and backward atmosphere left by General Rosas. Argentina had strong ties with Britain; London was the 'old world' centre for commerce; as Paris was for culture. But the United States represented all the drive and progress that could be attained in the 'new world'. One demonstration of this respect was the Argentine President's regular attendance at 4 July parties at the Legation and frequent meetings with leading figures in the North American community. The English-speaking Press acknowledged the gestures with praise. For example, *The Standard* of 6 July 1864 reported that 'The friends of the United States met at the American Minister's pursuant to invitation ...' and in the 'crowded salons' were 'H. E. Bartholomew Mitre, President of the Republic', and members of his Cabinet. The following year, on 5 July, the newspaper said that the United States' Independence Day anniversary would long be remembered because it was the first time the date had really been celebrated in Buenos Aires: the provincial government had declared the day a public holiday and administration buildings were illuminated for the occasion. The reports on the Legation party and the speeches filled the paper and most of the following day's issue as well.[1]

President Mitre's successor, President Domingo F. Sarmiento, previously Argentine minister in Washington, sought United States assistance in all fields. A treaty of friendship, commerce and navigation had existed since July 1853, signed in Entre Rios when General Urquiza moved the Argentine capital to the city of

Paraná. Removal of the capital followed the secession of Buenos Aires province from the Argentine Confederation which lasted until 1859. Sarmiento, who had at one time been sympathetic and later extremely critical of Urquiza, was determined to use the treaty to full advantage for Argentina. One of his main concerns was to improve education and build schools throughout the country. He offered qualified North American teachers fairly high wages to come to Argentina and managed to attract sixty-five trained women. Some left immediately, feeling cheated by the country they saw: a façade modelled by European influence in the city on the River Plate and a backdrop of prevailing disorder and backwardness in the provinces. But many of the teachers stayed for several years and some opened private schools in the provincial capitals.

The United States started to show its commercial drive at the Córdoba trade fair, which opened in October 1871. The North American consul rallied merchants to show they could compete with British goods. At the same time, in Córdoba, Sarmiento inaugurated the country's first astronomical observatory. While Argentina's minister in the United States, he had met Benjamin Apthorp Gould, a scientist and lecturer at the University of Harvard who owned a small private observatory and wanted to explore the sky south of the Equator. This had not yet been done to any great extent. In 1866 the Argentine Government had authorized Gould to travel to Córdoba and establish an observatory there.[2]

Sarmiento's good relations with the United States were shown again only a few weeks before his term ended, at the Independence Day reception at the United States Legation in 1874. *The Standard*'s list of guests was impressive. Besides the President, there was a former president, General Mitre, and a future president, Nicolás Avellaneda, at the party. General Thomas Osborne, the resident minister, wrote on the afternoon of 4 July to the commander of the United States war steamer *Wasp* to ask that the Argentine colours be saluted by the ship's guns on 9 July, the Argentine Independence Day.[3] The attention paid to the United States in Buenos Aires appears to be out of proportion with the size of the mission in the city: a small representation which complained about being understaffed and unable to handle the matters it was faced with, mainly to do with North American merchant shipping in the South Atlantic.

Among the first formally established United States community associations was the all-male American Society of the River Plate, inaugurated on 4 July 1905, which was very much a suburban merchants' social club in the city. The second oldest club, and the largest, is the American Club, founded in September 1914 as the American Luncheon Club. It became the American Commercial Club of Buenos Aires in January 1915; but dropped the commercial side when the United States Chamber of Commerce in Argentina was organized in November 1918. The Chamber was a result of the war. The United States wanted to increase trade with Latin America and secure the support of its back-door neighbours in future. It was also a form of competition with Britain which, having suffered heavy damage during the war, sought to increase trade with what was a traditional British market. In addition to numerous small social clubs, the North American community also produced its own news-sheet, *The American Weekly of Buenos Aires*, published every Saturday as from July 1923. It folded after a few years because the English-language Press was already supplying community news, in addition to world news coverage – a field the *Weekly* did not enter.

The Adventist Church opened a branch in Buenos Aires in 1891, the Baptists in 1903, the Disciples of Christ in 1905 and the United States Menonite Church opened in the town of Pehuajó in 1917. The North Americans also had their own school: the Ward College, founded in 1913, which eventually was to merge with the Lincoln School, founded in 1936, to form the American Community School in 1952.

The begining of baseball in Argentina is recorded by a newspaper notice on 30 May 1889 which said: 'Base Ball – The Buenos Aires Base Ball Club will play a match today with the Club of the United States sloop *Richmond*. Play will commence at 1.30 p.m. This is the first time that the members of the Buenos Aires club will have appeared in their new costumes, especially made for the game and, doubtless, there will be a considerable attendance.' In the *Standard* of 20 August 1889, a short notice reported that the first game of 'base ball between the Rosario and Buenos Aires teams took place on Sunday at the new cricket grounds at Rosario, and resulted in a victory for Buenos Aires by the score of 21 to 13'. Interest in the sport was not strong and it was not until 1921 that a four-team league was formed.

The failure to establish institutions such as those of the Britons in Argentina was due to the fact that the number of permanent North American residents in Argentina was small. Most people were short-term residents. The community's members' occupations centered on commercial activities, as were the importation of consumer goods. Such enterprises were run by locally employed people and only the management travelled from the United States.

As importers of heavy industrial goods the North Americans were competing with the British; but they were more often suppliers of goods to British building companies and the railways. North Americans entered banking, but had little to do with farming. Some individuals, however, entered farming in the sugar industry in Tucumán, and became prosperous local personalities. Their social life was with the British, as there was no United States community outside of Buenos Aires and, to some extent, Rosario. As competitors or associates the North Americans were always close to the British, usually overshadowed by the latter, larger and better-established group. The North Americans' turn would come after the 1930s, when the United States and Britain would change their roles in the world.

An incident that alarmed the entire English-speaking community in Buenos Aires and caused enormous embarrassment to the North Americans in the city was the most exciting account of Americans in Argentina. It is the story of Robert Leroy Parker, best known as Butch Cassidy, and a Pennsylvania German, an evil-tempered killer named Harry Longabaugh, known as the Sundance Kid, and their brief careers in Patagonia.

Cassidy joined the Sundance Kid and Etta Place, his girlfriend, a former schoolteacher, in New York, towards the end of 1901, on the eve of their departure to Argentina. Cassidy had staged some small hold-ups to raise the money for three fares to Buenos Aires, where they had chosen to go to escape very long gaol sentences or death by the increasingly organized band of lawmen who were imposing law and order on the last unruly corners of the North American frontier. As James Ryan and Mr and Mrs Harry A. Place the three bade farewell to New York in grand style: they went to the theatre and dined out, they bought Etta, described as the rather stunning daughter of an Englishman, jewellery at Tiffany's and sailed for Buenos Aires on the SS *Soldier Prince*.

Behind them were five years as active cowboy-outlaws – an occupation forced on many drovers by unemployment – in Cassidy's successful Train Robbers' Syndicate, also known as the Wild Bunch. The frontier lawmen, the high cost of keeping an efficient hold-up gang and the Pinkerton Agency – whose list of wanted men Cassidy headed – had forced them away. Patagonia, they had been told, still was a land of free men. On arrival in Buenos Aires they were awarded 12,000 acres of rough land in Cholilla, Chubut, in the Andes foothills, to work as farmers.

The three arrived in Trelew, in Welsh territory, on the east coast of Chubut, in 1902. They entered the small town very much as an ordinary group of foreign travellers, not an infrequent sight there. They took rooms at the Del Globo Hotel and only the bar-room gossip recorded their arrival. From the Atlantic coast they went west, to the land near Cholilla on the way to Leleque, neighbouring the property of the British-owned Argentine Southern Land Company Ltd, for many years the largest landholder in the area. Within the year they had built a brick house and a trading store which was managed by a resident from Esquel, Mansell Gibbon.

They were seen as peaceful settlers for the first couple of years, even if the anecdotes that they have given rise to throughout the century would deny this.

In 1903 they were joined by Harvey Logan, who had escaped from gaol in Knoxville, Tennessee, and fled to Argentina. Logan reached Cholilla under the name of Andrew Duffy. Together they reconstituted the Wild Bunch and as hold-ups were second nature to them, they returned to the old habit. The raid on the *Londres y Tarapacá* Bank, in Gallegos, in February 1905, when assistant manager Mr Bishop and his teller, Mr MacKerror, were robbed of twenty thousand pesos, was attributed to what was to be known, and is still remembered, as the *Banda Norteamericana.* Some months later they were attributed the hold-up of the branch of the

Banco de la Nación, at Villa Mercedes, in San Luis province. By then the Pinkerton Agency was closing in on them. Descriptions of Cassidy, the Kid and Etta had been sent to the Buenos Aires chief of police and Pinkerton detectives travelled to the Argentine capital to start the search for the Wild Bunch. But the detectives never went south to Patagonia, allegedly because the territory was described as extremely hostile to police.

In December 1907 Cassidy sold the land of Cholilla and announced that they were crossing into Chile. Some stories say that it was Etta Place who wanted to leave, having become pregnant in a brief affair with an English neighbour, John Gardner, and thereby upsetting the *ménage à trois* that she had been part of with Cassidy and the Kid.

The story goes on from there to dramatic deaths in San Vicente, Bolivia, after a train hold-up which went wrong. But this story, although taken to film, is probably bogus.

In December 1909 two North Americans, identified as Bob Evans and Willie Wilson, held up the *Compañia Mercantil de Arroyo Pescado*, a bank and general trading store in a cluster of houses and sheds set in isolation in the Patagonian barrenness. The bank was expecting a consignment of sovereigns to pay for the wool clip; but the hold up took place too soon. All that was in the safe were a few Argentine pesos belonging to local indians and which the thieves decided not to take. As they left, Wilson tripped and fell; the store-manager, a big Welshman from Bara, Llwyd Ap Iwan, tried to take the thief's gun. The manager was shot dead and the thieves fled.

The murder of Ap Iwan – well known in the region for his support for Welsh colonists and his sympathetic attitude towards the indians – shocked the local foreign community. Publications on Patagonia that had to mention the raid referred to the manager's murder, but not to the suspect murderers. It was a source of concern to the British community that people with Anglo-Saxon names should be mentioned by the Press as murderers and bank thieves and a source of embarrassment to the North American residents in Buenos Aires that such people should have come from their country. Talk of the attack and of the *Banda Norteamericana* was dropped whenever possible.

There is no clear identification of Wilson and Evans, though descriptions given by Pinkerton do make them appear similar to Cassidy and the Kid.

While Cassidy, a man who was said to dislike shooting although he was an expert at planning hold-ups – the shooting being left to the Kid and to Logan, the latter attributed with twenty-five murders – has been described as going home to the United States to settle quietly under an assumed name, being shot dead by Uruguayan police, retiring to Ireland, settling down as an engineer on the North American east coast, prospecting for gold with Wyatt Earp, or touring about the United States in style, the end of his story is uncertain. The Kid and Etta are mentioned as sharp-shooters, expert riders, frequenters of elegant company in the region, attending dances and being seen in the company of government officials. But they too vanished.[4]

The names of Wilson and Evans came to notice again in March 1911, when the ranch of Lucio Ramos Otero, at Cañadón del Tiro, San Martín, was robbed of valuables and, in April, of a few head of cattle. According to old police anecdotes, a manhunt was then ordered. The tracks of the fleeing gangsters were found at the *estancia* La Teka in June and a camp they had used was traced at Sierra de Rio Pico. But it was not until December that the two men were found. According to the stories, the man identified as Evans was shot dead as he sat over an open fire. Wilson resisted and killed a policeman; but another policeman put two bullets through his chest.

However, the story has no end there. The statements, by relatives of Cassidy and the Kid, leave no doubt that the men did return to the United States, emigrated elsewhere, but certainly survived. Etta Place has her own corner of Patagonian history, among stories of other English and North American women who cropped their hair and dressed like men to go out and lead a life of crime. These women were said to be good with a gun and in the saddle, their criminal actions prompted by greed, or by charitable decisions to help the poor, or to feed their children after being widowed or abandoned.

The North American Band of Patagonia are still a source of speculation.

16

The Age of Growth

The building of a new Argentina in the second half of the nineteenth century is invariably connected with the laying of the railway lines through the country, most of them by British engineering. After the fall of Rosas in 1852, liberal economic policies were introduced by men who had been forced to flee the country during the dictatorship and, in exile, had been in contact with European ideas and customs.

At hand in every event was a Briton. Britons placed more long-term investment in South America during the nineteenth century than in any other geographic region. Argentina, Brazil, Chile, Mexico and Uruguay received the lion's share.[1] Britain's interest in Spanish America had always been strong. After Lord Ponsonby's intervention in the creation of the state of Uruguay in 1826, his successors, Henry Fox, John Mandeville, William Gore Ouseley, Thomas Hood, Lord Howden and Henry Southern, all secured advances in Britain's relations with Buenos Aires. Treaties for communications, transport and navigation were signed in the 1850s, paving the way for a mass of investment that began with the railways.

Argentina's first railway was not built by a British concern, however; but the group of shareholders and engineers included Britons. Daniel Gowland, a Briton, was vice-president of the Western Railway Company, formed in 1855 with a capital of £28,000 to build the railway, from the Parque station, where the Colón Opera House of Buenos Aires stands today, to Flores, running over a distance of eight miles. The railway opened to the public in August 1857, after the society had borrowed another £24,000 from the government to complete work. The company's directors rode on horse alongside the track during the inaugural run, making a show of escorting the passengers, though in reality not sure of the safety of their own machine, which travelled at fifteen miles per hour. On the return to the Parque terminal one of the train's two coaches derailed and, although a minor accident, it caused considerable delay. The railway managers asked passengers not to report the mishap to those waiting at Parque, to avoid undue alarm. The news leaked out the following day; but by then the tales of the successful journey had caused a greater impression.

The train was pulled by an engine later named *La Porteña*, built by the Hunslet Engine Company of Leeds.[2] It had been built for war service in Crimea and had a 5 ft 6 in Russian gauge. When the war ended, the engines and carriages were offered for sale around the world.

Daniel Gowland Phillips, the Western Railway Company director, was one of two Gowland brothers, well known in Buenos Aires business circles for their commercial success and power. When Daniel was twelve years old and his brother Thomas nine, their father had taken them to Buenos Aires from England. On arrival, in 1812, their first impression could not have been worse: the body of a man executed for taking part in a conspiracy against the revolutionary government installed in May 1810 had hung in the Plaza Victoria. Daniel and Thomas were among the founders of the Strangers' Club. Daniel Gowland became a director of the Banco Nacional de las Provincias Unidas and throughout his life held many public posts, an achievement which was used in immigration promotion, as proof that Argentina was a land of success for Britons. In his last years, Daniel Gowland was considered something of a patriarch of the British community. At the time of the first run of *La Porteña*, the local Press recorded the fact that Gowland was the only Briton in Buenos Aires to have travelled on a train in Europe. His brother, Thomas Gowland, opened an auctioneer's room and later was the founder of the society of auctioneers; he was also among the founders of the Primitiva de Gas Company. He became the first naturalized foreigner to hold a seat on the City Council. Although this was a demonstration of involvement by expatriates in government and administration, it was not an indication of an interest in local politics. He had taken the seat by invitation from all sides of the council, because of his prominence in commerce.

The first line on which *La Porteña* ran was built by a British engineer, William Bragge, also among the founders of the Primitiva de Gas Company (Bragge, a collector of old manuscripts and first editions, died in Birmingham in 1884, after a career that put him among the wealthiest men in the River Plate). John Allan, an Englishman, was the first engine driver. Although he was well known and highly regarded for that first in his life, he would become better known still in 1870 and 1871 as the man in charge of the train which took the victims of a yellow-fever epidemic from the city's hospitals to the cemetery on the western outskirts.

Several small companies followed the creation of the Western Railway. The first was the Northern Railway of Buenos Aires, spanning eighteen miles into the suburbs, followed by the Buenos Aires and Ensenada Railway – the brainchild of a North American, William Wheelwright, who founded the Pacific Steam Navigation Company. Then came the East Argentine Railway which ran from Concordia, in Entre Rios, along the River Uruguay, to Caseros, in the province of Corrientes. The Buenos Aires to Campana Line ran over forty-two miles between the two cities. All were built with British funds by British engineers. The Northern, Ensenada, East Argentine and Campana lines were later absorbed by bigger companies, also British.

Argentina's two biggest railways were the British-built, owned and operated Central Argentine Railway Ltd and the Buenos Ayres Great Southern Railway Co. Ltd, with headquarters in London. They were started at the same time, but the Southern was made in sections, while the Central was planned as a great iron road to open almost four hundred miles of sparsely populated, rich land.

A decree dated in August 1863 authorized the construction of the Southern, based on a proposal by a group of people that included the already mentioned wealthy Irish merchant Thomas Armstrong and George Drabble, a pioneer in railways and in the frozen meat trade and one-time president of the Bank of London and River Plate who had arrived in Buenos Aires in 1848, Alfred Lumb, Henry Green, John Fair and Henry Harrat, merchants and landowners who were anxious to invest in a promising enterprise and to increase the value of their property by means of the new communications. The initial authorized capital was about £700,000. Lumb had the concession and the support of shareholders among whose names were Thomas Duguid, the Fair family, British Consul Frank Parish – later the Southern's chairman who, with Baring, bought into the Central – and David Robertson. They were all the élite of the British community and as such found no difficulty in selling shares to investors in London, Birmingham, Liverpool and Manchester. The company quoted on the London stock exchange.

The Standard of 4 August 1865 announced that 'The Southern Railway will be open for passenger traffic on Monday, the trains will leave in the morning and return at night – they will go to a station within three leagues of Chascomús', which became the terminal in December of that year. Those were the first eighty miles. Another 500 were added in the next twenty years.

The Central Argentine was not such an English line in appearance. The concession went to a North American, William Wheelwright, in May 1863. One year later another North American, Allan Campbell, presented the plans for a line running from Rosario to Córdoba over nearly 300 miles. Thomas Armstrong, who had acquired vast landholdings in the territory that the Central was to cross, became one of the railway's principal representatives. The line started with an authorized capital of £1.6 million and was completed in 1870. Extensions to the north followed as well as south to Buenos Aires, by absorption of smaller companies. The names of the Central's shareholders are repeated in company after company as if between them they had much of the country to themselves.

The period is one of apparently limitless money and wealthy men. One report, quoted in *The Times* of 21 March 1870, a survey of the cost of living in foreign cities, said:

> An old resident of Buenos Ayres assures Mr Stuart (a member of the British Legation's staff) that twenty years ago £1,000 a year was a good income there, and would maintain a numerous family, but that now a

newly-married couple with £1,000 a year would have to study the very strictest economy and perhaps retire altogether from society; but, on the other hand, money is earned with great facility now, and at this day there is an amount of wealth in Buenos Ayres which would then have appeared incredible.

The original Parque to Floresta line was extended with an 1881 loan of £200,000 from Baring Brothers and eventually linked with a new Western Railway, operated by the Buenos Aires Government at first but later sold to a British group. A company acting for Baring offered £7 million, which was rejected, and a month later the Bank of London and River Plate, in representation of an English consortium, paid £8.2 million at a time when the Buenos Aires province treasury was going through a severe financial crisis.

Another small line, built for the government with a contract clause which made it immediately saleable to a private group, was the Andine Railway, running from Villa María, in Córdoba, to Mercedes, in San Luis. In January 1887, Bayless Hanna, the United States consul in Buenos Aires, reported that the Andine, 'operating over 324 miles from Villa Mercedes' and a necessary link in the line from Buenos Aires to Valparaíso, Chile, called the Transcontinental Railway, had been sold to a British company, which had outmanoeuvred North American bidders. Two brothers, Mathew and John Clark, had bought it as a condition for continuing work on the international line.

It was just one brief chapter in a forty-year story of the brothers' effort to cut a hole in the Andes. Mathew Clark was sixty-seven when he saw the tunnel go through the Andes, forty years after he had started work on the idea in 1869. The railway line between both countries was completed in April 1910.

Everywhere in Argentina there are reminders of the British engineering pioneers: a bridge, a track, stamped in Birmingham, or the stamp of English builders, or the engineering of British companies, or even in the names of railway stations.

The railways attracted many Britons to Argentina. They never constituted a wave of immigrants, but made a constant and noticeable trickle. The railways were a secure and stable form of employment as the companies expanded, even though the Emigrants' Information Office, in London, cautioned throughout

the 1870s that:

It cannot be too clearly pointed out that this country is not one for British emigrants in speculative search of employment ... The class of British emigrant to which this country is suited is the one who has money to take up a holding and work it. With the rapid development and opening up of the country which is in progress this class of person may sometimes be able to make a good living ...

The growth of the railways naturally attracted commercial houses, funded and supported by trading concerns in London and in all the principal British ports. Insurance brokerages grew to take up most of the market, banking and finance enterprises grew with increased investment, and shipping lines added tonnage to their River Plate services to supply manufactured goods and machinery to the growing country. By the late 1870s there was a British middle class, comfortable, insular and looked up to by the *Criollo* population, which Britons looked down on – just as Britons looked down on their closest competitors, the German community, which had the disadvantage of its divisions and periodical disputes.

A volume titled *Twentieth Century Impressions of Argentina*, reviewing the last third of the nineteenth century, assured that 'Where the man from England has established himself he has done well'. The same volume said that 'The Briton in Argentina is not of Argentina. He always looks forward to returning some day to his northern isles to end his days among the associations of his youth. This is true more of the Englishman than of the Scotsman or Irishman'. The May 1910 Centenary Supplement of the newspaper *La Nación* praised the British 'who possess in the Republic an influence superior to the rest of foreign nationalities ... No matter to what part of the Republic you direct your view you will find British capital invested there.'

The railways produced a new social class. The middle-class family became stronger because of the stability of employment; the people who spoke English were a step ahead, because the language associated them with the management. A whole myth became solidly built around the British nature. The aforementioned *Twentieth Century Impressions of Argentina* said that there are current sayings which speak for themselves. If a verbal promise is made the native, to seal the contract, usually says *palabra de inglés* (word of an Englishman), meaning that he will act as an Englishman, whose word is his bond. If an appointment is made, and the hour fixed, it is usual for the natives to say *hora de inglés* (Englishman's time), meaning that the Englishman's hour, who is always on time, will be observed. If a native has a house to let he prefers a Britisher, and generally without contract or guarantee, knowing that the house will be cared for as if it were his own, and all other conditions fulfilled. The provisions dealers are delighted to deal with Britishers; they say they buy plenty and pay well. This does not mean to say that all English-speaking people maintain the above standards. Many times the natives are deceived.

As the British railways grew, many of their staff were specifically imported and trained for work in different sections of the companies. And as this crowd became larger, rows of English-looking terraced or semi-detached houses were built in front of stations on the suburban lines. The houses were often built with bricks imported from Britain and most of the fittings were British-made too. But those were the smaller imports: entire stations – from railway terminals to signal boxes – were also shipped from Britain. In one case, what is today the La Plata central station was intended for India; but was re-routed at the time of shipment on the reception of news of disturbances and economic difficulties on the Indian subcontinent.

Many people were drawn by the boom. The construction of the railways was followed by British participation or ownership in all the public utility companies and public works, such as gas, tramways, water supply, docks, telegraph and, eventually, telephones and a share in electricity supply. The British companies, in banking, insurance, land, water, shipping, etc., make a long list. Large family firms grew into small empires and the names of Drysdale, Duggan and Bell are now of historical note in Argentina's landowning and export business. Macadam and Maitland-Heriot were prominent in commerce; David Hogg, of Fife, operated a huge engineering supply company since 1874; James Smart made English tailoring a must in Buenos Aires as from 1888; Cassels was a name for gramophones and vacuum cleaners; Murchison and Whiting & Stevens were established ship-brokers; and a few more made 'high society' of their own.

Argentina's traditional salted-beef trade and old-time *saladero* got their revolution with the aid of British enterprise. It was George Drabble, of the Central Argentine Railway, who set up the River Plate Fresh Meat Company Ltd, in 1882, using refrigeration in his attempt to improve the dry- and salted-meat trade. Refrigeration had been tested in Australia and, on a small scale, by one man in Buenos Aires. Drabble built his plant at Campana and, in 1883, the first shipment was made. Shipowners had no knowledge of the new industry to induce them to overhaul vessels, so shippers had to provide the equipment and instal it themselves. The Houlder Brothers Line ship *Meath* was fitted and carried the first shipment to London, arriving in January 1884. The meat-packing business which was to make Argentina famous had begun.

Liebig's Extract of Meat Company had started in London in 1865 with a capital of £150,000. It produced 'Extractum Carnis Liebig', invented by Justus von Liebig, in Germany, in 1847. Georg Christian Giebert, a German railway engineer living in Uruguay, read about Liebig and his offer to give his formula to any person who wished to produce it in South America – because production was too costly in Europe, as thirty kilos of lean meat were required to make one of extract. Hamburg-born Giebert got the licence to produce the extract in 1865 and started the Societe de Fray Bentos Giebert & Cie., at Fray Bentos, on the River Uruguay. But he needed capital almost immediately and sought it in London. From 800 kilos in the first month of operations, production rose to 500,000 kilos ten years later. And in 1878 the company started to produce corned beef.

The origin of the Argentine Estates of Bovril Ltd is traced to those times. In October 1871 one Eustaquio de la Riestra put up a beef-salting plant at Santa Elena, on the River Paraná, with a partner named Federico Gonzales. This plant was bought in 1880 by the German Kemmerich Company and, in 1908, by Bovril, which also became a landowning and cattle-raising concern. These were followed, in 1910, by the La Plata Cold Storage Co., a United States company better known by its name as from 1916, The Swift of La Plata. Almost a decade later, the Vestey family group, Union International, opened the Anglo meat-packing company on the Buenos Aires South Dock.

The counter-part of the processors were the cattle raisers who organized the Argentine Rural Society at a meeting at the home of the Martínez de Hoz family, in Buenos Aires, in July 1866. Among the thirteen men at the meeting there were four Britons. One was George Temperley, landowner and a member of the board of several large British concerns; another was Richard Blake Newton, a strong landowner in the Chascomús area and responsible for introducing fencing of land in Buenos Aires; and brothers Claude and George Stegmann, cattle raisers, born in York and resident in Argentina since 1818.

As Britain's interests in Argentina grew, the visitors became less suspicious of the far-off, Spanish-speaking country and were more prominent. In December 1880, Prince George, the Duke of York, later King George V, accompanied by the Duke of Clarence and Prince Louis Battenberg, stopped in Buenos Aires for five days, three of which they spent at the *Estancia El Negrete*. A special train took them from HMS *Bacchante* to the ranch.

Argentina was in financial and political crisis, however, and would be for most of the next decade. Disputes over the creation of a federal capital in Buenos Aires were followed by a period of government which was notable for its corruption. In 1890, followers of the Civic Radical Union rose in revolt against the government, demanding a greater share in the public administration for the benefit of the middle class. British interests suffered in the crisis, which put Barings on the brink of bankruptcy. But the British were also on hand to enjoy what followed, the liberal and progressive presidency of General Roca whose term in office at the turn of the century is now referred to as Argentina's *belle époque*.

Those were the days when the Jockey Club, with a large British membership, was described as the wealthiest club in the world and the British-run Buenos Aires Rowing Club became the largest club of its kind in the world. All was superlatives as Argentina entered the twentieth century as a rich country, its wealth lying on the land and ready to be picked up and exported through British companies. Argentina's high society kept racing horses in Paris, houses in Switzerland, but they bought British engineering and banked in London – where the palatial Argentine Club was opened in March 1911. To speak English was not just a mark of education, it was a daily necessity. Britons shied away from anything more than dabbling in the Spanish language; to keep their shocking accent in the native Spanish tongue became a symbol of status, of power.

17

Close to the Change

British influence was reflected everywhere in Argentina before it suffered the jolt that reverberated world-wide – the First World War.

Community institutions flourished and ran through a wide range, from individual ventures to large groups. They organized social activities, sporting clubs and charity associations with a determination to get full benefit from their efforts. In those 'good old days' of the British in Argentina, the English Club occupied a large rambling house in the middle of the city of Buenos Aires. Originally it was called the Albion Club, a private club inaugurated in 1893 by a Mr Wilde. It became the English Club, an all-male social and billiards watering place, in April 1898. English Clubs opened in most towns which had a number of resident Britons. British papers and publications were subscribed to and English gin was always in stock.

The approach of the decimation of the big community was not apparent to its members. It was not apparent anywhere else either, for that matter. The Coronation of King Edward VII and Queen Alexandra, on 9 August 1902, was celebrated in Argentina on a scale that might have embarrassed more than one colonial authority in other parts of the world. *The Standard* remarked that 'The King would have felt proud of his subjects ... had he seen their celebrations'. These had their start with the end of war in South Africa, marked with a telegram expressing 'respectful and heartfelt congratulations to His Majesty' in June. The Union Jack flew atop railway buildings and clubs.

It is perhaps a mark of the size and power of a community

when it can organize large charitable societies of its own; and Britons in Argentina had many such organizations.

The community centralized its social and charitable efforts in the British Society, formed in May 1912, to replace the local branch of the League of Empire, which had opened in October 1907. The British Society's premises were the Prince George's Hall – named in honour of the royal visit in December 1880 – used also by a variety of community entities, from the Girl Guides to the British Saturday Football League and by several smaller charities.[1]

To mark the May 1910 centenary of the peaceful revolution against Spanish authority a replica of Big Ben was built on the Plaza Británica, in front of the Central Argentine Railway terminal, and a monument to the forceful diplomatic pioneer of Anglo-Argentine relations, George Canning, was also built on the same square. The British Chamber of Commerce was formed in July 1914. Then came the beginning of the end of an era.

> The British community awoke to read newspaper confirmation of the overnight intimation [August 5]. The British Empire was at war. True to their national characteristic, there was no outward semblance of undue excitement. The situation demanded something different to that. Ties of blood and kindred, and devotion to the Motherland, brushed all other considerations on one side. Even at this early stage, men of military age made preparations for going 'over there'; they needed no special call. Others moved in the direction of securing united cooperation of the community with patriotic objects in view,

the *Buenos Aires Herald* would say later.[2]

> During the whole of the day a continuous stream of British subjects presented themselves at the Consulate-General, Consulates and Vice-Consulates, offering their services to our King and Country. There one rubbed shoulders with reservists, old soldiers, old volunteers, many of whom had seen active service in the South African war, and others anxious to give the most practical evidence of their patriotism. Some, whose business affairs did not take long to arrange, sailed on the *Aragon*, on 7 August. On board were quite a number of RNR men and French reservists.

A post-war report on the community's activities during the war said that

To attract recruits there was not that magnetism of a prestige to uphold, the prestige of a Colony or Protectorate, such as stimulated recruiting in all parts of the Empire. Men spoke in undertone about recruiting in a neutral country, and care had to be taken to avoid infringement of neutrality laws. These things did not damp the patriotic spirit nor diminish the homeward flight.[3]

During that long war, 4852 resident Britons and Anglo-Argentines volunteered for service in Britain, as recorded by the British Society's publication *The British Magazine*. It was a considerable number in a community of nearly 30,000. Many who went to serve were employees of British companies, especially the railways, which gave 1062 men, of whom eleven per cent were killed. The largest number of volunteers from Argentina joined infantry regiments. These totalled 1394, while 847 men joined the Royal Engineers, 761 went into artillery corps, 222 to the Flying Corps, 215 to the first and second King Edward's Horse regiments and 186 to other cavalry regiments – which attracted riding men from the vast British-owned *estancias* who, more than any other, went with the idea of noble service for King and Country – while 146 went into the Royal Navy and Marines. The others were spread out in a variety of units. Between them they collected 503 honours and distinctions, ranging from one Victoria Cross to 102 mentions in despatches, plus forty-three foreign decorations. There were 1704 men who received commissions and 820 non-commissioned officers. About one-quarter of the men who went to that war returned to Buenos Aires.

The city of that time was one free of the ravages of war; a prosperous city, ready to ship grain and meat to the hungry of Europe. It was a city of wide avenues and elegant pedestrian walks; where the poor were barred because it was a rule that a man had to wear a coat to walk on the street in the shopping centre – and not many of the poor had a coat for everyday use. The buildings of Buenos Aires reflected the wealth of the land in the provinces; every building that rose above the old tenements was a grand design by an Italian or a French architect. Wide new avenues were planned and built in Parisian style.

In that city, between 1914 and 1919, the British community formed numerous committees which included Socks for the

Trenches, Fresh Egg Fund, Yerba Maté Fund, Queen Mary's Needlework Guild, British Patriotic Committee, and many others. From Río Gallegos, in Patagonia, to the central province of Córdoba, forty-one British sports and social clubs raised cash for the war effort.

One demonstration of British strength in Argentina was the Statutory [or 'Black'] List of 'enemy firms and persons in the Argentine Republic' with which trade was prohibited for Britons under the Trading with the Enemy Act, 1915. The list was first issued in March 1916 and withdrawn in April 1919. It had a devastating effect on the image of persons and companies included. During that time the commercial relations between the local British community and German interests ceased to exist, with intimidating effects on native merchants. 'Owing to their predominant position in Argentine trade this action of the British commercial community was a severe blow to enemy trade and influence, which was accentuated as allied and neutral commerce followed the lead of the British', the *Buenos Aires Herald* said.[4] The List was printed by one James McGough, a journalist who ran his own printing plant, The British Printery, contributed articles to the English language Press, sports features to just about every paper in Buenos Aires and made several attempts at publishing his own English-language magazines. He was supplied with the information necessary to compile the List, the names to include or remove, by the British minister, Sir Reginald Tower, and by the Legation secretary, Eugen Millington Drake. It was indeed a blow to the Germans who, since the turn of the century, had been increasing investment in Argentina and building a commercial network on the foundation provided by large family companies that had been established in the second half of the nineteenth century.[5]

After the war there was a change in the habits of the British in Buenos Aires. The railways had made living in the suburbs easier and so the community scattered. At the same time, a class division became noticeable. The management of the railways went to the northern suburbs; engine drivers and guards lived on the southern side of the city; while the wealthy and the landowners made a district of their own in the western suburbs. As they scattered the adventure that was being part of the British community in Argentina changed in character.

18

The Twentieth Century

The Great War did not eclipse the community's influence, but its outstanding situation suffered a reduction. However, while a return to pre-war levels of power was not possible, Britain held the status of most prominent foreign investor in Argentina.

The British Chamber of Commerce in Buenos Aires became the leading spokesman for British interests as from June 1919. It was supported by a high-powered mission, led by Sir Maurice de Bunsen, charged with promoting British exports. The Chamber had been granted its certificate of incorporation in July 1914, three weeks before Britain went to war; but there had been little chance to organize public-relations ventures in view of Argentina's determined neutrality, declared by President Hipólito Yrigoyen – whose Radical party had also campaigned for universal male suffrage and had given the middle class a voice in politics. The Chamber's drive to reconquer trade, neglected during the war, was given further support from London by a succession of trade missions.[1]

A gigantic but relatively shortlived British commercial and industrial empire in Argentina centred on the tanine business. This was its main operation until synthetic products replaced the tanine and the company wound up most of its interests in Argentina in the late 1950s and early 1960s. It was the Forestal Land, Timber and Railways Co., formed by Baron Emile Erlanger, in 1906, after the purchase of the Compañía Forestal del Chaco. The Company's property – forests and farmland – expanded and extended like a vast wedge from the Chaco down through Santa Fé. The town it created around its tanine industry at Villa Ana, in Santa Fé, although a shell now, a ghost town, shows all the ruins of a once prosperous place. It had its own currency, with values in 'kilos' on the paper money which could only be traded at the plant store. Its rule was almost feudal over territory that at one point exceeded five million acres. On Empire Day and on the King's Birthday, the Union Jack flew at all its plants and offices.

The Argentine Government showed its interest in and concern for British enterprise established in Argentina by, among other things, ordering troops to quell strikes: in 1920 at La Forestal, in Santa Fé, when 5400 head of cattle were stolen by strikers protesting over low pay and working conditions, several strike leaders were shot dead by the army. In 1922, in southern Patagonia, where sheep-farm workers, led by anarchist activists, struck for better pay against their English and Scottish employers, the army was sent in. Colonel Varela, the officer in charge, was cheered with a chorus of 'For he's a jolly good fellow ...' at the English Club in Río Gallegos. He had ordered the summary execution of the strike leaders. Neither army nor church – the two institutions which kept records of the incident – have released to date the full details or the death toll of that strike.

Not in the category of an ordinary trade mission, but with the same ultimate effect, was the visit of the Prince of Wales, the future Edward VIII, in September 1925. There had not been a visit by royalty to Buenos Aires since the end of 1880. The 1925 tour was made a lavish event, by order of President Marcelo de Alvear, though Congress vetoed appropriation of 400,000 pesos for the occasion. Alvear, born into one of Argentina's most aristocratic families, had a 'passion' for Paris, an admiration for Britain and a personal dislike for the United States. In 1922, as ambassador to Britain before taking office as President, he had been entertained at Buckingham Palace by George V who had invested him with the Grand Cross of the British Empire. In 1925 Alvear reciprocated with a spectacular welcome for the Prince.

The *Buenos Aires Herald* and *The Standard* reported every move of the visitor who, after suffering meetings with bank and railway directors, found it more entertaining to accept the invitations from the Argentine élite; the British community was given the briefest attention – as the princes did in 1880, when the community, having lost the princes to the *Estancia El Negrete*, had retaliated by giving a ball in honour of the 'Admiral and officers of the Flying Squadron'. In 1925 the Prince's Argentine hosts organized full-dress parades, fireworks, displays, polo matches and concerts at the Colón Opera House.

The grand British occasion to follow was the opening, in March 1931, of the British Trade Fair. This was a display of British commercial and industrial quality, quantity and power.[2]

Buenos Aires was a blaze of lights and flags for the Fair, opened by the Prince of Wales, who was accompanied by Prince George. The city was a beautiful sight, its huge palatial buildings – ministries today, private homes then – built by the then world-famous 'rich of Argentina', in French and Italian styles, stood in testimony of their fortunes made on grain and meat. Argentina had come into a prosperous new century. Influenced by Britain's planning and by Europe's need, Argentine leaders had set the country on a course towards economic prosperity by agricultural export. The Great War had tarnished some of the glitter and there had been a decline in trade figures due to European austerity; but Europe still had to eat and Argentina had the food.

When the princes visited Argentina in 1931, the country was seen as a rather special faraway colony, and the members of government behaved as colonial officials. There are still many English homes in Buenos Aires that have pictures on the walls to remind them of the occasion, even if the fading photographs are the closest their owners ever got to the visitors. The Prince of Wales planted trees, opened buildings. Besides the photographs there are the reminiscences, of balls and of minor scandals, never published unfortunately. It is now to faulty memory that the researcher must refer to know about the women the Prince danced with or went out with, and about the theft of his cigarette case by a souvenir hunter ... Families claim to know somebody who was given a champagne cork popped by the Prince on the special train that took him first down to an *estancia* in the southern lake district, on the border with Chile, and another special train – with luxuries installed for travel by railway directors – north through Chile. If he had popped all the corks attributed to him by British community gossip and diplomatic service legend he would still have a hangover today.

It was good to be British, to wave the flag and be subjects of the future monarch who was then visiting Argentina.

However, Noël Coward arrived in Buenos Aires in December 1931 and was told that the community had been neglected by the Prince.[3] The British Ambassador asked Coward if he would not mind opening a flower show and making speeches at one or two clubs because though the 'Princes had been an enormous success with the Argentines [they] had not paid quite enough attention to the English residents, causing some resentment'. Noël Coward found these official appearances quite painless and 'rather enjoyed them'.[4]

And yet ignorance about Argentina in Britain was impressive. One British Ambassador, Malcolm Arnold Robertson, who had worked towards greater understanding between both countries and had given much support to the Anglo-Argentine Cultural Institute, complained that at a luncheon in London he had been asked to speak about Argentina, his remarks being announced as 'now Sir Malcolm will tell us something about his little corner of the Empire'. On another occasion, at the Lord Mayor's Show, a much-ornamented East African paraded with a notice which read 'Argentina'. A photograph of the man and the sign was splashed over the front page of the Buenos Aires evening newspaper *Crítica* with a strap that read: 'This is how our English friends see us'. Apart from the stupidity of the mistake, the publication of the photograph and strap reflected the indignation which being mistaken with black Africans caused in white Argentina.

Argentina was governed by an army general, Uriburu, installed in September 1930 by his own coup – which unleashed a series of coups that continues today. Many of his officers had trained in Prussian schools. They were filled with admiration for the German military machine, the British Empire, and European aristocracy and rank. The government presented itself as the architect of a nationalist revolution, though it did nothing to change the country's dependence on its links with Britain.

The grain shipments and chilled-beef and frozen-meat business were booming. The meat trade had grown steadily from its humble start in the 1880s. Britain was Argentina's principal meat-export market. British and North American capital competed for Argentina's produce, eventually to control the market, set the prices and dictate the terms on which Argentina would sell. To Argentine historians the 1930s have become known as the 'infamous decade', a period in which foreigners ran Argentina's economy. Britain added the meat industry to the railways, tramways, gas service, the telephone utility, as well as holding a near monopoly in shipping, in the absence of an Argentine merchant navy. Franco-Swiss capital controlled the Buenos Aires electricity supply, one section in which the deciding interest did not lie with the British, though they were among the principal consumers and, hence, had an influential voice in the charting of electricity supplies in the city.

The meat-packing industry became the centre of British influence in the 1930s. The railways and the other utilities had grown into vast corporations, costly to run, with shrinking profit margins as operational deficits grew. Meat was a fast profit-maker and a currency earner, even if a politically delicate product.

To move meat to market, the British had the railways, which had extended into the country like the spokes of a wheel; the hub was the port on the River Plate, whence the meat was exported to Britain.

With the land to raise the cattle, the railways to carry them, the plants to pack the product, the ships to transport it, the market to buy it and the banks to finance operations, the export price was favourably negotiated. In January 1933 the Argentine Vice-President, Dr Julio A. Roca – who had taken office in elections held the year before and which had installed another general, Justo, as constitutional president – travelled to London for talks on a meat industry and trade agreement with the British Board of Trade chairman, Walter Runciman.[5] At a banquet in his honour, at the Dorchester Hotel, Roca said geographical limits did not put boundaries to economics and, economically, Argentina felt it was part of the British Empire. The newspaper *La Nación* reported the speech on 11 February without comment. It was the right thing to say in 1933 even if the Roca–Runciman pact was bitterly attacked by politicians in Argentina. The government was accused of a sell-out. One government critic, a member of parliament, was murdered in the Chamber of Deputies. The dispute precipitated the suicide of another leading parliamentarian – and cattle rancher – who shot himself in frustration at his failure to bring about any change in government policy.

The scandal hardly touched the British community. Residents lived under the impression that they were a power without the political responsibility, which was assumed for them in London. Nor were the British blamed; accusations were levelled at Argentines for putting personal interests, and those of foreign buyers, before the development of local industry and economic growth.

In that decade before the Second World War British residents left the city and became more a suburban community, broken into small groups forming a middle-class belt around the city. Loans from the British railways, British banks and British meat-packing companies to their managers and senior employees permitted this spread to new housing. The move was as much social – to escape the ever-growing big port city – as moral. Buenos Aires by then had become a centre of international ill-repute as a white-slave trade market exploited by a vernacular Italian Mafia. East European girls, many of them Polish, but also French and German girls, were promised marriage to rich Argentines or establ ed British expatriates in Buenos Aires, usually identified as railway engineers because the fame of the British railways had spread world-wide; on arrival the women were forced into prostitution.[6]

It was not difficult to promise the women lured to Buenos Aires a comfortable future in the home of an *inglés*. The city of Buenos Aires business directory read almost like that of a British colony. A majority of commercial enterprise, were it British or Italian or native *Porteño* attached the word 'Limited' to the company name. Later, when the women were working whores, the *inglés* won fame as good and kind customer.

The bars of Buenos Aires catering to the British thirst and which carried British names numbered in the dozens. Apart from the many port-side and seamen's bars, used by British *winos* – who scrounged drinks, cigarettes and money for drink from their better-off countrymen – there were some well-established enterprises that attracted British patronage. These included the Union Bar, Lloyd's Bar, No Name, and Criterion. All were close to the banking and commercial heart of the city; most have been closed by expired leases and changing rent laws. Two generations of British and North American male expatriates found the comfort of 'good women' at Fanny's Bar, run by an understanding Irishwoman. The Glue Pot, thus named by the wife of a patron, in Belgrano, closed in 1967 after sixty years of faithful alcoholic service and even organized an annual golf tournament at the San Andrés links. At one bar, in the city's centre, the Argentine Rugby Union committee – most of the members had some British connexion – met many years to plan the weekend fixtures. When one committee member died, the hearse was driven past the bar in the thickest of midday traffic for a salute by committee members lined on the pavement, pink gins and gin-and-tonics held high. It was a British eccentricity accepted by the Argentine population. The British knew what they were doing ... Bars were for the drinkers, of course; but the cocktail sippers were also catered to. The tea rooms at the railway terminals were much favoured, as were those at the large department stores, such as Gath & Chaves. Tea, or cocktails, at Harrods or Richmond's were a treat.

Even as the threat of war grew in Europe and the community shrunk in Buenos Aires, some British interests continued to expand. A return was no longer possible to the time, in 1900, when eighty per cent of foreign capital in Argentina was British; but expansion in the traditionally British corners of the market – manufacturing, transport, communications and commerce – was possible because it was not hindered by the Argentine upper class. This social group's interest in investment was limited to the land. Landowning marked a social status, its quick profits – from speculative land deals, from meat that had made Argentine beef famous and from wheat, which had made the country known as the 'granary of the world' – maintained that status; mercantile and industrial activities, transport, meat packing and shipping were left to foreign investors. The fact that the railways gave the land greater value and afforded the cattle and wheat quicker transport to market did not change that idea, rooted in the tradition of the Spanish upper classes: the railways were a low profit margin enterprise. So were all public utilities, even when financed by government bonds. Such development, and the bonds, were left to the British who approached the venture with a different social and educational preparation, a Protestant dedication to work, to reap slow, secure profit. Hence the British charted the railways as their own interests determined, without seeking the orderly and progressive development of the country, as the government would have liked the Argentine upper class to do and could not do itself.

Meanwhile, the influence of the United States began to grow, in Argentina and all of South America. British interests suffered in the face of increased competition in banking, commerce and capital goods imports, a field in which the United States decided forcefully to make its mark.

In June 1938 the British community began to feel the need for austerity in its organization, pressed by a decline in investment from Britain and political events in Europe. A meeting of British charity associations and social clubs at the British Embassy, chaired by the Ambassador, Sir Esmond Ovey, agreed to co-ordinate efforts to raise funds 'to avoid overlapping and waste of money and to ensure that appeals, whether for community entertainments or for raising funds for charitable purposes, be met on as wide a basis as possible. The full force of the community would thus be available', the Ambassador said. In May 1939 the British Community Council – an organization which is still the residents' standard bearer – was formed.

The Council's efforts were soon to be directed to raising contributions towards fighting a war which would once again deplete the great British colony in Argentina, this time for good.

After 3 September 1939 the announcement of the declaration of war took 1739 men and 541 women as volunteers from Argentina (197 men and seven women died in action). The British Community Council recorded the donations of 8000 British residents and their descendants. The community's two daily newspapers, *The Standard* and the *Buenos Aires Herald*, recorded the fund-raising social activities and the antagonism towards the German community – in which the Nazi dogma had grown and had been actively fostered from Germany. Every pro-British event was meticulously recorded, often including the full text of one or more speeches. Argentina was officially neutral: but the armed forces and upper class were divided. The country, under the leadership of a rising generation of young officers, did not disguise its sympathy for the Axis, while the traditional establishment kept staunchly pro-Allies and saw the growing power of the nationalistic army as a threat to its own interests.

The closest the war came to Buenos Aires was with the Battle of the River Plate, where the Royal Navy finally cornered the German pocket battleship *Admiral Graf Spee*.

British efforts to encourage support from Argentina were translated in December 1940 into a corporation to promote the import of British manufactured goods. Sir Granville Gibson and the Marquis of Willingdon were in charge of the organization of the corporation.

In the end the war effort made it increasingly difficult for Britain to manage overseas interests where no colonial authority was available to take some of the responsibility. It was a relief to the shareholders when they finally learned that Argentina, under an army general not particularly sympathetic to the British, Juan Domingo Perón, wanted to nationalize the railways, and all the other utilities. The railways were run down, costly to repair and modernize and, in a hostile political atmosphere, difficult to manage. Argentina's funds were blocked in London as a result of the war, which had left Britain with a debt of £125 million to Argentina. The railways seemed the best thing on which to spend unconvertible sterling. A sum of £150 million (2500 million pesos then) was agreed. After the railways, the other services followed.

There was another exodus of British subjects; there were many retirements from the public services and the community shrunk again. The 1950s became a period of retrenchment or of departure. Until General Perón's removal from office by a coup, in September 1955, the British in Argentina suffered the vituperation inevitably directed against a dispossessed colonial power. There was some harassment; the Buenos Aires Cricket and Rugby Club pavilion was burned to the ground to force the club to move, some concerns were forced out of business, critics were ruined.

After Perón's departure into exile for the next eighteen years there were brief, impractical references to how good things had been 'in the days of the English' and it would be good if they returned. But the Britain with a controlling interest had left the River Plate forever. The Bank of London and South America, formed by the absorption of several British banks established in the last century and today part of Lloyds International, stands as the last big living witness to bygone achievements.

The Duke of Edinburgh's visit to Buenos Aires in February 1962 was a very quiet event, primarily aimed at an attempt to fly the British commercial flag. He played polo, had an egg thrown at him outside the British Hospital and found himself falling between stools when an impertinently planned *coup d'état* removed his host, President Frondizi, from Government House. Prince Philip's visit in September–October 1966, when another general, Onganía, was in office, was more successful, if, again, quiet. He played polo with President Onganía and the British community delighted in the attention the Prince paid the community.

The 1960s made the British departure more evident. The Royal Mail Lines Company was taken over by Furness-Withy in May 1965 and, some time later, ceased services to the River Plate with the decline of the frozen and chilled beef trade. It was the end of a tradition in British shipping, social and commercial – the older newspaper reporters remembered the days when their editors sent them across the River Plate to Montevideo to meet the Royal Mail ship and to interview the British personalities aboard who had Buenos Aires as their destination. The Western Telegraph Company, which had pioneered the first cable under the River Plate in March 1866, closed in 1968 with the nationalization of international communications services. The last of the big British-owned packing companies, the Vestey Group's *Frigorífico Anglo*, closed in the early 1970s, after fifty years on Buenos Aires' South Dock. The Houlder Brothers shipping line, which had been prominent in the meat trade for almost one century, reduced its services and took smaller offices as Europe and South America changed the pattern of their commercial relations. The European Economic Community blocked meat imports from Argentina in June 1967. In December 1967 Britain stopped imports of meat for six months following an outbreak of foot-and-mouth disease; after this tonnages never reached their previous levels. Britain reintroduced the ban in May 1969 for several months.

The turbulent Argentine political life of the seventies pushed the British community into a defensive attitude, its members keeping very much to themselves. A few still dream of Britain as a land of Churchillian might which they have called 'home' or admire for being the home of their fathers. The loyalty to roots becomes more fervent as the domestic surroundings become more hostile. Individual male aspirations still aim for paid leave in Britain every few years, as a way to keep in touch. Young women of British descent often think in marriage terms that make a British husband a good match, to keep the blood pure.

In June 1976 Hansard recorded the number of British subjects in Argentina at 17,500, an impressive figure still; though deceptive, as it includes native-born Britons and their registered Argentine-born descendants up to two generations.

It is difficult to give such a community a tense. They once had great influence; yet this would appear to make them a thing of the past. In fact, they are still a significant presence, perhaps best expressed in one of their lesser achievements, the clubs. Club life has kept them a community, strong enough to send a selection to the international cricket championship in England in May–June 1979.

Occasional television documentaries and magazine features, as well as some academic research, has shown the British community of the last forty years in a negative light: a disbanding, unintellectual group, able to resist assimilation because the culture and institutions of the host country are not as strong as were those of this small group of foreigners. But whatever other conclusion, it can still be said that the British in Argentina have a strength which has made them survive the economic decline of their own distant country. They have a timeless element, a conviction that some of their way of life will never change because it has strong roots. The roots lie in the respect held for what the British built; the knowledge that much of modern Argentina exists because their fathers and grandfathers built it; and that many died making it – over 50,000 Britons were buried in cemeteries in Argentina, principally Buenos Aires, between 1860 and 1910.

It is right to speculate, even now, that Britain interfered in the Spanish South American colonies as a matter of pride; as a way to find compensation for the humiliating loss of the North American colonies. Failure to understand the Latin mind, formed by three centuries of Spanish rule, meant an incapacity to seize colonial political administration. Instead there was the imposition of unparalleled economic might and that did colonize Argentina.

The story of the British in Argentina now comes to an end, as that of Empire and colonial power did too. This is, perhaps, the last story of Empire that remained to be told; the last tale of British greatness and world influence; the story of a Forgotten Colony in Argentina.

Notes

Introduction

1. The September 1887 population census showed that 49·8 per cent of British men married non-British women. As British males outnumbered females by a little more than two to one, this was inevitable. However, based on this figure it may be said that fifty per cent of British males did start assimilation.
2. Oxford University Press, 1960.
3. An Argentine might well argue that local politics were in part corrupted by British commercial interests. Several texts on this, from a variety of political angles, are given in the Bibliography list.

1 The Earliest Visitors

1. Patagonia was then described by some Spanish seamen as a land of giants where the natives were eight feet tall with soles as wide as the length of an ordinary European's foot, a story that no English voyager was able to confirm. The legend of the large natives is attributed to the fact that the Spaniards were said to be rather short; medical history has also explained the apparently large feet as being due to flat-footedness. The story of Patagonia is cloaked in such mariner's myths.
2. Dewhurst, Kenneth and Doublet, Rex: Thomas Dover and the South Sea Company, *Medical History*, Volume 18, No. 2, April 1974.
3. That journey has won its place in literary history too, because in February 1710 Rogers rescued a Scot, Alexander Selkirk, of Largo, Fife, from the Isle of Más a Tierra, in the Juan Fernandez Archipelago 360 miles from the coast of Chile. Selkirk boarded the ship in goatskins, after spending four years and four months alone as

a result of a dispute with his captain. He was to provide Daniel Defoe with the inspiration for the adventures of *Robinson Crusoe.*

4. It is strange that today there is almost no trace of the black man in Buenos Aires. Africans formed a large community right through the nineteenth century. Their disappearance is attributed principally to their recruitment into the provincial armies and to their death in battle. Within this theory it is held that the greatest decimation of blacks took place in the war with Paraguay, in 1865. However, another theory, as yet not substantiated, holds that when the United Provinces declared the freedom of the offspring of slaves in 1813 many people sold their slaves to Brazil.
5. The coast of Mar del Plata, a city founded in February 1873, had been described by a British seaman, John Bukeley, as a safe one, in 1742, when he was on his way to the Pacific.
6. The details of these conversions and information on Falkner were taken by the late Father Guillermo Furlong, for his writings on the priest, from the original records, before these were destroyed by arsonists who attacked several churches in Buenos Aires in June 1955 (see Bibliography).

2 The Invasion that Failed

1. Colonia was snatched by the Spanish in 1763, lost to Brazil soon after, to be taken permanently from the Portuguese a few years later.
2. See Chapter 4.
3. Cañas, Jaime E.: *Espionaje en la Argentina*, Buenos Aires, 1969.
4. Fortescue, J. W.: *The history of the British Army*, London, 1910.
5. Roberts, Carlos: *Las invasiones inglesas al Rio de la Plata*, Buenos Aires, 1938.
6. Hudson, E. R. B.: The English invasion of the River Plate, 1806–1807, *The Army Quarterly and Defence Journal*, Vol. 71, London, 1955.
7. Belgrano, Manuel: *Autobiografía, Escritos Económicos*, Raigal, Buenos Aires.
8. The song, which praised Popham, was illustrated with a picture of a young sailor smoking a pipe, with a cup in one hand; he sat on a barrel with the inscription 'dollars' and behind him was a sketch of troops storming a castle. The song-sheet was published by T. Evans of 79 Long Lane, London. One of the surprising aspects of the 1806–7 military expeditions is the quantity of personal literature they produced. The outburst of military literacy in Britain which is associated with the Peninsular Wars – to which Beresford and Pack

went on to fight in – is preceded by numerous volumes written by officers who went to Montevideo and Buenos Aires. The reason for an increase in military writing might be considered twofold: the start of the age of the appeal to a spirit of adventure and the demand for information about South America, after the traumatic loss of the North American colonies, at a time when Napoleon, by the Continental System, was ordering the closure of European ports to Britain. A third reason, it might well be argued, was that the army had grown in size and there were, therefore, more officers with more varied interests, some of these being interested in writing about their experiences.

9. Belgrano, Manuel: op. cit.
10. The flag of the 71st is still at the Nuestra Señora del Rosario Church in Buenos Aires.
11. Scalvini, Jorge: *Historia de Mendoza*, Spaldoni, Mendoza, 1965.
12. In 1809, in a gesture of compensation, Pack sent a large clock to the priests of the Bethlemite order as a token of gratitude for the care they had given his men wounded in battle. The clock remains at a church in San Telmo, Buenos Aires. However, as regards the actual accusation of breaking parole, published by *The Times* on 28 September 1807, in a report taken from *La Gaceta de Madrid*, which in turn reproduced it from *El Publicista*, of Buenos Aires, this was refuted in a letter from Pack and Beresford – who said Liniers broke the parole agreement – published by *The Times* on 30 September 1807.
13. Illio is probably Captain Elío, later Governor of Montevideo.
14. Roberts, Carlos: *Las invasiones inglesas al Río de la Plata*, Buenos Aires, 1938.
15. Ferns, H. S.: *Britain and Argentina in the nineteenth century*, Oxford, 1960.
16. Argentina's national hero, General José de San Martín, would reach a similar conclusion forty years later. The authorities could evacuate the town and leave the invader in an empty city; the civilian population could survive in the Pampas and a foreign invader would not venture far from the city limits. San Martín made such a remark in his old age, in exile in France, at the time of an Anglo-French blockade of Buenos Aires.
17. *The Times*, 5 December 1806, includes a cutting poem on Popham, whom the paper blamed, on 22 September 1807, for the failure of the South American venture.
18. See Bibliography.
19. Battolla, Octavio C.: *Los primeros ingleses en Buenos Aires*, Muro, Buenos Aires, 1928.
20. Murga, Ventura: Las invasiones inglesas y Tucumán, *Revista de la*

Junta de Estudios Históricos de Tucumán, San Miguel de Tucumán, 1968.

3 The British Merchants of Buenos Aires

1. Roberts, Carlos: *Las invasiones inglesas al Rio de la Plata*, Buenos Aires, 1938.
2. Tjarks, German O. E.: *El Comercio inglés y el contrabando*, Buenos Aires, 1962.
3. Ruiz Guiñazú, Enrique: *Lord Strangford y la Revolución de Mayo*, Buenos Aires, 1937.
4. Mackinnon's grandson, also Alexander, served as British minister in Uruguay seventy years later.
5. Cottrell, P. L.: *British Overseas investment in the nineteenth century*, Macmillan, London, 1975. (Although the figure is not a big one, it is nevertheless considerable in contrast to British exports and substantial if the colonial status of Buenos Aires is borne in mind.)
6. The Rooms' records report activities only after 20 July 1822, when Thomas George Love became chairman. Members met every three months at Faunch's English restaurant, famous for its steaks, until the group split in 1829 over whether or not to accept native merchants as members. Love formed a new group, the Buenos Aires Commercial Rooms, which accepted native-born members. The old association soon disappeared as members drifted away. Love was best known as the founder-editor of *The British Packet and Argentine News*.
7. Fitte, Ernesto J.: *Los Comerciantes ingleses en visperas de la revolución de mayo*, Buenos Aires, June 1967.
8. Fitte, Ernesto J.: *El precio de la libertad*, Emece, Buenos Aires, 1965.
9. *The Times*, 2 July 1810, reported the 19 April revolt against Spain in Caracas.
10. Belgrano, Manuel: *Autobiografía*, Ediciones Raigal, Buenos Aires.
11. In 1820 about thirty English shopkeepers and mechanics formed a light cavalry volunteer bodyguard for the Governor, turning out on special occasions in uniforms provided by each guard. But the following year the government ordered all foreigners to report for military service. The British community reported instead to a visiting Royal Navy ship, which arrived in the River Plate, and after some correspondence on the matter between the commander and the local authorities, the call-up of Britons was cancelled.
12. The British community set up their first subscription library in 1815. It lasted for over ten years. In 1826 an English library was opened by

a Mr Herve and after that there was a British Union Library and Reading Room, in 1831, and a Buenos Aires British Library, in 1841. But the most famous, until recently open for business, was that of George Mackern, born in Limerick in 1814. He opened a bookstore with his brother, Hector, in April 1849 and Mackern's Library soon became a rendezvous for the British residents, through a mixture of the proprietors' commercial cunning, good stocks and ample space in which visitors could gather in conversation. For many years George Mackern ran his bookstore with a near monopoly of English-language books. He lived to be eighty-three and to hold the status of a kind of elder in the community.

13. Fitte, Ernesto J.: Crónica de un cónsul oficioso británico, *Boletín de la Academia Nacional de Historia*, Buenos Aires.
14. Britain started to recognize the independence of the South American nations, as a result of a policy launched by Canning, in October 1823. The United States also announced such recognition, under the principles of the Monroe Doctrine of non-intervention, in December 1823.
15. Barber Beaumont became best known as an English traveller in the River Plate for his book *Travels in Buenos Aires and the adjacent provinces of the Rio de la Plata* (London, 1828). His father, John Thomas, also tried to promote immigration to the United Provinces in 1821 and together they made an attempt to raise investments for Argentina with Hullet Brothers & Co., the government's agent in London. Through the *Asociación Agricola del Rio de la Plata* about 600 immigrants were introduced; but, because of a lack of planning and bad agency, they rapidly disbanded and no organized community could be established.
16. After Staples left Buenos Aires, British interests relied on the Royal Navy commanders in the area for protection.

4 North Americans

1. See Chapter 2 for details of White's contact with officers during the British invasions.
2. Espil, Courtney Letts de: Las memorias y cartas de David Curtis De Forest, *La Nación*, Buenos Aires, 26 November 1944.
3. President Madison declared war on Britain in June 1812. The Anglo-United States war was ended by the Treaty of Ghent in December 1814.
4. See Bibliography for title of the report.
5. See Bibliography: Un Inglés: *Cinco años en Buenos Aires,*

1820–1825, Buenos Aires, 1970.

6. A memorial stone to Rodney stands in front of the Cathedral of St John, Buenos Aires.
7. *The Times* for 21 March 1828, under 'Parliamentary intelligence' reports Lord Strangford's fear of damage to British trade interests caused by the war. Earl Dudley said that 'the practice of privateers and the blockade' were causing the damage. 'Government had received certain information that privateers had been fitted out under letters from Buenos Ayres, with the capital and under the management of persons in no way connected with the country ... instruction had been sent out to His Majesty's Admiral in those quarters to take such energetic measures as would put a stop to that practice and to punish the persons employed. With respect to the blockade, he knew that Government had received complaints that that blockade, which was very pernicious to commerce, considering that there was a very large quantity of British capital, was not an actual blockade, but only a paper one ... Whenever the blockade of Buenos Ayres should turn out to be not an efficient blockade, orders would be given that it should no longer be respected.' *The Times* for Saturday, 20 December 1828, reproduces the preliminary peace treaty between the Republic of the United Provinces of the River Plate and the Empire of Brazil, signed in Rio de Janeiro on 27 August 1828. 'We cannot but observe that, though on both sides all right to the possession of the disputed territory of Monte Video is renounced, yet that both retain just so much power of interference in its concerns as may ultimately embroil them with it, and with each other.'
8. See Chapter 5, 'Mercenaries and Heroes', for records of foreigners who served in the Buenos Aires forces.
9. See Chapter 9, 'The Islands Issue'.
10. Hale died in Buenos Aires on 11 September 1888, the same day as his close friend and regular visitor at the Hale home, former Argentine President Domingo F. Sarmiento, in Paraguay.
11. See Chapter 12, 'The Welsh ...'
12. Morrell, Benjamin: *A narrative of four voyages to the South Sea, North and South Pacific Ocean, Indian and Antarctic Ocean*, New York, 1832.
13. Captain Fitzroy, of the HMS *Beagle*, had surveyed the coast of Patagonia and Tierra del Fuego between 1828 and 1830 and had attempted to take some rudiments of European religion to the natives.
14. Charles Darwin, travelling on the second voyage of the *Beagle*, in 1833, described the Patagonian and Fueguian natives as being closer to wild animals than to civilized humans.

15. Coan calls María a 'queen' and remarks that her only royal attribute was a horse. The royal rank may have been Coan's assumption, not based on fact. The tribes had chiefs and not monarchs.
16. Nash reached the Falkland Islands two days later to take on provisions and there established contact with an outlaw, who could have been Antonio Rivero, a *gaucho* whom British forces were hunting for leading a rebellion, on 26 August 1833, and for the murder of island officials. Nash agreed to pay the outlaw five dollars a head for a fat cow and six steers. But when the captain informed the British authorities of this deal he was forbidden to make the purchase. The *Antarctic* then sailed for Rio de Janeiro. See Chapter 9, 'The Islands Issue'.
17. Coan, Titus: *Adventures in Patagonia, a missionary's exploring trip*, New York, 1880.

5 Mercenaries and Heroes

1. Parish Robertson, John and William: *Letters on South America*, comprising travels on the banks of the Paraná and Río de la Plata, London, 1843.
2. See Chapters 1 and 4.
3. A contemporary writer had this to say of Buenos Aires' fortifications: 'Of the public buildings the Fort is the seat of government; it is situated near the river, with residences inside. Though surrounded by a ditch, with cannon mounted on the ramparts, draw-bridges, etc., it could make but little defence against a serious attack. One would suppose that those who chose the spot on which the city is built, had had in view the prevention of attack by hostile fleets, the shallowness of the water being a defence against any danger of this kind.' *An Englishman's impressions of Buenos Aires, 1820–25*; see Bibliography under 'Un Inglés ...' See also Chapter 2, Part II, Note 16.
4. See Chapter 4, Part I, Note 7. Also see Chapter 6: The Treaty of Friendship, Navigation and Commerce, between Great Britain and the United Provinces of the Rio de la Plata, in 1825, agreed that slavery and privateering should no longer be encouraged by signatory governments.
5. See Chapter 8 for a fuller explanation of the civil war, between December 1828 and December 1829, and of the rival factions.
6. Foreign Office correspondence from Mandeville, the British minister in Buenos Aires, records the start of the French blockade thus (F.O. 6/63, 27 March 1838): Admiral Leblanc sent an aide on 24 March to demand that the law of the Argentine Republic towards foreigners be

no longer applied and that French nationals and their property be treated 'as are treated the persons and properties of the most favoured nation (meaning us) until the intervention of a treaty'. The Buenos Aires authorities were instructed to agree within forty-eight hours, under threat of blockade, to the demand that there should be no compulsory military service for Frenchmen resident in Buenos Aires and that the authorities should recognize France's right to claim 'indemnities in favour of Frenchmen who have suffered unjustly in their persons or in their properties'.

7. A good description of Garibaldi's residence in Uruguay and his participation in the Anglo-French attack on Buenos Aires is to be found in Jasper Ridley's *Garibaldi* (Constable, London, 1974). See also Chapter 8.
8. O'Brien's brother, George, served in Chile, with Lord Cochrane, and took part in the capture of the Spanish frigate *Esmeralda*, on 5 November 1820, under the full force of the batteries of the Fort of Callao, an action which was a severe blow to Spanish morale as it was an attack at the Crown's colonial stronghold. Foreign Office correspondence (F.O. 63) reports the parole of General O'Brien on Christmas Eve 1837, arrested while carrying a letter from General Santa Cruz, of Bolivia, to the Buenos Aires authorities. However, he was accused of being an agent to buy ships and guns for Bolivia.
9. *Gaucho* is the name given the man who traditionally rides the open spaces with complete freedom, more at home on a horse than anywhere else. South American folklore has made him a hero, a descendant of the old Spaniard or European creole, or *Criollo*, mixed with the native, nomadic indians. He is attributed the inheritance of the nobility of the former and the cunning of the latter. In fact, he is an anti-hero; city dwellers considered the *gaucho* an ignorant, erratic social outcast, good as a cattle driver, bad as a farmhand. The *gaucho* is rescued for traditional symbolism as the individual pursuing freedom, yet suffering the persecution of progress.
10. This changing of sides was not uncommon in the country's factional fighting. There are many examples among foreigners serving in many provincial armies and with privateers working for the then newly independent republics. A civilian case is more rare. However, one case is that of Domingo Cullen, born in 1780, the son of the British consul in the Canary Islands, who arrived in the River Plate during Spanish colonial rule and adjusted rapidly. He later supported the conspiracy that led to the change in May 1810. In 1814 he was granted officer's rank and made chief of the Customs in recognition of his support. As a result of disagreement with senior military authorities he moved to Santa Fé, where he became a confidant of the

local *caudillo*, Estanislao López. He later reestablished contacts with Buenos Aires groups in a conspiracy against the government. He was executed by order of the Buenos Aires Government in 1839. It must be borne in mind that Coe's changes of allegiance were for money; Cullen's, because of his political involvement.

11. Grenón, SJ, Pedro: Internación de los prisioneros ingleses, 1806–1807, *Documentos Históricos del Archivo de Córdoba*, Córdoba, 1929. In private correspondence Father Grenon told the author about the deduction concerning the origin of the name of Reynafé – whose three sons were born in Tulumba between 1796 and 1799. However, 'Queen Faith' seems a strange name and its origins must be open to speculation.
12. *Camp* from the Spanish word *campo* (field; Latin *campus*) is one of the few really Anglo-Argentine words. It is used to refer to the large *estancias* or ranches in Argentina.

Note: This chapter has concentrated on English-speaking men in the army and navy. The air force is another story, of course, and a much later one. In this case there is one prominent name to record. It is that of Jorge Alejandro Newbery, born in Buenos Aires in May 1875 of a North American father, Ralph Newbery, a dentist with a practice in Buenos Aires, and an Argentine mother. Newbery became the prototype dandy in his time; an all-round sportsman, electrical engineer in the navy, lecturer and communications expert, as well as a flying enthusiast. After a first flight in a balloon in 1907, he started a career as a civilian and military flier; his daring adventures gave him public prominence. He was killed while on a trial flight in Mendoza, in March 1914.

6 The Opening of the Colony

1. *An Englishman's impressions of Buenos Aires, 1820–1825.* See Bibliography under 'Un Inglés ...'
2. The book's author is anonymous; however, it is generally thought that Thomas George Love, founder and editor of *The British Packet and Argentine News*, is responsible.
3. There was also Jackson's Hotel and Smith's, two restaurants with predominantly European clientele. The exchange rate at the time was about four shillings to the 'Spanish dollar', as the author refers to the local currency; a house rent cost between sixty and eighty dollars a month; board and lodging at a coffee-house cost about forty dollars.
4. In 1820 *Picturesque Illustrations of Buenos Ayres and Montevideo*, by artist Emeric Essex Vidal, was published in London. The watercolours are to this day one of the most valuable documents on the

appearance and style of those two towns immediately after independence and at the start of the decade of contrasts that were the 1820s. Vidal was born into a family of French origins at Brentford, Middlesex, in 1791. He joined the navy as a purser in 1806 and made his first contact with South America in 1808. He was on a Brazilian station up to September 1813 and from there went to Montevideo and Buenos Aires, where he spent several years. His *Illustrations* are necessary complement to the writings of the English travellers.

5. Caldcleugh, Alexander: *Travels in South America*, Murray, London, 1825.
6. One of Bevans' daughters married a French architect, Carlos Pellegrini, also under contract to Rivadavia. One of their sons, also Carlos Pellegrini, would become an Argentine president. Bevans died in 1832, according to a notice in the English-language weekly published in Buenos Aires, *The Cosmopolitan*, of 4 April. Probably by coincidence, the death notice was followed by another which said that a Mr William S. Wilson was starting in business in Buenos Aires as an undertaker.
7. Britons were generally well represented in the early years of the bank – which is today the state-owned Buenos Aires Province Bank – among the shareholders. Admiral William Brown was a director of the bank between 1830 and 1831.
8. Fitte, Ernesto J.: *Historia de un empréstito, la emisión de Baring Brothers en 1824*, Emecé Editores, Buenos Aires, 1962.
9. Not all was well. The community lost one of its most distinguished members, Hugh Dallas, in December 1824. His business had fared badly and he was heavily in debt with the bank, after failing to collect from government contractors for equipment supplied. In desperation, he cut his throat. The other sad news in the community that year was the (natural) death of Jack Hall, a rumbustious, heavy-drinking undertaker, who had previously run a laundry and, prior to that, a house-decorating service.
10. See Chapter 3, Part II; and Chapter 5.
11. Frank, the son born in Buenos Aires, later returned to the River Plate as a British consul and became a director of one of Argentina's first railways.
12. Another British physician, John Sullivan, was responsible for the autopsy on Belgrano.
13. Fletcher, H. R. and Brown, W. H.: *The Royal Botanic Garden Edinburgh, 1670–1970*, HMSO, 1970. Contains information on Gillies and another Scottish botanist, Tweedy, active in Argentina. (See Chapter 11 of this book, on the Scottish settlers.) Before Redhead went to Salta there were two other doctors there, Robert

Martin Miln and Joseph Todd. Both were thought to be Scots, but both were registered as born in Boston. They settled in Salta about 1805. A later arrival in Salta was John H. Scribiner, born in 1806, who reached the province in 1825. Four years later he went to Peru, but returned to live in Paraná and later, as British consul, in Buenos Aires. He was commended for his work in a cholera epidemic. He died in Britain in 1881.

14. Oughan had arrived in Buenos Aires in 1817 and, having almost immediately joined General San Martín in the preparation of the latter's expedition to Peru, had some social standing in local society. This standing he used to object to Parish's dictation of community organization. Amid growing hostility between the two men, Parish discovered that Oughan had failed to pay a debt to a local creditor. Convinced that such matters were damaging to the image of the entire British community, Parish used his power to order the auction of Oughan's furniture, in January 1826. After this he also succeeded in getting Oughan deported, for 'some eccentricities in his conduct' according to *The British Packet and Argentine News.* Oughan sued Parish successfully, for invasion of privacy, and returned to Buenos Aires a few years later.
15. Lord John Ponsonby (1770–1855), a baron, elevated to Viscount in 1834, wrote to Governor Manuel Dorrego from aboard HMS *Thetis*, as the British diplomat left Buenos Aires, bound for Rio de Janeiro, on 8 August 1828: 'Your Excellency cannot have any respect for the doctrine set up by some crude theorists "that America ought to have a political existence separate from the political existence of Europe". Commerce and the common interest of individuals have formed ties between Europe and America which no Government nor perhaps any power possessed by Man can now unloose, and whilst they exist Europe will have the right and certainly will not want the means, nor the will to interfere with the policy of America, at least so far as shall be necessary for the security of European interests.'
16. Governor Rosas resigned in December 1832 after failing to convince the Chamber of Representatives to grant him extraordinary powers. When the Chamber came round to accepting Rosas's terms, he took office in April 1835 and remained there until February 1852. See Chapter 8.
17. See Chapter 13, on sports and entertainments.

7 Preachers, Churches and Schools

1. M. G. Mulhall, in *The English in South America* (1878), says there

were 3500 Britons in and around Buenos Aires in 1823, which is a figure substantially higher than that given by Parish. And even Parish's figures are confusing. In April 1824, one month before his letter on the need for a clergyman, the consul had written to Canning reporting that there were 1355 British residents in Buenos Aires. This might have been in the city itself, without the outskirts. In 1831 the consul estimated that there were 4072 Britons in Buenos Aires and probably one thousand more not registered. However, any of the figures represent a considerable community in relation to the total population: 50,000 in 1824 and about 60,000 in 1833.

2. The Consular Chaplaincy Act ran from 1826 to 1875, when it was repealed by the British Parliament.
3. See Chapter 11 on the Scots.
4. See Chapter 11 on the Scots.
5. Hodges, Reverend W. H.: *History of the Anglican Church of St John the Baptist*, Buenos Aires, 1931. The church's neo-classical lines made it a gloomy place when it was first built; but in reforms after 1875 windows were added, increasing the light which formerly came from plain clerestory windows. In the evenings the church was lit by two candelabra, suspended by a long chain from the ceiling. A meeting of seat holders in the church, held on 16 July 1875 – after the repeal of the Chaplaincy Act – drew up a new constitution after which the church was known as the Anglican Church of St John. Baptist was dropped from the name, though the word was restored in 1922. With the end of the chaplaincies, the Vestry took over administration of the church. This led to a dispute with the Bishop of the Falkland (Malvinas) Islands, W. H. Stirling, who had authority over the Buenos Aires church yet had never visited the town. British residents were reluctant to accept his authority and only did so after what church records describe as a 'long and painful' meeting at which the bishop was strongly criticized. In 1910 the church was raised to the rank of pro-cathedral, as part of the Falkland (Malvinas) Islands and East South America Diocese.
6. Lafone later moved with his wife to Montevideo, where he became a strong critic of the Buenos Aires Government. His commercial house became steadily stronger and in 1845 he bought 600,000 acres in the Falkland (Malvinas) Islands (an area known as Lafonia). He sold this land to the Falkland Islands Company in 1851. In Uruguay, Lafone was a powerful landowner, responsible for introducing European immigrant-colonists on to his land. He was one of the founders of the Comercial del Uruguay Bank; he built the first steam mill in Uruguay; owned a beef-salting plant on the Bay of Montevideo; owned all the peninsula which is now the Punta del Este resort; he

owned the Cuñapirú mines in Uruguay and also held mining interests in Argentina, in the provinces of Córdoba and Catamarca. During the *Guerra Grande* – the dispute between Buenos Aires and the Banda Oriental which lasted from 16 February 1843 to 3 October 1851 – Lafone helped to finance the Montevideo Government's civil service expenses. The Buenos Aires Government accused Lafone of being part of a syndicate of English merchants, which also owned the journal *Britannia*, a weekly publication that was constantly at war with its Buenos Aires counterpart, *The British Packet and Argentine News.* Lafone and his syndicate also helped to arm a group of 600 British civilians who formed the English brigade that joined other foreign brigades to defend Montevideo against attack from Buenos Aires. (The most famous officer of these brigades was the leader of the Italians, Giuseppe Garibaldi. The English were led by a Scot, one Joseph Mundell, described several times as a savage by *The British Packet and Argentine News.*) Lafone later invested in war supplies for Crimea (1853–6) but there he lost much of his fortune. He moved to Catamarca, in Argentina, in 1869, and died soon after. The only memorial to him to be found today is in the annex of the Holy Trinity Church building, in Montevideo.

7. Charles Ridgely Horne, born in Baltimore in 1801, had reached Montevideo in 1819. He had married in that city, in 1826, and had crossed to Buenos Aires in 1830, where he became a partner in a shipping business that made much of its profit from smuggling and gun-running. When he inherited his mother's fortune he bought the mansion on the south side of Buenos Aires, then owned by a Scot, Alexander W. Mackinlay, in 1846. Widowed in 1851, Horne married the sister of the late General Juan Lavalle, a prominent figure in the independence and civil wars (see Chapter 8). In 1852 all his property was confiscated because of his friendship with the government of General Rosas, who was overthrown. His mansion, known as 'Horne's Hill' in the English-speaking community, was sold to a member of the locally prominent Lezama family who eventually donated it to make it Argentina's National History Museum. Horne ended his days, aged eighty-three, as the Montevideo agent of the Lamport and Holt Shipping Company.
8. Lafone's son, Samuel A. Lafone Quevedo, was born in Montevideo in February 1835. He was educated in Britain and obtained his MA at Cambridge University. His father gave him his mining property in Catamarca province, in Argentina, and there the young Lafone created a community with the native indians. This venture became bankrupt and Lafone worked as an archaeologist and natural historian. He later became a lecturer at the University of Buenos Aires

and director of the Museum of Natural History, in La Plata, until his death in July 1920.

9. In January 1869 a committee of Britons, North Americans and Germans reached agreement with the Municipality of Buenos Aires to move the cemetery to a new site. This did not take place until November 1892, when the Chacarita Cemetery, still used today, was inaugurated.
10. See Chapter 11 on the Scots.
11. In the second half of the nineteenth century the Anglican Church spread to the provinces. The first service of the British Episcopalian Church in Rosario was held in May 1863. An Anglican church was built south of Buenos Aires, in the district of Lomas de Zamora, and was inaugurated in January 1873. The All Saints Church, also in the southern suburbs, in Quilmes, was consecrated in August 1893. In each case the building of churches outside Buenos Aires was justified by rapidly expanding communities of residents who clustered around the newly built depots of the railways. The most beautiful of non-Catholic churches in Buenos Aires is St Saviour's Church, on the north side of the city, consecrated in November 1896.

    On the western limits of the city, St Peter's, in San José de Flores, was inaugurated in June 1889. This church's congregation was formed in January 1872 by people who had fled Buenos Aires to higher, healthier ground when the plague struck in 1871. The district became a place favoured by the British – who had once made the southern side, Barracas, their residential area – because of the expanding Western Railway.
12. In 1977 and 1978 Picton Island was one of three tiny isles in the Beagle Channel at the centre of a boundary dispute between Argentina and Chile.
13. British schools in Argentina still catering for large numbers of students include St Andrew's; St George's College for Boys, which opened in October 1898, founded by Canon J. Stevenson; Quilmes High School, for girls, opened in March 1907; St Alban's College for boys, founded in 1907; the co-educational Belgrano Day School, started with two pupils in February 1912; St Hilda's school for girls, inaugurated in 1912; Northlands School for girls, founded by Winifred Brightman in 1920; Barker's College for girls, administered by a British education committee since 1938; as well as St John's School, Michael Ham Memorial College, Leach Institute, St Catherine's School, St Brendan's School, St Patrick's School, etc. The main organization teaching English in Argentina is the Association of English Culture, founded in November 1927 by the British Ambassador in Buenos Aires.

8 Governor Rosas and the British Doctors

1. See also Chapters 6 and 7.
2. Public Record Office files, F.O. 27, Parish to Aberdeen.
3. See Chapter 5.
4. Public Record Office files, F.O. 6/67.
5. See Chapter 7 for details on Lafone and Chapter 5.
6. Mackinnon, Lachlan B.: *Steam warfare in the Paraná*, a narrative of operations by the combined squadrons of England and France. Charles Ollier, London, 1848.
7. Towards the end of the nineteenth century Britons formed a small community of dairy farmers and railwaymen in Tandil, but at the time of MacCann's visit there were only about half a dozen families there with British names.
8. Lepper born in County Tyrone, Ulster, in 1785, had been a Royal Navy surgeon before he arrived in Buenos Aires on half-pay in January 1822. He was among the fifteen founding members, who included Dr Dick, of the Academy of Medicine, in April 1822. His first practice in Buenos Aires was awarded by government decree in April 1824.
9. Rosas named Lord Palmerston his executor and ordered that his body should not be returned to Argentina until all charges against him were removed. This referred to a bill passed in July 1857 by the Buenos Aires legislature which declared the former governor a traitor. It was not until 30 October 1973 that the same legislature voted to end the sanction. The then President María Estela Perón decreed the repatriation of the remains from the Southampton cemetery on 21 October 1974, but no action was taken.

9 The Islands Issue

1. The formula for naming the islands, 'Falkland (Malvinas) Islands', is used here because it was the one agreed on by both governments in talks held under the auspices of the United Nations. Less publicized but none the less disputed, are the South Shetland Islands, South Sandwich and South Georgia Islands, in the South Atlantic. The Georgias were first claimed and named by Captain Cook, aboard HMS *Resolution*, in January 1775.
2. Consul Parish informed the Foreign Office in November 1830 that Spain had paid Bougainville £618,018 to establish the colony.
3. The settlers' plaque was found by a Spanish officer in January 1776, during an inventory of the islands' installations. He tore it down and

took it to Buenos Aires, only to be recovered by the British during General Beresford's invasion in 1806.

4. Jewett was born at New London, Connecticut, in June 1772. After studying law and navigation he joined the navy at nineteen. He was axed in 1801 and first appeared in the River Plate in June 1815, ready to 'support the cause of independence', according to his assurance to the Buenos Aires authorities. He was granted a privateer's licence, to use with his own ship, and two years later declared that he had captured four Spanish merchant ships. In 1822, aboard his own ship, Jewett went to Rio de Janeiro where he entered the service of the Emperor of Brazil with the rank of 'Captain on Land and Sea'.
5. There is still some controversy concerning the historical role of Rivero: whether he was a heroic figure, determined to fight the usurper, or merely a thug and a murderer seizing the apparent advantage of the absence of authority to rustle cattle and rob property, killing those who might bear witness against him. Some Argentine nationalist historians see him as a hero and see in the British court's failure to convict him a tacit recognition of the fact that Britain had no right over the islands. A more liberal historical school, while in no doubt as to Argentina's rights over the islands, dismiss Rivero as a minor figure, a product of the circumstances, and cast some doubt on his actual revolutionary zeal. See Chapter 4 for a further reference to Rivero.
6. In recent years, the diplomatic dispute has become more intense. Current negotiations on sovereignty over the islands started in 1965 following the vote of the United Nations decolonization committee, in September 1964, inviting both countries to seek a peaceful solution to the problem. The committee asked that both sides take into consideration the territorial claims of Argentina, the interests of the 2000 islanders and the British precedent.

   The suspicion of the existence of vast oil deposits in the sea around the islands – compared in some reports with the North Sea deposits – has given a new political intensity to diplomatic contacts, although evidence of the existence of oil is not conclusive. The first mineral survey of the islands was carried out in 1920–2 by a Mr H. A. Baker, who recommended test drilling in Shallow Cove, on the East Falkland. Baker's exploration was carried out at the request of the Falkland Islands Company, which today still owns forty-six per cent of the land on the islands (its parent company is Charringtons Industrial Holdings). In 1945, the United Engineering Corporation of New York, test drilling in the Magellan area, planned a survey of the Falklands, but this was never carried out. Since then, international companies periodically express interest in exploration of the area and such expressions led, in 1971, to rumours – that remain unfounded – of existence of a 'new Kuwait' off the Falklands. In January 1976, Lord Shackleton visited the islands to prepare a report on the economic potential of the Falklands – the report was published in February 1977. The report found good possibilities for the fisheries, mutton, alginate and oil industries. The Argentine authorities considered the Shackleton mission a political affront and asked Britain to recall her ambassador in Buenos Aires in January 1976. In April 1977 both governments announced plans for a series of meetings between representatives of both sides to exchange views on matters stemming from the dispute. The appointment of new ambassadors by both countries was only completed in November 1979.

10 The Irish

1. The census results were 15,719 Spaniards, 544 indians, 674 mestizos, 3153 mulattoes and 4115 blacks.
2. *The Kilrane Boys* was attributed to a schoolmaster, Walter Cormack. The following is an extract:

> On the thirteenth day of April in the year of Forty Four,
> With the bloom of Spring the birds did sing around green Erin's shore,
> The feathered train in concert their tuneful notes did strain
> To resound with acclamation that echoed through Kilrane.
>
> Foul British laws are the whole cause of our going far away;
> From the fruits of our hard labour they defraud us here each day.
> To see our friends in slavery tied, with taxes for to pay,
> Ere we'll be bound to such bloodhounds we'll plough the raging sea.
>
> There's William Whitty and his bride their names I will first sound,
> John Murphy and John Connors from Ballygeary town,
> William Lambert and John Donnelly, two youths that none could stain,
> Nicholas Kavanagh and Tom Saunders, four more from Ballygillane.
>
> From Ballyhire Nick Leary a most superior man,
> James Pender, Patrick Howlin, John Murphy from Hayesland,
> Larry Murphy from Kilrane joined them in unity
> They're bound for Buenos Aires the land of liberty.

3. Two examples might be useful to reflect the extent of Irish dispersion in Argentina, apart from the occupations in farming and business. There were a number of merchants named Lynch in the Spanish colony. The family of one of them left the country in the 1840s to escape the Rosas regime and joined a fairly large settlement of Argentine gold-hunters in California. The daughter of one of those Lynch, born in the United States, returned to Argentina and would be the grandmother of Dr Ernesto Guevara, better known as 'Che' after the Cuban revolution in 1959. His political acquaintances included two other Argentines of Irish descent: John William Cooke, a trusted lieutenant of the late Juan Domingo Perón, and Peronist ideologue; and Joseph Baxter, leader of an extreme nationalist revolutionary organization. Another Lynch, Patrick, of Lydican, Galway, arrived in Buenos Aires in the eighteenth century and became an established merchant. One of his descendants, Benito Lynch (1880–1951), is placed among Argentina's leading writers, his best-known books being *El inglés de los güesos*, *Los caranchos de la Florida* and *Raquela*.

11 The Scottish Settlers

1. St Andrew's Society started in January 1888, in the English Literary Society rooms.
2. Mackinlay's son, Alexander, sold the house to Charles Ridgely Horne in 1846. See Chapter 7.
3. The *chacra* was in what are today the districts of Lomas de Zamora and Esteban Echeverría.
4. The *Edinburgh Weekly Journal* of Wednesday, 25 May 1825; and the *Edinburgh Evening Courant* of 23 May only record the ship's date of sailing in the shipping lists.
5. Dodds, James: *Records of the Scottish settlers in the River Plate and their churches*, Buenos Aires, 1897.
6. The Reverend William Brown was born at Leuchars, Fifeshire, and was a graduate of St Andrew's and Aberdeen universities. He arrived in Buenos Aires in 1826.
7. William Grierson was the grandfather of Dr Cecilia Grierson, author of a book on the Scottish colony and a doctor at the British Hospital. See Chapter 8.
8. This remark is to be found in *Twentieth century impressions of Argentina* (1911), edited by Reginald Lloyd and others.
9. See Chapter 7.
10. Richard Adams died in August 1835, soon after he had built the

Scots church. He had been known in Buenos Aires as a competent portraitist and artist.

11. The Scots church had a fairly large congregation. Mulhall, in *The English in South America*, estimated that the number of Scots in the country in 1885 was two thousand. Adams' building remained in use until demolished in 1893, to make way for the *Avenida de Mayo.* The Scots' church was paid £25,000 compensation and another church was built, in April 1896, on *Avenida Belgrano*, where it stands today.
12. Edward Taylor (1801–68) became well known for his work and was invited to Paraguay to build the government palace for the dictator, Carlos Antonio López, and the railway terminal building. The dictator's son and successor, Francisco Solano López, who took a dislike to foreigners because he suspected them of being spies, became irritated by Taylor, whom he one day had pegged and chained to the ground. Taylor was freed later without explanation or apology. He returned to Buenos Aires, where he was said to have become quite unbalanced, and died there.
13. The church is used only once a year now. It retains an atmosphere of peace and beauty as a monument to the pioneering Scots.

12 The Welsh Settlers and Other Colonists

1. This was reported in the newspaper *La Tribuna* of Buenos Aires on 26 July 1863.
2. Newton, Ronald C.: *German Buenos Aires, 1900–1933. Social change and cultural crisis*, University of Texas Press, Austin, 1977.
3. In 1876 Edwards went to Buenos Aires to get married. While he was away his farm was burned to the ground by the indians, in revenge for some of his raids against them.
4. The letters ranged through domestic issues, to elementary political comment, remarks on the weather and orders for equipment required on the farms; and usually all was told in long breathless paragraphs. Here is one sample, a letter from one Arthur Mildred, a settler, to Edmund Goodhall, dated 17 January 1873: '... You will have heard accidentally of the indians down here. I wlll tell you as well as I can what is really true. There were a gang of fifteen of them in the *Sierras* robbing. An *alferez* [junior army officer] came across them and killed three, also losing a soldier I believe. They attacked *Pavón* [a farmer] and lost another. They came for Edwards' trot horse and Walker shot one in the back and the natives [the farmhands] finished him [the indian shot by Walker]. On their way back *Heralde* [a farmer]

met them on the other side of the *Sierra*, and killed six, and yesterday I heard that some of them came back with some more and that they killed four. This I give you for what it is worth. I know it is the truth. We spent a very pleasant Xmas day. The three Cobbolds were here and one or two others and we got up some races. I was very successful I have lately made $700 in racing ...' These letters have never been published and the owner, Miss E. M. Brackenbury, allowed the author, among other researchers, to take copies. She had kept them after Goodhall's death. Among the more special souvenirs in this correspondence is a letter dated in New York, 15 July 1888 and addressed to the British Consulate in Bahía Blanca – Goodhall was the Consul. 'I venture to trouble you with this note to ask you if you could inform me if it would be feasible to engage a hand of say twenty Patagonian or Pampa indians and some ½ doz or doz *Gauchos* to join Colonel Cody's (Buffalo Bill's) show and if Bahía Blanca would be a good place to make my starting point to get them from ... would engage them on a two-years contract giving first class guarantees for their good treatment and return at end of contract ... I would be obliged if you would find out for me amongst some of the old time *estancieros* such as *Facón Grande* if the scheme is feasible ...' Unfortunately the file did not contain a reply or the story of what happened.

5. Williams, Glyn: *Welsh settlers and native Americans in Patagonia.* Journal of Latin American Studies, London, 1979.
6. Souter, Gavin: *A peculiar people, the Australians in Paraguay*, Angus & Robertson, Sydney, 1968.

13 The Sporting Life and Entertainments

1. The quotation is from *Twentieth Century Impressions of Argentina*, by Reginald Lloyd and others, published in London in 1911.
2. The name of Palermo has only indirect links with the Sicilian city. It was named after a Spanish Sicilian merchant, Juan Dominguez Palermo, owner of the land in the early seventeenth century. It was later called San Benito de Palermo because of a shrine to a saint worshipped by the former slaves in Buenos Aires.
3. Buenos Aires rejoined the Argentine Confederation in 1859 after the defeat of the Buenos Aires secessionist army by an army of provincial troops at the battle of Cepeda.
4. In 1948 the clubhouse was burned down, allegedly by arsonists acting under orders of some officials in the Peronist Government. After that the club moved to its present field in Don Torcuato.

5. See Chapter 6.
6. The many societies and clubs were the forerunners of what would become the Jockey Club, started in April 1882 by a group of Turf enthusiasts and horse breeders, among whom were several Britons. Newton, Jorge: *Historia del Jockey Club*, Buenos Aires, 1966.
7. *El Negrete* was owned by David Anderson Shennan in partnership with C. H. Krabbe and John Hannah, who started the *estancia* – one of the more famous in Anglo-Argentine 'folklore' – in 1836. It was the site of Argentina's first sheep-dip. With the *Estancia Los Sajones*, owned by Peter Sheridan, John Hannah, and James Lawrie, it was considered the cradle of commercially and technically planned sheep farming in Argentina.
8. The club in Flores was 'near Mr Leslie's *quinta*' according to an announcement of a match in *The Standard* in June 1885. Neither the club nor Mr Leslie's residence remain.
9. In 1885 Lomas Polo Club opened with a match Railway *v.* Club. Rosario got its own club in 1887; the now well-known Hurlingham Polo Club was founded about 1888 and the Belgrano Polo Club started in 1891. On 4 March 1892, the River Plate Polo Association was formed as a governing body. The sport spread until Argentina became internationally renowned for its polo playing. Between 1893, when the local open polo championship started, and 1913, there were few Argentine names among the winners. The First World War put an end to that, as the British clubs were depleted. The sport regained strength after the war; and for many years English surnames, accents and public schools predominated in the Argentine clubs.
10. *Alumni* won the championship nine times up to 1911, coming second to Belgrano in 1904 and 1908. In 1912 Quilmes took the cup, marking the last year of British supremacy. The war affected most teams and *Alumni* was dissolved. British community interest in soccer was renewed in 1921, when a British Saturday League was organized and continued through the 1930s.
11. Mulhall, M. G.: *The English in South America*, Buenos Aires, 1878.
12. During the war of the Triple Alliance, when Paraguay fought the combined forces of Argentina, Uruguay and Brazil.
13. Theatre groups renewed their work after the war. These included the Buenos Aires Amateur Theatrical Society, which lasted a few seasons as from 1923; the Quilmes Musical and Dramatic Society, which closed in 1929; and the Lomas Choral Society, which had started in 1895. In more recent years there has been an annual operetta by the Gilbert and Sullivan Society; an annual pantomime by the Mordino Company; several performances a year by the English Speaking

Theatre Club; the Southern Theatre Group; the Suburban Players; and the Eaglets, among others.

14. One of the individuals who has gone down in Argentine history among the more famous of comic entertainers was Frank Brown, who became the best-known clown in the River Plate. Born in England in September 1858, he was apprenticed to the Holborn Amphitheatre from where he joined Cookes Royal Circus, in Edinburgh. He travelled all over Europe and the United States, finally to start his career as a clown in Mexico after one occasion when the public was in stitches on hearing his Spanish spoken with an English accent. With this he made his way through South America, reaching Buenos Aires in 1884, when he married a local actress. Brown started his own circus in Buenos Aires in 1889 and led it until his death in April 1943. Cuneo, Dardo: *Frank Brown*, Buenos Aires, 1944.

14 Travellers' Tales and Other Writings

1. The most important of the locally published guides was the Mulhall brothers' *Handbook of the River Plate.* See Chapter 10.
2. A theoretical end of the period of this kind of literature is marked by Thomas Woodbine Hinchliff's *South American Sketches, or a visit to Rio de Janeiro, the Organ Mountains, La Plata and the Paraná* (London, 1863); British consul Thomas Hutchinson's *Buenos Aires and Argentine gleanings, with extracts from a diary of Salado Expedition in 1862 and 1863* (London, 1865); and George Chaworth Musters' *At home with the Patagonians: a year's wanderings over untrodden ground from the Straits of Magellan to the Rio Negro* (London, 1871). There were followers of the old line, of course. One was Lucas Bridges, the Argentine-born son of a British minister, the Reverend Thomas Bridges of the South American Missionary Society. In *The Uttermost Part of the Earth* (London, 1948), Lucas Bridges gives a first-hand account of Patagonia, which he lived and farmed in, and of life among the now extinct Yagán indians of Tierra del Fuego, a subject that had not been dealt with at all since Darwin's diaries. Bridges has a special corner in Argentine writing: his one non-fiction book gave him renown for presenting a still little-known area.
3. *The Times*, obituary, 19 August 1922.
4. Municipal boundary changes situate the house today in Florencio Varela. The house, a museum today, is of mud and wattle, with a primitive thatch roof. It looks far from a comfortable home and must have been crowded, even when bearing in mind that there was an

outside kitchen and toilet. The *rancho* was occupied by squatters until the early 1960s, when a successful campaign won approval for the creation of a museum.

5. The memories of this period are to be found in one of his best-known works, *Far away and long ago* (London, 1918).
6. Hudson's production includes the novel *Green Mansions* (1904) which lacks any spark; a collection of short stories titled *El Ombú* (1902); a long story and poems in *A little boy lost* (1905). He is best remembered as a naturalist for *The Naturalist in La Plata* (1892), *Idle Days in Patagonia* (1893), *British Birds* (1895), *Birds in London* (1898), *Nature in Downland* (1900), *Birds and Man* (1901), *Afoot in England* (1909), *A Shepherd's Life* (1910), *Adventures among Birds* (1913), *Birds in Town and Village* (1919) and *Birds of La Plata* (1920).
7. This was 'confessed' by Carlos Leumann, in an article in *La Prensa* of Buenos Aires in August 1941.
8. Watts, Cedric: *Cunninghame Graham, a critical biography*, Cambridge, 1979; and Walker, John: *South American Sketches of R. B. C. Graham*, Oklahoma UP, 1979.
9. Babington Smith, C.: *Masefield, a Life*, Oxford, 1979.
10. Watts, Cedric: *Cunninghame Graham, a critical biography.*
11. Wilde had two sons, Diego Wellesley Wilde, who followed a military career; and José Antonio Wilde, who became a physician, publisher, writer and director of the Argentine National Library.
12. See Chapter 10.
13. Lloyd, Reginald and others: *Twentieth Century Impressions of Argentina.*
14. In 1968 the Charleston Publishing Company, of Charleston, South Carolina, bought the majority stock holding in the *Buenos Aires Herald.* The change of ownership coincided with a change of editor. Norman Ingrey, editor for almost forty years, retired, making way for Robert John Cox. Both of them Britons, they ran an outspoken general news daily which catered to all foreign communities and Argentines who read English. And in keeping with the line set at the start of *The Herald*, the paper's critical view of government affairs and policy won it a wide readership (17,000 copies). In December 1979, Robert Cox, an award-winning journalist who had been decorated with an OBE by Queen Elizabeth II, left Argentina after numerous threats against him and his family.

15 North American Businessmen and Bandits

1. Two months before, the Buenos Aires North American community

had received the news of the assassination of President Lincoln. *The Standard*, on 10 May, carried a full report of a meeting of residents and sympathizers called by the United States minister. The meeting decided that, 'We gratefully accept as a compliment to our country and to ourselves the voluntary and considerate action of the authorities here on Sunday, the 28th April, in causing all the national and provincial flags to be hoisted to half mast, as a token of grief at the untimely loss'. And they also resolved that 'Governor Saavedra and the Legislature are equally entitled to our thanks for their complimentary resolution of last evening, declaring that the next new town or city which shall be organised within the province shall be designated Lincoln'. The town was founded soon after.

2. Gould, born in Boston in September 1824, returned to the United States to become director of the Dudley Observatory in Albany.
3. General Osborne was responsible for the arbitration that split Patagonia between Argentina and Chile. See Chapter 12.
4. This brief description of the Wild Bunch is taken from many sources that tried to reconstruct the tale of Butch Cassidy and the Sundance Kid. One of the best, recent, descriptions is contained in Bruce Chatwin's book *In Patagonia* (Picador 1979).

16 The Age of Growth

1. Cottrell, P. L.: *British Overseas Investment in the Nineteenth Century*, Macmillan, London, 1975.
2. Between 1874 and 1948 Hunslet sold 650 engines of various models to Argentina.

17 Close to the Change

1. Among the most important of the individuals operating charities was one William Case Morris, philanthropist and educator, who made the ragamuffins of Buenos Aires his main concern and through pressure and pleading drew funds from the wealthy and the government. He was born in the Isle of Ely, in 1864, was taken to Argentina at the age of seven, then to a farming colony in Paraguay. Morris returned to Buenos Aires to work as an office clerk and part-time decorator. In 1892 Morris collected fifty copybooks, some chairs and a kitchen stove and opened a classroom in the Boca district, where he took in children from the street. Three years later he was ordained as a preacher in the Anglican Church. In 1897 he established the

Christian Mission, in the Boca, on the south side of the city of Buenos Aires, where he opened two day-schools and a Sunday school. He started an orphans' home with eighteen urchins and by the end of 1898 had 200 children in the home and 588 at the schools. He went on to open several schools and a technical college; but the financial burden of running them became too great and the State was asked to subsidize them. A school and a home are the memorial to his work in Buenos Aires. He died in England in September 1932.

2. 3. 4. *Buenos Aires Herald*: *Activities of the British Community in Argentina during the Great War*, Buenos Aires, 1919.

5. Newton, Ronald C.: *German Buenos Aires, 1900–1933*, University of Texas Press, 1977. However, the German community boasted that not a single company was forced into bankruptcy by the British, even if trade was seriously affected. The Germans used front companies led by Argentines and Spaniards which were created as fast as British agents could detect them. In the absence of British coal to fuel the German-owned electricity supply company, CATE, the management ordered the burning of 2500 tons a day of surplus corn and bran, as well as charcoal and *quebracho* wood from the northern Argentine tanine plants, to keep electricity services going. When the British-owned gas supply company had to curtail services in 1917 because of a shortage of coal, CATE took over the city's lighting, until then fuelled by gas.

18 The Twentieth Century

1. The first post-war president of the Chamber, Joseph Macadam, was a middle-aged merchant who had made a fortune with his own trading company, opened in 1899, who knew the local market well from his passage through banking, as a clerk, and the railways, as guard and fireman, and from working as a stockbroker's assistant; his family business lasted into the 1960s.
2. There would be no other British fair in Buenos Aires for forty years and the later one, opened by Princess Alexandra, would only be a shadow of the earlier occasion.
3. Lesley, Cole: *The life of Noël Coward*, Penguin 1976.
4. A line in 'Mad dogs and Englishmen go out in the midday sun'; which runs 'Hindus and Argentines sleep firmly from twelve to one/But Englishmen detest a siesta', appears to have been inspired by Coward's visit to Buenos Aires.
5. The treaty was signed on 27 April 1933.

6. Their story was told in the book, *The road to Buenos Ayres*, by a French journalist, Albert Londres, published in London by Constable in 1930.

Chronology

1492 – Christopher Columbus reaches the American continent.
1536 – Buenos Aires is founded by Pedro de Mendoza (the town is later destroyed by the indians).
1580 – Buenos Aires is founded a second time by Juan de Garay.
1617 – The River Plate province is given boundaries and government.
1776 – The River Plate province is declared a Viceroyalty.
1806 – First British invasion.
1807 – Second British invasion.
1810 – Buenos Aires is declared autonomous of Spain.
1813 – Slavery is abolished in the River Plate Provinces.
1816 – The River Plate provinces declare their independence from Spain.
1818 – Chile is declared independent of Spain.
1822 – Perú is declared independent of Spain.
1823 – The United States recognizes independence in the River Plate.
1824 – Great Britain recognizes independence in the River Plate.
1825 – Brazil declares war on Buenos Aires.
1826 – Rivadavia becomes the first president of the River Plate provinces.
1829 – Juan Manuel de Rosas becomes governor (up to 1832).
1833 – The Falkland Islands are occupied by Britain.
1835 – Rosas starts his second term in government.
1838 – France blockades Buenos Aires (up to October 1840).
1845 – Anglo-French blockade of Buenos Aires (up to November 1849).
1852 – Rosas is overthrown. The Argentine Confederation is created.
1865 – War of the Triple Alliance; Argentina, Brazil and Uruguay against Paraguay (up to 1870).
1880 – Buenos Aires is declared Argentina's federal capital.
1890 – Economic crisis and recovery; beginning of the '*belle époque*'.
1914 – War; end of Argentina's '*belle époque*'; many British leave Argentina.

1930 – General Uriburu leads a coup against President Hipólito Yrigoyen (of the Civic Radical Union party) and instals a military government for two years.

1931 – British trade fair in Buenos Aires. The Prince of Wales visits Argentina during the South American tour.

1933 – Anglo-Argentine meat trade pact, signed by Vice-President Roca of Argentina and Walter Runciman, chairman of the British Board of Trade.

1943 – A military coup overthrows the civilian government and paves the way for Colonel Juan Perón to take office three years later.

1947 – Nationalization of the British railways in Argentina is announced (legal transfer is completed in 1949).

1955 – A military *coup d'état* overthrows President Juan Perón.

1962 – Prince Philip, the Duke of Edinburgh visits Argentina; a military coup removes President Frondizi (a civilian).

1966 – Prince Philip visits Argentina; General Onganía is President, having led a coup against a civilian government in June.

1973 – General Juan Perón returns from exile in Spain to become Argentina's president; he dies in July 1974, aged seventy-nine, in office; he is succeeded by his wife.

1976 – An armed forces coup removes Mrs María Estela Perón from the Presidency and instals General Jorge Videla as President.

Bibliography

Abeijón, Asencio: *Recuerdos de mi primer arreo*, Editorial Galerna, Buenos Aires, 1975. (Includes recollections about Butch Cassidy in Patagonia.)

Aguilar, Antonio: *Dr Guillermo Rawson (Hombres de San Juan)*, Editorial Sanjuanina, San Juan, 1971. (Short biography of William Rawson.)

Albanelli MacColl, Norah: *Bibliografía selecta sobre inmigración en la República Argentina*, Recopilación, Washington, 1953. (Specialized reference on immigration.)

Alberdi, Juan B.: Rosas y los ingleses, *El Nacional*, Montevideo, 19 December 1838. (Contemporary attack on Rosas for his close links with British interests.)

Alen Lascano, Luis C.: *Imperialismo y comercio libre*, A. Peña Lillo, editor, Buenos Aires, 1963. (A discussion of trade between Britain and Argentina, and others.)

Almeida, Juan Lucio: *Qué hizo el Gaucho Rivero en las Malvinas*, Introduction by A. A. Piñeiro, Editorial Plus Ultra, Buenos Aires, 1972. (Rivero's revolt against the British in the Falkland Islands.)

Andreasen, José Christian: Currents of friendship between the United States and Argentina in the XIXth century. *Comments on Argentine Trade* (US Chamber of Commerce in Argentina), July 1976.

Andrews, Joseph: *Las provincias del norte, 1825*; Ediciones Sesquicentenario, Universidad Nacional de Tucumán, 1967. (Extracts from *Journey from Buenos Aires through the provinces of Córdoba, Tucumán and Salta to Potosí*, Murray, London, 1827).

Araoz Alfaro, Gregorio: *Rawson, ministro de Mitre*, Institución Mitre, Buenos Aires, 1938.

Babington Smith, C.: *John Masefield, a life*, Oxford University Press, 1978.

Bagú, Sergio; Barba, Enrique M.; Irazusta, Julio; Goróstegui de Torres, Haydé: Rosas, su figura, su actitud frente a los intereses británicos, *Revista Polémica*, Centro Editor de América Latina, Buenos Aires, 1970.

Bailey, John P.: *Immigration and ethnic relations. The British in Argentina*, La Trobe Sociology Papers, La Trobe University Press, 1978.

Baines, Thomas: Observations on the present state of affairs of the River Plate, *The Times*, Liverpool, 1845. (Off-print of a lengthy newspaper article.)

Bateman, John Frederic: *City of Buenos Aires improvements*, report of the drainage and sewerage and water supply of the city, 21/9/1871, Buenos Aires 1871. (Study of the city after the yellow-fever epidemic.)

Battolla, Octavio C.: *Los primeros ingleses en Buenos Aires, 1780–1830*, Editorial Muro, Buenos Aires, 1928. (A collection of anecdotes about early British residents in Buenos Aires.)

Baudizzone, M. Luis: *Buenos Aires visto por viajeros ingleses, 1800–1825*, Emece, Buenos Aires 1945.

Bauer, John E.: The Welsh in Patagonia: an example of nationalistic migration, *Hispanic American Historical Review*, Duke University Press, November 1954.

Bayer, Osvaldo: *Los vengadores de la Patagonia trágica*, Editorial Galerna, Buenos Aires, 1971. (A history of the anarchist strikes against British landowners in Patagonia in the 1920s.)

Beaumont, John A. Barber: *Viaje por Buenos Aires, Entre Ríos y la Banda Oriental – 1826–1827*, Translation by José Luis Busaniche, Editorial Solar Hachette, Buenos Aires 1957. (Originally *Travels in Buenos Aires and the adjacent provinces*, James Ridgway, London 1828.)

Beck-Bernard, Lina: *Le Rio Parana. Cinq années de séjour dans la République Argentine*, Paris 1864. (Translated by José Luis Busaniche as *Cinco años en la Confederación Argentina*, Buenos Aires 1935.)

Beverina, Juan: *Las invasiones inglesas al Rio de la Plata*, Buenos Aires 1939.

Beverina, Juan: Montevideo o Buenos Aires? Un problema para los comandos en la primera invasión inglesa, *La Prensa*, Buenos Aires, 21 March 1937.

Beyhaut, Gustavo: Inmigración y desarrollo económico. *Jornadas argentinas y latinoamericanas de sociología*, Buenos Aires, 1961.

Blasco Ibañez, Vicente: *Argentina y sus grandezas.* Editorial española americana Madrid, 1910.

Blondel, J. M.: *Almanaque político y de comercio de la Ciudad de Buenos Aires para el año 1826*, Ediciones de la Flor, Buenos Aires, 1969.

Bloomfield, Paul: *The essential Cunninghame Graham*, Cape, London, 1956.

Borrero, José María: *La Patagonia Trágica*, Editorial Americana, Buenos Aires, 1967. (History of the anarchist uprisings in Patagonia, 1919–21. See also Bayer, Osvaldo.)

Bourne, Benjamin Franklin: *The captive in Patagonia*, Gould & Lincoln, Boston 1853.

Bowen, E. G.: The Welsh in Patagonia 1865–1885; a study in historical geography, *Geographical Journal*, Vol. 132, Part 5, March 1966.

Boyson, V. F.: *The Falkland Islands*, Oxford University Press, 1924.

Brackenridge, Henry Marie: *Voyage to Buenos Ayres performed in the years 1817 and 1818, by order of the American Government, in the frigate Congress*, Sir R. Phillips & Co., London 1820.

Brand, C.: *Journal of a voyage to Peru*, Henry Calburn, London 1828.

Braun Menéndez, Armando: Patagonia, mitos y leyendas, *Boletín de la Academia Nacional de la Historia*, No. 41, Buenos Aires, 1968.

Braun Menéndez, Armando: *Pequeña historia patagónica*, Buenos Aires, 1936.

Braun Menéndez, Armando: *Pequeña historia magallánica. Las cuatro fundaciones magallánicas*, Buenos Aires 1937.

Braun Menéndez, Armando: *El reino de Araucanía y Patagonia*, Emecé Editores, Buenos Aires, 1945.

Braun Menéndez, Armando: *Pequeña historia fueguina*, Buenos Aires, 1939 (Editorial Francisco de Aguirre, Santiago, Chile, 1971.)

Bridger, Kenneth: *North and South, a history of the annual cricket classic in Argentina*, Buenos Aires, 1976.

Bridges, E. Lucas: *Uttermost part of the earth*, Hodder & Stoughton, London 1948. (A classic on life in southern Patagonia and Tierra del Fuego.)

British Community Council in the Argentine Republic: *Activities of the British Community in the Argentine Republic during the 1939–1945 war*, Buenos Aires, July 1953.

Bruce, Rev. Douglas W.: *To Scots in Argentina, sermons and lectures*, Buenos Aires, 1933.

Bunkley, Allison Williams: *The life of Sarmiento*, Princeton University Press, 1952.

Burgin, Miron: *The economic aspects of Argentine federalism, 1820–1852*, (Cambridge, Massachusetts, 1946). Translated as *Aspectos económicos del federalismo argentino*, Editorial Solar/Hachette Buenos Aires.

Burnet-Merlin, Alfredo R.: *Cuando Rosas quiso ser inglés, historia de una anglofilia*, Ediciones Libera, Buenos Aires 1974.

Burton, Sir Richard Francis: *Letters from the battlefields of Paraguay, with a map and illustrations*, Tinsley Brothers, London, 1870.

Buschiazzo, Mario J.: *La arquitectura en la República Argentina, 1810–1930*, Editorial MacGaul, Buenos Aires, 1971.

Cady, John F.: *Foreign intervention in the Rio de la Plata, 1838–50*, University of Pennsylvania Press, Philadelphia, 1929.

Caillet-Bois, Ricardo: *Una tierra Argentina: las islas Malvinas*, Ediciones Peuser, Buenos Aires, 1948.

Caillet-Bois, Ricardo: *Nuestros corsarios, Brown y Bouchard en el Pacífico, 1815–1816*, Instituto de Historia Argentina Dr Emilio Ravignani, Buenos Aires, 1930.

Caldas Villar, Jorge: *Nueva historia argentina* (4 vols.), Editorial Granda, Buenos Aires.

Caldcleugh, Alexander: *Travels in South America*, Murray, London, 1825.

Canclini, Arnaldo: Diego Thomson, pedagogo de América, Revista *Todo es Historia*, No. 52, Buenos Aires, agosto 1971.

Canclini, Arnaldo: *Hasta lo último de la tierra. Allen Gardiner y las misiones en Patagonia*, Editorial La Aurora, Buenos Aires, 1951.

Cañas, Jaime E.: *Qué hicieron los agentes secretos en el Río de la Plata*, Editorial Plus Ultra, Buenos Aires, 1970. (Report on secret agents at work during the Spanish administration and after.)

Cañas, Jaime E.: *Espionaje en la Argentina*, Editorial Mundo Actual, Buenos Aires, 1969. (Spies at work in Argentina, principally in the nineteenth century, many of them British.)

Carranza, Angél Justiniano: *Campañas navales* (2 vols.), Buenos Aires, 1914/16. (Argentina's principal naval battles, with much about Admiral Brown.)

Carreño, Virginia: *Estancias y estancieros*, Editorial Goncourt, Buenos Aires 1968. (Anecdotes and family ties on old farming establishments.)

Ceres, Hernán: William Morris, el apóstol de la niñez, *Todo es Historia*, No. 66, Buenos Aires, Agosto 1972.

Chatwin, Bruce: *In Patagonia*, Jonathan Cape, London, 1977. (Good descriptions of Patagonia and accounts of Scots and their recollections.)

Chiaramonte, José Carlos: *Nacionalismo y liberalismo económicos en la Argentina, 1860–1880*, Editorial Solar/Hachette, Buenos Aires, 1971. (A discussion of economic development under British influence.)

Christelow, A.: Great Britain and the trades from Cadiz and Lisbon to Spanish America and Brazil, *Hispanic American Historical Review*, Duke University Press, 1947.

Christie, E. W. Hunter: *The Antarctic problem*, Allen & Unwin, London, 1951. (A view of the Antarctic and Falkland Islands from a British angle.)

Coan, Titus: *Adventures in Patagonia, a missionary's exploring trip*, Dodd Mead and Co., New York, 1880.

Coghlan, Eduardo A.: *Los irlandeses*, Buenos Aires, 1970. (A private edition which includes much useful reference material on early Irish settlers in Argentina.)

Cole, Lesley: *The life of Noël Coward*, Jonathan Cape, London, 1976. (Includes remarks on Coward's encounter with the British community in Buenos Aires in 1931.)

Coleman, Arturo: *Mi vida de ferroviario inglés en la Argentina, 1887–1948*, Bahía Blanca, 1949.

Cordero, C. J.: *Los relatos de los viajeros extranjeros, posteriores a la Revolución de Mayo, como fuentes de historia Argentina*, ensayo de sistematización bibliográfica, Institución Mitre, Buenos Aires, 1936. (A good bibliography and discussion of the books of early British and European travellers to the River Plate. See also Uriburu, J. E.)

Cordero, Héctor Adolfo: En torno a los indios en las invasiones inglesas, *La Prensa*, Buenos Aires, 27 June 1971.

Correa Falcón, Edelmiro J.; Klappenbach, Luis J.: *La Patagonia argentina, estudio gráfico y documental del Territorio Nacional de Santa Cruz*, Buenos Aires, 1924.

Cottrell, P. L.: *British overseas investment in the nineteenth century*, Studies in economic and social history, Macmillan Press, London 1975.

Crawford, Robert: *South American sketches*, Longman, Green & Co., London, 1898.

Crawford, Robert: *Across the Pampas and over the Andes*, Longman, Green & Co., London, 1884.

Critchell, James Troubridge; Raymond, Joseph: *A history of the frozen meat trade, an account of the development and present day methods of preparation, transport and marketing of frozen and chilled meats*, Constable, London, 1912.

Cuccorese, Horacio Juan: *Historia de los ferrocarriles en la Argentina*, Ediciones Macchi, Buenos Aires, 1969.

Cuneo, Dardo: *Frank Brown*, Colección Mar Dulce, Editorial Nova, Buenos Aires 1944.

Cunningham, Robert Oliver: *Notes on the natural history of the Strait of Magellan and West coast of Patagonia, made during the voyage of H.M.S. 'Nassau' in the years 1866–69*, Edmonton & Douglas, Edinburgh, 1871.

Currier, Theodore S.: *Los cruceros del 'General San Martín', investigación sobre el corso norteamericano realizado con bandera de las Provincias Unidas*, Instituto de Historia Argentina, Buenos Aires, 1944.

Currier, Theodore S.: *Los corsarios del Río de la Plata*, Instituto de Investigaciones Históricas, Facultad de Filosofía y Letras, Buenos Aires, 1929. (Both books by Currier are essential reference on English and North American corsairs working for the Buenos Aires Government.)

Cutolo, Vicente Osvaldo: *Nuevo diccionario biográfico argentino (1750–1930)*, Author's edition, Buenos Aires.

Dampier, William: *A voyage around the world*, Cassells, London. (Abridged version of the mariner's writings, used here for its reference to Dr Dover and Alexander Selkirk.)

Danero, E. M. S.: *Toda la historia de las Malvinas*, Editorial Tor, Buenos Aires, 1964.

Darwin, Charles: *Charles Darwin's diary of the voyage of the H.M.S. Beagle*, Cambridge University Press, 1933.

Darwin, Charles: *Un naturalista en el Plata*, Editorial Arca, Montevideo, 1968. (Section of the diary on the River Plate which includes useful notes to the translation.)

Davie, John Constanse: *Letters from Paraguay*, Robinson, London 1805.

de la Cruz Mendoza: *Historia de la ganadería argentina*, Buenos Aires, 1928.

del Carril, Bonifacio: *Monumenta iconográfica*, Emecé Editores, Buenos Aires, 1964. (Probably the most complete collection of reproductions of illustrations of nineteenth-century Buenos Aires.)

De Paula, SJ, Alberto: Templos rioplatenses no católicos, *Anales del Instituto de Arte Americano*, No. 15, 1962; No. 16, 1963; No. 17, Buenos Aires, 1964.

De Paula, SJ, Alberto: El arquitecto Richard Adams y la colonia escocesa de Santa Catalina, *Anales del Instituto de Arte Americano e Investigaciones Estéticas*, No. 21, Facultad de Arquitectura y Urbanismo, Buenos Aires, 1968.

Destefani, Capitán Laurio H.: El pabellón argentino en las Malvinas, *La Prensa*, Buenos Aires, 1 November 1970.

Destefani, Capitán Laurio H.: *Los marinos en las invasiones inglesas*, Comando General de la Armada, Buenos Aires, 1975.

Dewhurst, Kenneth E.: *The quicksilver doctor*, John Wright & Sons Ltd, Bristol 1957. (A biography of Dr Dover.)

Dewhurst, Kenneth; Doublet, Rex: Thomas Dover and the South Sea Company, *Medical History*, Vol. 18, No. 2, April 1974.

Dirección General de Cultura y Educación: *Semblanza y evocación de la epopeya galesa en Chubut*, Provincia de Chubut, 1961. (Official pamphlet on the Welsh.)

Dobie, J. Frank: *The Gauchos and horses in Hudson and Graham*, Little, Brown, Boston, 1975.

Dobson, A. G.: *A short account of the Leach Bermejo expedition of*

1899, with some reference to the flora, fauna and indian tribes of the Chaco, Buenos Aires, 1900.

Dodds, James: *Records of the Scottish settlers in the River Plate and their churches*, Introduction by Rev. J. W. Fleming, Grant & Sylvester, Buenos Aires, 1897.

Drees, Dr Charles W.: *Americans in Argentina*, a record of past and present activities of Americans in Argentina, Rodney to Riddle, Buenos Aires, 1922.

Escobar Bavio, Ernesto: *Alumni, cuna de campeones y escuela de hidalguía*, Editorial Difusión, Buenos Aires, 1953. (A tribute to Watson Hutton and his English High School soccer team.)

Escudé, Carlos: Perón, Miranda y la compra de los ferrocarriles británicos. *Todo es Historia*, No. 142, Buenos Aires, March 1979.

Espil, Courtney Letts de: *La segunda presidencia de Roca vista por los diplomáticos norteamericanos*, Editorial Paidos, Buenos Aires, 1972.

Espil, Courtney Letts de: John Pendleton and his friendship with Urquiza, *The Hispanic American Historical Review*, Vol. 33, Duke University Press, February 1953.

Espil, Courtney Letts de: Las memorias y cartas de David Curtis De Forest, *La Nación*, Buenos Aires, 12 November 1944.

Espil, Courtney Letts de: Las invasiones inglesas y el comercio en el Río de la Plata, *La Nación*, Buenos Aires, 26 November 1944.

Espil, Courtney Letts de: Los patriotas y el nacimiento de una nación, *La Nación*, 10 December 1944.

Espil, Courtney Letts de: Los veinticinco de mayo en New Haven, Connecticut, *La Nación*, Buenos Aires, 26 December 1944.

Espil, Courtney Letts de: *Noticias confidenciales de Buenos Aires a USA, 1869–1892*, Editorial Jorge Alvarez, Buenos Aires, 1969.

Espil, Felipe A.: *Once años en Buenos Aires (1820–1831). Las crónicas diplomáticas de John Murray Forbes*, Editorial Emecé, Buenos Aires.

Espinoza, Enrique: *Tres clásicos de la Pampa, F. B. Head, W. H. Hudson, R. B. Cunninghame Graham*, Colección del Tajamar, Babel, Santiago de Chile, 1951.

(The) Falkland Islands Co. Ltd., 1851–1951, Falkland Islands Co. Ltd, London, 1951.

Falkner, P. T.: *Descripción de la Patagonia y de las partes contiguas de la America del Sur*, Second Edition, Hachette, 1974. (A good translation with many notes to the eighteenth-century original.)

Feldman Josín, Luis: Centenario de la enseñanza en el Chubut, *Cuadernos de Historia del Chubut*, No. 7, October 1970. (Includes notes on the origins of Welsh education in Chubut.)

Ferns, H. S.: *Gran Bretaña y Argentina en el siglo XIX*, Editorial Solar/Hachette, Buenos Aires, 1968. (Translation of the book published by OUP in 1960.)

Ferns, H. S.: Beginnings of British investment in Argentina, *Economic History Review*, Cambridge University Press, 1952.

Ferns, H. S.: Investment and trade between Britain and Argentina in the nineteenth century, *Economic History Review*, Cambridge UP, 1950.

Ferns, H. S.: *The Argentine Republic*, David & Charles, Devon, 1973. (A brief economic history.)

Ferns, H. S.: *Argentina*, Ernest Benn, London.

Fitte, Ernesto J.: *Historia de un empréstito, la emisión de Baring Brothers en 1824*, Emecé Editores, Buenos Aires, 1962.

Fitte, Ernesto J.: Los primeros misioneros protestantes en la región magallánica, *Boletín de la Academia Nacional de la Historia*, No. 35, Buenos Aires, 1964.

Fitte, Ernesto J.: Diplomáticos norteamericanos acreditados en Buenos Aires durante el siglo XIX, *Boletín de la Academia Nacional de la Historia*, No. 40–4, Buenos Aires, 1967–8.

Fitte, Ernesto J.: *El precio de la libertad (la presión británica en el proceso emancipador)*, Emecé Editores, Buenos Aires, 1965.

Fitte, Ernesto J.: Los comerciantes ingleses en vísperas de la revolución de mayo, *Investigaciones y ensayos II*, Academia Nacional de la Historia, pp. 69–139, Buenos Aires, Jan.–June 1967.

Fitte, Ernesto J.: Crónica de un cónsul oficioso británico, *Boletín de la Academia Nacional de Historia*, No. 34, Buenos Aires (p. 719).

Fitte, Ernesto J.: *La disputa con Gran Bretaña por las islas del Atlántico sur*, Editorial Emecé, Buenos Aires, 1968.

Fitte, Ernesto J.: *La agresión norteamericana a las islas Malvinas*, Editorial Emecé, Buenos Aires, 1966.

Fitte, Ernesto J.: Malvinas, de Puerto Stanley a Puerto Luis, *La Prensa*, Buenos Aires, 10 November 1968.

Fitte, Ernesto J.: Malvinas, la reclamación diplomática de las Provincias Unidas, *La Prensa*, Buenos Aires, 29 June 1969.

Fitte, Ernesto J.: *Dignificación de mayo y el encono de un comodoro inglés*, (*Comodoro Peter Heywood*), Buenos Aires, 1960.

Fitzroy, Robert: *Narrative of the surveying voyages of H.M. ships 'Adventure' and 'Beagle' between the years 1826 and 1836*, H. Colburn, London, 1839.

Fletcher, H. R.; Brown, W. H.: *The Royal Botanic Garden of Edinburgh, 1670–1970*, HMSO, London, 1970. (Page 70 includes notes on Tweedie and the Scottish colony at Monte Grande.)

Ford, A. G.: *Argentina and the Baring crisis of 1890*, Oxford Economic Papers, Clarendon Press, 1956.

Ford, A. G.: *The gold standard, 1880–1914. Britain and Argentina*, Oxford, 1962.

Fortescue, The Hon. J. W.: *The history of the British army, Vol. V, 1803–1807*, Macmillan, London, 1910. (Includes the history of the 1806–7 British invasions of the River Plate.)

Furlong, SJ, Guillermo: *Tomás Falkner y su 'Acerca de los Patagones' 1788*, Librería del Plata, Buenos Aires, 1954.

Furlong SJ, Guillermo: *La personalidad y la obra de Thomas Falkner*, Instituto de Investigaciones Históricas, No. XLVIII, Facultad de Filosofía y Letras, Buenos Aires, 1929.

Furlong, SJ, Guillermo: San Telmo y el reloj de los ingleses, Revista *Todo es Historia*, No. 55, November 1971 Buenos Aires.

Furlong, SJ, Guillermo: *Samuel A. Lafone Quevedo*, Ediciones Culturales Argentinas Buenos Aires, 1965.

Furlong, SJ, Guillermo: *Tomás Fields S.J. y su 'Carta al prepósito general'*, Casa Pardo, Buenos Aires, 1971.

Furlong, SJ, Guillermo: *Historia social y cultural del Río de la Plata, 1536–1810*, Tipográfica Editora Argentina, Buenos Aires, 1969.

Gallo, Ezequiel: *El gobierno de Santa Fé vs. El Banco de Londres y Río de la Plata – 1876*, Instituto Torcuato Di Tella, Buenos Aires, 1972.

Gallo, Ezequiel: *Conflictos socio-políticos en las colonias agrícolas de Santa Fé, 1870–1880*, Instituto Torcuato Di Tella, Buenos Aires, 1973.

Gardiner, Allen: *A voice from South America*, Seeley, Burnside and Seeley, London, 1847.

Geoghegan, A. R.: *Bibliografía de Guillermo Furlong, S.J.*, Buenos Aires, 1957.

Germani, Gino: *Política y sociedad en una época en transición, de la sociedad tradicional a la sociedad de masas*, Editorial Paidos, Buenos Aires, 1965. (Page 179 includes notes on British immigration.)

Gesualdo, Vicente: *Cómo fueron las artes en la Argentina*, Editorial Plus Ultra, Buenos Aires, 1973.

Giberti, Horacio C. E.: *Historia económica de la ganadería argentina*, Editorial Solar/Hachette, Buenos Aires, 1970.

Gibson, Herbert: *The history and present state of the sheepbreeding industry in the Argentine Republic*, Ravenscroft and Mills, Buenos Aires, 1893.

Gillespie, Alexander: *Gleanings and remarks collected during many months' residence at Buenos Ayres and within the upper country*, Leeds, 1819.

Gonzalez Arrili, Bernardo: El General Ignacio H. Fotheringham y el más famoso de sus olvidos, *La Prensa*, Buenos Aires, 5 September 1971. (Anecdotes on an English general in the Argentine army.)

Gonzalez Climent, Aurelio y Anselmo: *Historia de la marina mercante argentina*, Buenos Aires, 1972.

Gonzalez Garaño, Alejo B.: E. E. Vidal autor de las 'Picturesque illustrations of Buenos Aires and Montevideo,' *La Nación*, 6 April 1930, Buenos Aires.

Gonzalez Garaño, Alejo B.: *Iconografía argentina anterior a 1820*, Buenos Aires 1943. (Includes references to E. E. Vidal.)

Gonzalez Lonzieme, Enrique: *Martín Jacobo Thompson, ensayo para la biografía de un marino criollo*, Comando General de la Armada, Buenos Aires.

Goodwin, Paul B.: *Los ferrocarriles británicos y la U.C.R. – 1916–1930*, Ediciones la Bastilla, Buenos Aires, 1974.

Gordon Davis, Jorge: *Memorias. La ganadería argentina, sus orígenes y algunos datos históricos*, Buenos Aires, 1960.

Gori, Gastón: *Inmigración y colonización en la Argentina*, EUDEBA, Buenos Aires, 1971.

Gori, Gastón: *La Forestal*, Editorial Proyección, Buenos Aires. (A nationalist view of the British company.)

Gorostegui de Torres, Haydee; Sampay, Arturo E.: Las ideas políticas de Rosas, *Revista Polémica*, No. 19, Centro Editor de América Latina, Buenos Aires, 1970.

Graham, María: *Diario de mi residencia en Chile en 1822*, Translation from the English by José Valenzuela Dooner, Editorial Francisco de Aguirre, Santiago, Chile, 1971. (A fascinating view of South America's independence leaders by the widow of an English sea captain.)

Graham, Richard: *Britain and the onset of modernisation in Brazil, 1850–1914*, Cambridge Latin American Study Series. Cambridge University Press, 1970.

Graham, R. B. Cunninghame: *The conquest of the River Plate*, Heineman, London 1924.

Graham, R. B. Cunninghame: *The horses of the conquest*, Heineman, London, 1930. (Translated into Spanish by Justo Saenz, Editorial Kraft, Buenos Aires, 1946.) (For biographical and bibliographical notes on Graham see P. Bloomfield, R. Curle, A. Jurado, J. Meyers, J. Polwarth, A. F. Tschiffely, J. Walker, H. F. West and C. Watts.)

Graham-Yooll, Andrew: Chascomús Scots' church is still there, *Buenos Aires Herald*, 24 November 1973.

Graham-Yooll, Andrew: Quinta Santa Coloma, Whitelocke slept here, *Buenos Aires Herald*, 24 February 1973.

GGraham-Yooll, Andrew: William Case Morris, The prince of beggars, *Buenos Aires Herald*, 30 May 1975.

Graham-Yooll, Andrew: Caledonian Ball: golden anniversary, *Buenos Aires Herald*, 10 July 1975.

Graham-Yooll, Andrew: ... and of so many years ago, *Buenos Aires Herald*, 15 September 1975.

Graham-Yooll, Andrew: Llegaron los escocéses. A 150 años del arribo del

'Symmetry', *Clarín*, Buenos Aires, 21 August 1975.

Graham-Yooll, Andrew: Rosas y los ingleses. La Batalla de Caseros vista por The Times, *La Opinión*, Buenos Aires, 13 February 1977.

Graham-Yooll, Andrew: Times-eye view of 1816, *Buenos Aires Herald*, 9 July 1977.

Graham-Yooll, Andrew: La batalla de la Vuelta de Obligado vista por The Times, *Todo es Historia*, No. 138, Buenos Aires, November 1978.

Graham-Yooll, Andrew: *Así vieron a Rosas los ingleses*, Editorial Rodolfo Alonso, Buenos Aires, 1980.

Grant, Robert (publisher): *The Argentine yearbook 1913*, London, 1913.

Grenon, SJ, Pedro: Internación de los prisioneros ingleses, 1806–1807, *Documentos Históricos del Archivo de Córdoba*, Vol. 15, Códoba, 1929.

Grierson, Cecilia: *Colonia de Monte Grande; primera y única colonia formada por escoceses en la Argentina*, Peuser, Buenos Aires, 1925.

Guastavino, Juan Estevan: San Martín y los británicos en la emancipación sudamericana, *La Prensa*, Buenos Aires, 9 March 1941.

Guedalla, Philip: *Argentine tango* (a novel), Hodder & Stoughton, London, 1932.

Gurney, R. E.: *Pasado, presente y porvenir. Centenario del Ejército de Salvación en la Argentina.* Talleres Gráficos El Faro, Buenos Aires, 1964.

Haigh, Samuel: *Sketches of Buenos Ayres and Chile*, J. Carpenter & Sons, London, 1829.

Hakluyt, Richard)Hakluyt's voyages. The principal navigations, voyages and discoveries of the English nation. Made by sea or over land to the remote and farthest distant quarters of the earth at any time within the compass of these 1600 years; by Richard Hakluyt, preacher and some time student of Christ ochurch in Oxford. Introduction by Irwin R. Blacker. Viking Press, New York, 1967.

Hanson, Simon G.: *Argentine meat and the British market*, Stanford University Press, 1938.

Hartingh, Charlotte: *Servitor on an outer plane, the biography of Walter Owen*, Instituto Cultural Walter Owen, Buenos Aires, 1966.

Hasbrouck, Alfred: *Foreign legionnaires in the liberation of South America*, Columbia University Press, New York, 1928.

Head, F. Bond: *Rough notes taken during some rapid journeys across the Pampas and among the Andes*, John Murray, London, 1861.

Head, F. Bond: Reports relating to the failure of the Río de la Plata Mining Association, formed under the authority and signed by His Excellency, Don Bernardino Rivadavia, London, 1827.

Helms, Anthony Zachariah: *Travels from Buenos Ayres by Potosí to Lima*, Richard Phillips, London, 1806.

Hicks, Agnes: *The story of the Forestal*, London, 1956. (The Forestal company's own story of its work; for opposition see G. Gori.)

Hidy, R. W.: *The house of Baring in American trade and finance*, Cambridge, Mass., 1949. (For other views see E. Fitte, R. Ortega Peña, etc.)

Hinchliff, Peter: *The Anglican church in South America*, Darton, Longman and Todd, London, 1963. (Among other stories, pp. 21–2 include notes on Allen Gardiner, for which also see A. Canclini, E. Fitte, A. Gardiner, J. Marsh, etc.)

Hinchliff, Thomas Woodbine: *Viaje al Plata en 1861*, Hachette, Buenos Aires 1961. (Translation of *South American sketches*, or a visit to Rio de Janeiro, the Organ mountains, La Plata and the Paraná, Longman, London, 1863.)

Hirst, W. A.: *Argentina*, with an introduction by Martin Hume, South American series, Fisher Unwin, London, 1910.

Hodges, William Herbert: *History of the Anglican church of St John the Baptist*, Buenos Aires, 1931.

Hoffman, F. L.: The financing of San Martín's expeditions, *Hispanic American Historical Review*, Duke University Press, 1952.

Hogg, Ricardo: Las tertulias de antaño y los ingleses, *La Prensa*, Buenos Aires, 22 December 1940.

Hogg, Ricardo: Los organizadores de nuestra primera industria, *Anales* de la Sociedad Rural Argentina, Buenos Aires, August 1923. (Article on the origins of the meat trade.)

Hogg, Ricardo: El combate de Perdriel, *Anales* de la Sociedad Rural Argentina, Buenos Aires, December 1962. (Includes notes on British in the army.)

Hogg, Ricardo: *Yerba Vieja*, Julio Suarez Editor, Buenos Aires, 1945. (Book of stories and anecdotes from English farms.)

Holder, Arthur L.: *Activities of the British Community in Argentina during the Great War, 1914–1919*, The British Society in the Argentine Republic, printed at the *Buenos Aires Herald*, Buenos Aires, 1920.

Holland, Col. Lancelot: *Expedición al Rio de la Plata*, Introduction by Andrew Graham-Yooll, EUDEBA, Buenos Aires, 1975.

Holmberg, Adolfo M.: *Cree Ud. que los ingleses nos devolverán las Malvinas? Yo no.* Grandes Temas Argentinos, Buenos Aires, 1979.

Hudson, E. R. B.: The English invasion of the River Plate, 1806–1807, *The Army Quarterly and Defence Journal*, Vol. 71, Oct. 1955–Jan. 1956, London.

Hudson, W. H.: *153 Letters from W. H. Hudson*, Edited by Edward Garnett, Nonesuch Press, London, 1923.

Hudson, W. H.: *Far away and long ago*, Dent, London, 1962.

Hudson, W. H.: *Letters to R. B. Cunninghame Graham*, Edited by Richard Curle, Golden Cockerel Press, London, 1941.

Hudson, W. H.: *The naturalist in La Plata*, Chapman & Hall, London, 1892.

Hudson, W. H.: *Letters to E. Garnett*, Dent, London, 1925.

Hudson, W. H.: *Idle days in Patagonia*, Chapman & Hall, London, 1893.

Huergo, Luis A.: *El puerto de Buenos Aires, historia técnica*, Imprenta de la Revista Técnica, Buenos Aires, 1904.

Hughes, William M.: *A orillas del río Chubut en la Patagonia*, Comisión Oficial de los Festejos del Centenario de Chubut, 1967. (Reprint of recollections of the early days of the Welsh in Chubut.)

Huhn, Eduardo A.: *Reseña de Venado Tuerto en sus primeros cincuenta años de vida*, Imprenta Amorortu, Buenos Aires, 1933.

Humphreys, Robert Arthur: *Tradition and revolt in Latin America and other essays*, Weidenfeld & Nicolson, London, 1969.

Humphreys, Robert Arthur: *Liberation in South America, 1806–1827. The career of James Paroissien*, Athlone Press, London, 1952.

Humphreys, Robert Arthur: *British consular reports on the trade and politics of Latin America, 1824–1826*, Royal Historical Society, London, 1940.

Hunt, Rev. R. J.: *The Livingstone of South America.* The life and adventures of W. Barbrooke Grubb among the wild tribes of the Gran Chaco in Paraguay, Bolivia, Argentina and the Falkland Islands and Tierra del Fuego, Seeley Service & Co., London, 1933.

Hutchinson, Thomas J.: *Buenos Aires y otras provincias Argentinas con extractos de un diario de la exploración del Río Salado en 1862 y 1863*, translated from the original by Luis V. Varela, Buenos Aires, 1866. (*Buenos Aires and Argentine gleanings with extracts from a diary of Salado expedition in 1862 and 1863*, Edward Stanford, London, 1868.)

Hutchinson, Thomas J.: *The Paraná, with incidents of the Paraguayan war, and South American recollections from 1861 to 1868*, Edward Stanford, London, 1868.

Ibarguren, Federico: *Así fue Mayo (1810–1814)*, Ediciones Theoria, Buenos Aires, 1966.

Irazusta, Julio y Rodolfo: *La Argentina y el imperialismo británico*, Buenos Aires, 1934.

Irazusta, Julio: *La influencia económica británica en el río de la Plata*, EUDEBA, Buenos Aires, 1969. (Irazusta's books present a nationalist's view of British influence in Argentina.)

Isherwood, Christopher: *The condor and the cows*, Methuen, London, 1949. (A novelist/traveller's impressions of Argentina.)

Jackman, Sydney: *Galloping Head*, Phoenix, London, 1958. (Life of

Sir Francis Bond Head.)

Jalikis, Marino: *Historia de los medios de trasporte y de su influencia en el desarrollo urbano de la ciudad de Buenos Aires*, Compañía de Tranvías Anglo-Argentina Ltda., Buenos Aires, 1925.

James, Colonel L.: *The history of King Edward's Horse*, London, 1921.

Jofré Barroso, Haydée M.: *Genio y Figura de Guillermo Enrique Hudson*, EUDEBA, Buenos Aires, 1972.

Johnson, H. C. Ross: *A long vacation in the Argentine Alps or where to settle in the River Plate state*, London, 1868.

Johnson, John J.: *Political change in Latin America, the emergence of the middle sector*, Stanford, California, 1958.

Johnson, Samuel: Thoughts on the late transactions respecting Falkland Islands, 1771, *The political writings of Dr Johnson*, selection by J. P. Hardy, Routledge & Kegan Paul, London, 1968.

Jones, Lewis: *Una nueva Gales en Sud America*, Comisión Oficial de los Festejos del Centenario de Chubut, 1967.

Jones, Tom B.: *South America rediscovered*, University of Minnesota Press, 1949. (A wide ranging compilation and report on books by early travellers.)

Joslin, David: *A century of banking in Latin America*, Oxford University Press, 1963. (The history of the Bank of London and South America.)

Jurado, Alicia: *Vida y obra de W. H. Hudson*, Fondo Nacional de las Artes, Buenos Aires, 1971.

Jurado, Alicia: *El escocés errante, R. B. Cunninghame Graham*, Emecé, Buenos Aires, 1978.

Justo, Liborio: *Nuestra patria vasalla (de los Borbones a Baring Brothers)*, Editorial Schapire, Buenos Aires.

King, Col. John Anthony: *Twenty-four years in the Argentine Republic*, embracing the author's personal adventures, with the civil and military history of the country, its political condition, before and during the administration of Governor Rosas, his course of policy, the courses and character of his interference with the government of Monte Video, New York, 1846.

Knight, E. J.: *The cruise of the Falcon, a voyage to South America in a 30-ton yacht*, Thomas Nelson & Sons Ltd., London, 1883.

Koebel, W. H.: *Argentina past and present*, Kegan Paul, London, 1910. (Includes an interesting chapter with advice to British emigrants.)

Krüger, D. W.: Afrikaners in Argentina, *Standard Encyclopedia* of Southern Africa, Vol. 5, Nasou Limited, South Africa.

Lamb, John S.: *River Plate personalities, a biographical dictionary*, Imprenta Lamb & Co., Buenos Aires, 1939.

La Nación, Un día en 1875, Buenos Aires, 31 August 1975. (On the origins of Polo.)

Lanuza, José Luis: *Un inglés en San Lorenzo y otros relatos*, Libros del Caminante, EUDEBA, Buenos Aires, 1964. (Includes several stories of early British settlers.)

La Prensa, Antiguos libros ingleses que tratan de América, Buenos Aires, 13 February 1927.

Larden, Walter: *Argentine plains and Andine glaciers*, Fisher Unwin, London, 1911.

Latham, Wilfred: *Los estados del Rio de la Plata, su industria y su comercio*. Translated from the English, *The states of the River Plate*, Longmans, London, 1866, by Luis V. Varela, Buenos Aires, 1867.

Lenzi, Juan Hilarión: *Antecedentes y proyecciones de la colonia galesa de Chubut* (Lecture), Buenos Aires, 1965.

Leumann, Carlos Alberto: La conquista inglesa de Buenos Aires trazada en 1711, *La Prensa*, Buenos Aires, 5 November, 1933.

Leumann, Carlos Alberto: Hudson y Tagore, *La Prensa*, Buenos Aires, 3 August 1941.

Levene, Ricardo: *Historia de la República Argentina* desde sus orígenes hasta la organización definitiva de 1862, 14 vols., Buenos Aires 1936–50.

Lloyd, Reginald, and others: *Twentieth Century impressions of Argentina*, its history, people, commerce, industries and resources. Lloyd's Greater Britain Publishing Co. Ltd, London, 1911. (An excellent work of reference of over 800 pages, published to mark Argentina's centenary, and probably an essential document for the researcher on Argentina at the turn of the century.)

Lopez, Lucio V.: *La Gran Aldea (1861)*, Centro Editor de América Latina, Buenos Aires, 1967. (An essential guide to the history of Buenos Aires.)

Luiggi, Alice Houston: *Sesenta y cinco valientes, Sarmiento y las maestras norteamericanas*, Editorial Agora, Buenos Aires, 1959.

Lynch, J.: *Spanish Colonial administration (1783–1810)*, London, 1958.

Lynch, J.: *Spanish American revolutions, 1808–1826*, Weidenfeld & Nicolson, London 1973 (pp. 37–126 cover Argentina and Uruguay.)

McCann, William: *Viaje a caballo por las provincias argentinas*, Editorial Solar/Hachette, Buenos Aires, 1969. (Translation of *Two thousand miles' ride through the Argentine provinces* – with a historical retrospect of the Río de la Plata, Monte Video and Corrientes, Smith, Elder, London, 1853.)

McGann, Thomas F.: *Argentina, the United States and the Inter-American system, 1880–1914*, Cambridge, Mass., 1957. Translated by Germán O. E. Tjarks into Spanish and published by EUDEBA, Buenos Aires, 1965.

Mackellar, C. D.: *A pleasure pilgrim in South America*, John Murray,

London, 1908.

Mackinnon, L. B.: *Steam warfare in the Paraná*: a narrative of operations by the combined squadrons of England and France, Charles Ollier, London, 1848. Translated as *La escuadra anglo-francesa en el Paraná, 1846*, Hachette, Buenos Aires, 1957.

Mackinnon, L. B.: *Some account of the Falkland Islands*, from a six months' residence in 1838 and 1839, A. H. Baily, London, 1840.

McNeil, R. A. and Deas, M. D.: *Europeans in Latin America, Humboldt to Hudson*, Bodleian Library, Oxford, 1980.

Madero, Eduardo: *Historia del Puerto de Buenos Aires*, Ediciones Buenos Aires, 1939.

Madero, Guillermo: Sobre algunos hacendados del siglo pasado, *Anales* de la Sociedad Rural Argentina, Buenos Aires, January 1962.

Mansfield, C. B.: *Paraguay, Brazil and the Plata, Letters 1852–3*, Cambridge, 1856.

Mansilla, Lucio V.: *Una excursión a los indios ranqueles* (2 vols.), Centro Editor de América Latina, Buenos Aires, 1967.

Marechal, Leopoldo: *Historia de la calle Corrientes*, Editorial Paidos, Buenos Aires, 1967.

Mariluz Urquijo, José M.: *Los matrimonios entre personas de diferente religión ante el derecho patrio argentino*, Buenos Aires, 1948. (Notes on Lafone's marriage to Queredo.)

Marsh, J. W.; Stirling, W. H.: *The story of Commander Allen Gardiner, R.N.*, with sketches of missionary work in South America, James Nisbett & Co. Ltd, London.

Marsh, J. W.: *Rays of sunlight in darkest South America*, or, God's wondrous working on southern shores and seas, Wells, Gardner, Darton & Co., London.

Masefield, John: *Collected poems*, Heineman, New York, 1923. (Includes the poems 'Rosas' and 'The daffodil fields'.)

Matthews, Rev. Abraham: *Crónica de la colonia galesa de la Patagonia*, Editorial Raigal, Buenos Aires, 1954. (Reprint by the Saint David Society, Trelew, Chubut, 1975.)

Medina, J. T.: *La expedición del corso Comodoro Guillermo Brown en aguas del Pacífico, octubre 1815–junio 1816*, Instituto de Historia, Facultad de Filosofía y Letras, Buenos Aires, 1928.

Merchant, Ronald M. and others: *St Andrew's Scots Presbyterian church, Chascomus, 1857–1957*, McCorquodale & Co., Buenos Aires, 1957.

Metford, J. C. J.: The recognition by Great Britain of the United Provinces of the Rio de la Plata, *Bulletin of Hispanic Studies*, London 1952.

Meyers, Jeffrey: The genius of failure, R. B. Cunninghame Graham, *London Magazine*, London, Oct./Nov. 1975.

Miers, John: *Viaje al Plata, 1819–1824*, Solar/Hachette, Buenos Aires, 1968. (Translation by Cristina Correa Morales de Aparicio of *Travels in Chile and La Plata*, including accounts respecting the geography, geology, statistics, government, finances, agriculture, manners and customs and the mining operations.)

Miller, John: *Memorias del General Miller al servicio de la República del Perú*, Translated by General Torrijos, Biblioteca Ayacucho, Editorial América, Madrid. (Originally published by Longman, in London, 1829.

Miro, R. R.: Viajeros ingleses en la Argentina, *La Nación*, Buenos Aires, 17 August, 1925.

Mitre, Bartolomé: *Historia de Belgrano y de la independencia argentina*, (4 vols.) Buenos Aires, 1927.

Mitre, Bartolomé: *La inmigración expontanea en la República Argentina*, speeches in the Senate 23–24 September, 1870 (against immigration promotion). Buenos Aires, 1870.

Monacci, Gustavo A.: *La colectividad británica en Bahía Blanca*, Universidad Nacional del Sur, Bahía Blanca, 1979.

Moneta, José Manuel: *Nos devolverán las Malvinas?* Buenos Aires, 1970.

Montieth Drysdale, J.: *A hundred years in Buenos Aires, 1829–1929*, being a brief account of St Andrew's Scots Church and its work during the first century of existence, Buenos Aires, 1929.

Monteith Drysdale, J.: *One hundred years old, 1838–1938*, a record of the first century of St Andrew's Scotch School, Buenos Aires, 1938.

Montenegro, Ricardo: Quiénes pretenden la Antártida Argentina? *Todo es Historia*, No. 142, Buenos Aires, March 1979.

Montoya, Alfredo J.: *Historia de los saladeros argentinos*, Editorial El Coloquio, Buenos Aires, 1970.

Moore, Guillermo H.: *Colección cronológica de visitas de Buenos Aires*, Kraft, Buenos Aires, 1939.

Moorehead, Alan: *Darwin and the Beagle*, Penguin, London, 1978.

Moreno, Juan Carlos: *La recuperación de las Malvinas*, Editorial Plus Ultra, Buenos Aires, 1973.

Morrell, Benjamin: *A narrative of four voyages to the South Sea, North and South Pacific Ocean, Indian and Antarctic Ocean, from 1822 to 1831*, New York, 1832.

Morris, John: *Argentine Republic, the forced metal laws of 1885 and gold contracts*, London, 1891.

Mulhall, E. T.: *Saudades* (obituaries), Buenos Aires, 1923.

Mulhall, M. G. & E. T.: *Handbook of the River Plate (1885)*, Standard office, Buenos Aires; Trubner & Co., London, Ballantyne Press, Edinburgh.

Mulhall, M. G.: *The English in South America*, Standard Office, Buenos Aires, 1878. (Stanford, London.)

Muñoz Aspiri, José Luis: *El poema Rosas de John Masefield*, EUDEBA, Buenos Aires, 1970.

Murga, Ventura: Las invasiones inglesas y Tucumán, *Revista de la Junta de Estudios Históricos de Tucumán*, Año I, No. 1, pp. 123–38, San Miguel de Tucumán, March 1968.

Murray, Thomas: *The story of the Irish in Argentina*, P. J. Kennedy & Sons, New York, 1919.

Musiker, R. & N.: Allen Francis Gardiner, *Standard Encyclopedia* of Southern Africa, Vol. 5, Nasou Ltd, Cape Town.

Musters, C. G.: *At home with the Patagonians*, a year's wanderings over untrodden ground from the Straits of Magellan to the Río Negro, Murray, London, 1871. (Translated into Spanish by Arturo Costa Alvarez as *Vida entre los patagones*, Solar/Hachette, Buenos Aires, 1964.)

Navarro Viola, Jorge: *El club de Residentes Extranjeros, 1841–1941*, breve reseña histórica en homenaje a sus fundadores, Buenos Aires, 1941.

Nevin, Kathleen: *You'll never go back*, a novel about the Irish in Argentina, Bruce Humphries, Boston, 1946.

Newton, Jorge: *Diccionario biográfico del campo argentino*, Buenos Aires, 1972.

Newton, Jorge: *Historia de la Sociedad Rural Argentina*, Librería Goncourt, Buenos Aires, 1966.

Newton, Jorge: *Historia del Jockey Club*, Buenos Aires, 1965.

Newton, Ronald C.: *German Buenos Aires, 1900–1933*, University of Texas, 1977.

Noailles, Alicia: *Eduardo T. Mulhall, un nexo con Gran Bretaña, siglo XIX*, Introduction by Jorge Luis Borges, Buenos Aires, 1970.

Noble, Julio: *Los británicos en la Argentina y en la guerra* (lecture), Buenos Aires, 1941.

Notes on the Viceroyalty of La Plata in South America, J. J. Stockdale, London, 1808.

Novillo Quiroga, Diego: Los primeros ganaderos extranjeros, *Anales* de la Sociedad Rural Argentina, Buenos Aires, March 1961.

Nuñez, Luis F.: *Los cementerios, almario de Buenos Aires*, Ministerio de Cultura y Educación, Buenos Aires, 1970.

Oliver, María Rosa: *Mundo, mi casa* (memoirs of Buenos Aires and of some resident Britons), Falbo, Buenos Aires, 1966.

Olivera, Eduardo A.: *Historia de la ganadería, agricultura e industrias afines de la República Argentina, 1515–1927*, Corporación Histórica Americana, Buenos Aires, 1928.

Olmos, Pbro. Ramón Rosa: *Historia de Catamarca*, La Unión, Catamarca, 1957. (Includes a history of the British invasion prisoners, Chapter XIII.)

Oría, Jorge S.: *Relaciones comerciales argentino-británicos*, (lectures) Buenos Aires, 1969.

Ortega Peña, Rodolfo; Duhalde, Eduardo Luis: *Baring Brothers y la historia política argentina*, Editorial Peña Lillo, Buenos Aires, 1973.

Ortíz, Fernando F.; De Paula, Alberto and others: *La arquitectura del liberalismo en la Argentina*, Editorial Sudamericana, Buenos Aires, 1968.

Ortiz, Ricardo M.: *El valor económico de los puertos argentinos.* Editorial Lozada, Buenos Aires, 1943.

Ortiz, Ricardo M.: *Historia económica de la Argentina.* Plus Ultra, Buenos Aires, 1974.

Ortiz, Ricardo M.: Política ferroviaria argentina; consideraciones sobre el vencimiento de la Ley Mitre; la nacionalización de los ferroccariles. *Colegio Libre de Estudios Superiores.* Bahía Blanca, 1946.

Osler, William: Thomas Dover M.B. (of Dover's powder), physician and buccaneer, *Bulletin of the Johns Hopkins Hospital*, Baltimore, January 1896.

Owen, Geraint D.: *Crisis in Chubut, a chapter in the history of the Welsh colony in Patagonia*, C. Davies, Swansea, 1977.

Page, Jesse: *Captain Allen Gardiner of Patagonia*, Pickering & Inglis, London.

Page, Jesse: *Captain Allen Gardiner, sailor and saint*, S. W. Partridge & Co., London.

Page, Thomas Jefferson: *Notas de viaje por la Confederación Argentina, 1853–1855*, (Tucumán-Santiago del Estero), Comisión Nacional de Museos y Monumentos Históricos, Serie III, No. 4, Paraná, 1954. (Translation of *La Plata, the Argentine Confederation and Paraguay*, Trubner, London, 1859.)

Parish, Woodbine: *Buenos Aires y las provincias del Río de la Plata*, Hachette, Buenos Aires, 1958. (Translation of *Buenos Aires and the provinces of the Rio de la Plata*, Murray, London, 1838.)

Parle, Estevan: *Registro de marcas de hacienda de la provincia de Buenos Aires*, Brown & Rawcliffe, Liverpool, 1885. (A curiosity: a register of sheep and cattle brands in Buenos Aires.)

Payne, John R.: *W. H. Hudson, a bibliography*, Dawson, Archon, 1977.

Pellegrini, Carlos: *Británicos en la Argentina*, Lecture at Prince George's Hall, Buenos Aires, 28 November 1905. (National Library, Buenos Aires, Cat. 514872.)

Peña, Enrique: *Documentos y planos*, relativos al período edilicio colonial de la ciudad de Buenos Aires, Buenos Aires.

Pendle, George: *Argentina*, Oxford University Press, 1961. (Includes a good general bibliography.)

Pendle, George: Railways in Argentina, *History Today*, February, 1958, London.

Perkins, Carmen Peers de: *Eramos jóvenes el siglo y yo*, Editorial Jorge Alvarez, Buenos Aires, 1969. (Recollections of Argentina and some of its characters in the early part of the twentieth century.)

Perkins, Guillermo: *Las colonias de Santa Fé*, su orígen, progreso y actual situación, con observaciones generales sobre la emigración a la República Argentina, Imp. El Ferro Carril, Rosario, 1865.

Peters, H. E.: *Foreign debt of the Argentine Republic*, Baltimore, 1934.

Peterson, Harold F.: *La Argentina y los Estados Unidos, 1810–1860*, EUDEBA, Buenos Aires, 1970.

Phillips, G. W.: *The missionary martyrs of Tierra del Fuego*, being the memoir of Mr J. Garland Phillips, late catechist of the Patagonian, or South American Missionary Society, Wertheim, MacIntosh and Hunt, London, 1861.

Phipps, Colin: What future for the Falklands?, *Fabian Tract 450*, London, 1977.

Piccirilli, Ricardo; Gianello, Leoncio: *Biografías navales*, Depto. de Estudios Históricos Navales, Secretaría de Estado de Marina, Buenos Aires, 1963.

Piccirilli, Ricardo; and others: *Diccionario histórico argentino*, Ediciones Históricas Argentinas, Buenos Aires, 1953.

Piccirilli, Ricardo: *Lecciones de historia naval argentina*, Depto. de Estudios Historicos Navales, Secretaría de Estado de Marina, Buenos Aires, 1967.

Pillado, Antonio: *Diccionario de Buenos Aires o sea guía de forasteros*, Buenos Aires, 1864.

Pillado, J. Antonio: *Buenos Aires colonial*, Editorial Bonaerense, 1943.

Pillado, José A.: Orígenes del ganado argentino, *Anales* de la Sociedad Rural Argentina, Buenos Aires, March–October 1910.

Pilling, William: *Near the lagunas*, or scenes in the states of La Plata, Buenos Aires, 1895.

Pineda Yañez, Rafael: *Cómo fué la vida amorosa de Rosas*, Editorial Plus Ultra, Buenos Aires, 1973. (Introduction by Armando A. Piñeiro.)

Piñeiro, Armando Alonso: *Dramas y esplendores de la historia argentina*, Editorial Platero, Buenos Aires, 1974.

Pla, Josefina: *The British in Paraguay, 1850–1870*, Translation by B. C. MacDermot, Richmond Publishing Co., Richmond, 1977.

Platt, D. C. M.: Britain's informal Empire in Argentina, 1806–1914, *Past and Present*, Vol. 1:4, 1953.

Platt, D. C. M.: *Latin America and British Trade, 1806–1914; The merchant adventurers*, A. & C. Black, London 1972.

Polwarth, Lady Jean: *R. B. Cunninghame Graham*, Lecture at the Anglo-Argentine Society, London 24 January 1979.

Potash, Robert A.: *El ejército y la política en la Argentina, 1928–1945, de Yrigoyen a Perón*, Sudamericana, Buenos Aires 1971.

Pratt, E. J.: Anglo-Argentine commercial and political rivalry on the Plata, 1820–1830, *Hispanic American Historical Review*, Duke Univ. Press, 1931.

Proctor, Robert: *Narrative of a journey across the Cordillera of the Andes*, Constable, London, 1825.

Pueyrredón, Carlos A.: Un inculpado de alta traición, la fuga de Beresford, *La Nación*, July 1930.

Radaelli, Sigfrido: *Buenos Aires visto por viajeros ingleses, 1806–1826*, Emece, Buenos Aires, 1945.

Raed, José: *Rosas y el cónsul general inglés*, Buenos Aires, 1965.

Random sketches of Buenos Aires with explanatory notes, William P. Nimmo, Edinburgh, 1868. (Anonymous sketches of Buenos Aires, including several of events concerning Britons, and attributed to a Scots artist in Buenos Aires.)

Ratto, Héctor R.: *Almirante don Guillermo Brown*, Buenos Aires, 1934.

Ratto, Héctor R.: *Batallas navales*, Rio Santiago, 1945.

Ravignani, Emilio: *El virreinato del Río de la Plata (1776–1810)*, Buenos Aires, 1938.

Ravignani, Emilio: *Historia constitucional de la República Argentina* (3 vols.), Buenos Aires, 1938.

Ravignani, Emilio: La Revolución de Mayo y los intereses británicos en el Plata, *La Nación*, Buenos Aires, 24 May 1931.

Read, Jan: *The new conquistadors*, Evans, London, 1980.

(A) Relation of R.M.'s voyage to Buenos Ayres, and from thence by land to Potosí, John Darby, London, 1710.

Reyes, Tte. Col. Marcelino: *Bosquejo histórico de la provincia de La Rioja, 1543–1867*, Buenos Aires, 1913.

Richards, Dr José E.; Gaynor, Juan S.: *El Padre Fahy.* Homenaje de la Asociación Católica Irlandesa en el centenario de su fallecimiento, 1871–1971, Editorial Irlandesa, Buenos Aires, 1971.

Rickard, Major F. I.: *The mineral and other resources of the Argentine Republic (La Plata) in 1869*, Longman, Green & Co., London, 1870.

Ridley, Jasper: *Garibaldi*, Constable, London, 1974. (Includes interesting notes on the British in Montevideo and Buenos Aires during the Anglo-French blockade.)

Riopardense de Macedo, Francisco: *Ingleses no Rio Grande do Sul*, Ediçoes a Naçáo, Porto Alegre, 1975.

Rippy, J. Fred: *La rivalidad entre Estados Unidos y Gran Bretaña por América latina*, EUDEBA, Buenos Aires, 1964.

Riveros Tula, Anibal M.: *Historia de la Colonia del Sacramento*, Montevideo.

Roberts, Carlos: *Las invasiones inglesas del Río de la Plata, 1806–1807*, y la influencia y organización de las provincias del Río de la Plata, Peuser, Buenos Aires, 1938. (A book long-considered essential reference on the invasions.)

Roberts, F. Evelyn: El espíritu del Eistedvod, *Jornada*, Trelew, 5 November 1970.

Roberts, Morley: *W. H. Hudson: a portrait*, Nash & Grayson, London, 1924.

Roberts, Tegai: Editor. *Camwy*, published by the Gaiman Museum, Chubut, 1974.

Robertson, J. P. & W. P.: *Letters on South America*, comprising travels on the banks of the Paraná and Río de la Plata, London, 1843.

Robertson, J. P. & W. P.: *Letters on Paraguay*, Comprising an account of four years' residence in that Republic, under the government of Dictator Francia, London, 1838.

Robertson, Malcolm A.: *Argentina and Great Britain*, Institute of Hispanic Studies, Liverpool, 1935. (Lecture by a former ambassador.)

Robertson, P.: *Letters from Buenos Aires and Chile*, London, 1819.

Robertson, S. R.: *Making friends for Britain, an incursion into diplomacy*, Kraft, Buenos Aires, 1948. (Memoirs of a press attaché at the British Embassy in Buenos Aires.)

Rochel, W. H.: *Argentina past and present*, London, 1914.

Rodney, C. A.; Graham, John: *The reports of the present state of the United Provinces of South America*, with their accompanying documents, occasional notes by the editor, and an introductory discourse, intended to present, with the reports and documents, a view of the present state of the country and of the progress of the independents, London, 1819.

Rogers, Woodes: *A cruising voyage around the world*, A. Bell & Co. Ltd, London, 1712.

Rogind, William: *Historia del Ferrocarril del Sud*, Establecimiento Gráfico Argentino, Buenos Aires, 1937.

Romero Sosa, Carlos Greogrio: Nuevas investigaciones sobre Redhead, el médico de Belgrano y de Güemes, *Revista Argentina de la Historia de la Medicina*, Vol. V, No. 1, Buenos Aires, 25 April 1946. (Also in *Actualización*, Facultad de Filosofía y Letras, Documentos T.XII; Territorio y Población, Buenos Aires, 1919, Emilio Ravignani.)

Roncoroni, Atilio: *Historia del Municipio de Dolores*, Dolores, 1967.

Rosa, José María: *Historia Argentina*, Editorial Oriente, Buenos Aires.

Rosa, José María: El triste destino de quienes se adelantaron al Congreso de 1816, *La Opinión*, Buenos Aires, 9 July 1971.

Rothenstein, William: *Men and memories, 1900–1922*, Faber, London, 1932. (Includes notes on W. H. Hudson.)

Rugeroni, J. J.: *Gran Bretaña en la evolución de la economía argentina*; el comercio, la industria y la producción del país; published by the *Buenos Aires Herald*, 1945.

Rugeroni, J. J.: *Una contribución a la confraternidad argentino-británica*, *Buenos Aires Herald*, Buenos Aires, 1946.

Rugeroni, J. J.: *Los ferrocarriles de capital británico en el progreso argentino*, *Buenos Aires Herald*, 1947.

Rugeroni, J. J.: *Vinculación argentino-norteamericana*, *Buenos Aires Herald*, 1945.

Ruiz Guiñazú, Enrique: Lord Strangford y la independencia argentina, *Boletín de la Academia Nacional de la Historia*, No. 34, Buenos Aires.

Ruiz Guiñazú, Enrique: *Lord Strangford y la Revolución de Mayo*, Editorial La Facultad, Bernabé & Cia., Buenos Aires, 1937.

Saenz, Jimena: Camila O'Gorman, Love story, 1848, *Revista Todo es Historia*, No. 51, Buenos Aires, 1971.

Saldías, Adolfo: *Historia de la Confederación Argentina*, EUDEBA, Buenos Aires, 1968.

Saldías, Adolfo: *Por qué surgió Rosas*, Editorial Plus Ultra, Buenos Aires, 1973.

Salesky Ulibari, Aurelio: *Una escuela y un maestro en la colonización Boer*, Cuadernos de Historia del Chubut, No. 7, Trelew, October, 1970.

Sanguinetti, Manuel J.: *San Telmo y su pasado histórico*, Ediciones República de San Telmo, Buenos Aires, 1965.

Santillán, Diego Abad de: *Historia argentina*, Tipográfica Editora Argentina, (5 vols.), Buenos Aires, 1961–1971.

Sarmiento, Domingo F.: Frank Brown, *El Censor*, Buenos Aires, 24 July 1886.

Scalabrini Ortiz, Raúl: *Historia de los ferrocarriles argentinos*, Editorial Plus Ultra, Buenos Aires, 1973.

Scalabrini Ortiz, Raúl: *Política británica en el Río de la Plata*, Editorial Plus Ultra, Buenos Aires, 1973.

Scalvini, Jorge M.: *Historia de Mendoza*, Editorial Spadoni, Mendoza, 1965. (pp. 97–100 cover the history of the British in Mendoza.)

Scenna, Miguel Angel: Palermo, *Revista Todo es Historia*, No. 36, Buenos Aires, April, 1970.

Scenna, Miguel Angel: *Cómo fueron las relaciones argentino-norteamericanas*, Plus Ultra, Buenos Aires, 1970.

Scobie, James R.: *La lucha por la consolidación de la nacionalidad argentina, 1852–1862*, Editorial Hachette, Buenos Aires, 1964.

Scobie, James R.: *Argentina: a city and a nation*, New York, 1964.

Scobie, James R.: *Revolución en las pampas*, Editorial Solar/Hachette, Buenos Aires, 1968. Translation by Floreal Mazia from *Revolution on the Pampas, a social history of Argentina wheat, 1860–1910*, Austin, Texas, 1964.

Segreti, Carlos S. A.: Las relaciones entre los Estados Unidos y el Río de la Plata, 1810–1816, y la finalidad de la Revolución de Mayo, *Revista de la Junta de Estudios Históricos de Tucumán*, (pp. 9–51) No. 2, San Miguel de Tucumán, July 1969.

Seymour, Richard Arthur: *Pioneering in the Pampas or the first few years of a settler's experience in the La Plata*, London, 1869. Translated by Justo P. Saenz as *Un poblador de las pampas, vida de un estanciero de la frontera sudeste de Córdoba, entre los años 1865 y 1868*, Editora del Plata, Buenos Aires, 1947.

Shipton, Eric: *Tierra del Fuego, the fatal lodestone*, Charles Knight, London 1973.

Shipton, Eric: *Land of tempest, travels in Patagonia, 1958–1962*, Hodder & Stoughton, London 1963.

Shrubsall, Dennis: *W. H. Hudson, writer and naturalist*, Compton Press, Salisbury, 1978.

Shuttleworth, Nina E.: *A life of Sir Woodbine Parish*, Smith, Elder & Co., London, 1910.

Smith, Peter H.: *Carne y política en la Argentina*, Paidos, Buenos Aires, 1968.

Socolow, Susan Migden: *The merchants of Buenos Aires, 1778–1810*, Cambridge Latin American Studies, 1978.

Solanas, Saul: Un joven y brillante médico escocés, *La Nación*, Buenos Aires, 7 March 1973.

Solari, Juan Antonio: *Esteban Echeverría; Asociación de Mayo, su ideario*, Buenos Aires, 1949.

Solari Yrigoyen, Hipólito: *Musters en el Chubut*, Cuadernos de Historia del Chubut, No. 4, Junta de Estudios Históricos del Chubut, Trelew, September 1968.

Solberg, Carl: *Immigration and nationalism, Argentina and Chile, 1890–1914*, University of Texas Press, Austin, 1970.

Souter, Gavin: *A peculiar people, the Australians in Paraguay*, Angus & Robertson, Sydney, 1968.

Sporleder, Carlos R.: Las invasiones inglesas, ensayo sobre dos aspectos de la Reconquista, *La Nación*, Buenos Aires, 6 August 1939.

Stevens, Edward F.: *One hundred years of Houlders*, a record of the history of Houlder Brothers & Co. Ltd, 1849–1950, The Mendip

Press, London, 1950.

Stevenson, J. T.: *The history of St George's College, Quilmes, Argentina*, Society for the Promotion of Christian Knowledge, London, 1936.

Steward, C. S.: *Brazil and La Plata, the personal record of a cruise*, New York, 1856.

Stewart Taylor, Margaret: *Focus on the Falkland Islands*, Hale, London 1971.

Stirling, Alfred: *Gang forward*, a history of the Stirlings, Hawthorn Press, London, 1972. (Includes a biography of Bishop Stirling, of the Falkland Islands.)

Strange, Ian, J.: *The Falkland Islands*, David and Charles, London 1972.

Strasser, María Pía L.: *Chubut, ensueño y realidad*, Comodoro Rivadavia, 1962. (A rather patronizing, but rich in anecdotes, history of Chubut, including the Welsh colonization.)

Street, J.: *British influence in the independence of the River Plate provinces*, Cambridge, 1950. (Partly reproduced as *La influencia británica en la independencia de las provincias del Río de la Plata, con especial referencia al período comprendido entre 1808 y 1816*, Revista Histórica, Montevideo, 1953–7.)

Street, J.: Lord Strangford and Río de la Plata, 1808–15, *Hispanic American Historical Review*, Duke University Press, 1953.

Strong, L. A. G.: *Doctor Quicksilver*, Melrose Press, London, 1956 (on Dr Dover).

Studer, Elena F. S. de: *La trata de negros en el Río de la Plata durante el siglo XVIII*, Instituto de Historia Argentina Dr Emilio Ravignani, Facultad de Filosofía y Letras, Buenos Aires, 1958.

Tallon, A. G.: *Historia del Metodismo en el Rio de la Plata, 1836–1936*, Imprenta Metodista, Buenos Aires 1936.

Tarragno, Roberto: *Sarmiento, los liberales y el imperialismo inglés*, A. Peña Lillo, Buenos Aires, 1963.

Taullard, A.: *Los planos más antiguos de Buenos Aires, 1580–1880*, Peuser, 1940.

Temperley, H.: The foreign policy of Canning, 1822–1827, *The Cambridge History of British Foreign Policy*, London, 1925.

Tesler, Mario: Nuestro primer comisionado en las islas Malvinas, el corso David Jewett, *Mayoría*, Buenos Aires 26 November 1973. Los ingleses piden permiso, *Mayoría*, Buenos Aires, 30 November 1973. Jewett no fue gobernador, *Mayoría*, Buenos Aires, 5 December 1973.

Thomas, Donald: *Cochrane*, Andre Deutsch, London, 1978.

Thomson, Basil: *Ramón Writes*, Buenos Aires Herald, 1979. (A sample of Spanglish.)

Thomson, James: *Letters on the moral and religious state of South*

America, written during a residence of nearly seven years in Buenos Aires, Chile, Peru and Colombia; London, 1827.

Thomson, R. W.: *Land of tomorrow, a story of South America*, Duckworth, London, 1936.

Tjarks, German O. E.; Vidaurreta, Alicia: *El Comercio inglés y el contrabando.* Nuevos aspectos en el estudio de la política económica en el Río de la Plata, 1807–1810; Buenos Aires, 1962.

Tobal, Gastón F.: *Evocaciones porteñas*, Kraft, Buenos Aires, 1944.

Torre Revello, J.: *Crónicas del Buenos Aires colonial*, Bajel, Buenos Aires 1947.

Townsend, B. J.: *The history of Holy Trinity Church*, Lomas de Zamora, 1936.

Troncoso, Oscar A.: El negocio de las carnes, el Pacto Roca-Runciman, *Revista Polémica*, No. 65, Centro Editor de América Latina, Buenos Aires, 1971.

Tschiffely, A. F.: *This way southward*, Heineman, London, 1940.

Tschiffely, A. F.: *Don Roberto* (a life of R. B. Cunninghame Graham), Heineman, London, 1937.

Truscott, Basil R.: *Sixty years of Christian service*, Lomas de Zamora, 1956,

Udaondo, Enrique: *Diccionario Biográfico Argentino*, Institución Mitre, Edición Coni, Buenos Aires, 1938.

Un inglés: *Cinco años en Buenos Aires, 1820–1825*, Solar/Hachette, Buenos Aires 1970.

Ure, John: *Cucumber sandwiches in the Andes*, Constable, London, 1977. (Chapter 7 includes notes on life in Mendoza at the time of San Martín's expedition and references to the British there.)

Uriburu, José Evaristo: *La república Argentina através de las obras de los escritores ingleses*, (Compilación), Buenos Aires, 1948.

Vacarezza, Oscar A.: De la vida y de las cosas del Académico Lepper, médico de caudillos, *Boletín de la Academia Nacional de Medicina*, No. 44, Buenos Aires, 1966.

Varios autores: *Buenos Aires visto por viajeros ingleses*, Colección Buen Aire, Emecé, Buenos Aires, 1941.

Vedoya, Juan Carlos: Rivadavia y el empréstito Baring, *Revista Todo es Historia*, No. 57, Buenos Aires, January 1972.

Vedoya, Juan Carlos: *La verdad sobre el empréstito Baring*, Editorial Plus Ultra, Buenos Aires, 1971.

Vedoya, Juan Carlos: Los Andes, entre el túnel y el Cristo, *Revista Todo es Historia*, No. 72, Buenos Aires, April 1973.

Vedoya, Juan Carlos: Monopolios y chacareros, *Revista Todo es Historia*, No. 71, Buenos Aires, May, 1973.

Vercellana, Juan F.: A más de cien años del tendido de los ferrocarriles,

La Nación, Buenos Aires, 27 February 1966.
Vergara, Ignacio: *El protestantismo en Chile*, Editorial del Pacífico, Santiago de Chile, 1962 (p. 19, notes on Allen Gardiner).
Vidal, Emeric Essex: *Picturesque illustrations of Buenos Aires and Montevideo*, Ackerman, London, 1820.
Villafañe, Benjamín: *Motivos de la selva y la montaña*, Buenos Aires, 1952 (a collection of stories and recollections of different personalities in Argentina; p. 37 has an anecdote about a British diplomat buried in the Quebrada de Humahuaca).
Villalobos, R. Sergio: *Comercio y contrabando en el Río de la Plata y Chile*, EUDEBA, Buenos Aires, 1971.
Villalpando, Waldo Luis; and others: *Las iglesias del trasplante, protestantismo de inmigración en la Argentina*, Centro de Estudios Cristianos, Methopress, Buenos Aires, 1970.
Vizoso Gorostiaga, Manuel: *Camila O'Gorman y su época*, Santa Fé, 1943.
Walker, John: *The South American Sketches of R. B. Cunninghame Graham*, University of Oklahoma Press, 1978.
Walker, John: *R. B. Cunninghame Graham, gaucho apologist and costumbrist, of the Pampa*, Hispania, Vol. 53, No. 1, March 1970.
Walker, John: A chronological bibliography of works on R. B. Cunninghame Graham (1852–1936), *The Bibliothek*, Vol. 9, No. 2/3 Edinburgh 1978.
Walker, John: Cunninghame Graham and the River Plate region, *The Bulletin*, Vol. XXII, No. 8, Buenos Aires, April 1977.
Walker, John: R. B. Cunninghame Graham: an annotated bibliography of writings about him, *English Literature in Transition*, Arizona State University, Vol. 22, No. 2, 1979.
Walker, John: English-speaking writers of the River Plate, *Buenos Aires Herald*, 13 February 1977.
Walker, John: Walter Owen: the Latin American epic and the art of translation, *Latin American Literary Review*, Vol. III, No. 5, 1974.
Walker, John: Walter Owen: Cultural envoy, *Buenos Aires Herald*, 6 August 1977.
Watts, Cedric: *Joseph Conrad's letters to R. B. Cunninghame Graham*, Cambridge, 1969.
Watts, Cedric: *Cunninghame Graham, a critical biography*, written in collaboration with Lawrence Davies, Cambridge, 1979.
Watts, Cedric: *Conrad and Cunninghame Graham*, J. Conrad Society, London, 1978.
Webster, Charles Kingsley: *Britain and the independence of Latin America, 1812–1830*, Oxford University Press for the Ibero-American Institute of Great Britain, London, 1938.

West, Herbert Faulkner: *A modern conquistador*, Cranley & Day, London, 1932 (on R. B. Cunninghame Graham).

Wheelwright, W.: *Ferrocarril a Ensenada*, Informes de Santiago Bevans, Antonio Toll, José Murature, Francisco Segui, Juan Coghlan; Buenos Aires, 1870.

Whitaker, Arthur Preston: *Estados Unidos y la independencia de América latina, 1800–1830*, EUDEBA, Buenos Aires, 1964.

White, Ernest William: *Cameos from the silverland*, or the experiences of a young naturalist in the Argentine Republic; J. van Voorst, London, 1881.

Whitington, G. T.: *The Falkland Islands*, compiled from ten years' investigation of the subject; London, 1840.

Wilcksen, Guillermo: *Las colonias*, informe sobre el estado actual de las colonias agrícolas de la República Argentina, presentado a la comisión central de inmigración; Buenos Aires, 1873.

Wilcocke, Samuel Hull: *History of the viceroyalty of Buenos Ayres*, Symonds, London, 1807.

Wilde, José Antonio: *Buenos Aires desde setenta años atrás, 1810–1880*, EUDEBA, Buenos Aires, 1961.

Wileman, Henry St John: *The growth and manufacture of cane sugar in the Argentine Republic*, London, 1884.

Williams, Glyn: *The desert and the dream*, University of Wales Press, Cardiff, 1976. (Probably the most comprehensive social history of the Welsh in Chubut.)

Williams, Glyn: Welsh settlers and native Americans in Patagonia, *Journal of Latin American Studies*, London, May, 1979.

Williams, Glyn: *Bibliography on the Welsh in Chubut*, British Lending Library, HR 3686.

Williamson, James A.: *A short history of British expansion – the old colonial empire*, Macmillan, London, 1968.

Wilson, George F.: *A bibliography of the writings of W. H. Hudson*, Bookman's Journal, London, 1922.

Winkler Bealer, Lewis: *Los corsarios de Buenos Aires, sus actividades en las guerras hispanoamericanas de la independencia, 1815–1821*, Instituto de Historia Argentina Dr Emilio Ravignani, Facultad de Filosofía y Letras, Buenos Aires, 1937.

Wright, Winthrop R.: *British-owned railways in Argentina: their effect on the growth of economic nationalism, 1854–1948*, Univ. of Texas Press, 1976.

Yaben, Jacinto R.: *Biografías argentinas y sudamericanas*, Editorial Metropolis, Buenos Aires, 1938.

Yates, William: *José Miguel Carrera, 1820–1821*, Translation by José Luis Busaniche, Imprenta Ferrari, Buenos Aires, 1941.

Zampini, Virgilio: *Trelew, biografía de una ciudad*, Trelew, Chubut, 1972.

Zampini, Virgilio: *Significación de la colonización galesa en el desarrollo del Chubut*, Cuadernos de Historia del Chubut, No. 1, October 1970.

Zar, Marcos A.: Un libro sobre la segunda invasión inglesa, *La Prensa*, Buenos Aires, 19 June 1932.

Zeballos, Estanislao S.: La nacionalidad de los hijos de extranjeros, *Revista de Derecho, Historia y Letras*, Buenos Aires, 1906.

Zeballos, Estanislao S.: The British mission to South America, *Revista de Derecho, Historia y Letras*, Buenos Aires, 1918.

Newspapers and Periodicals

(Numbers in brackets are those of the National Library, Buenos Aires, catalogue.
The dates given are those of the start and, sometimes, where known, end of publication.)

The Argentine Magazine (July 1925 to 1928, continued as *Ourphun*) (30385)
The Argentine News (December 1890) (30572)
The Argentine News (December 1940) (208139)
Britannica (January 1943) (207393)
The British Packet and Argentine News (1826–1858) (30610, 20634; La Plata 123)
Buenos Aires Christian Advocate and Home Messenger (January–Dec. 1933) (201084)
Buenos Aires Herald (started as *The Herald*) (1876) (30428)
Buenos Ayres Herald (1852–1853) (30439)
Central Argentine Railway Magazine
The Cosmopolitan (November 1831–January 1833) (30741/7)
El Regional, special historical edition, Gaiman, Chubut, July 1975
The Review of the River Plate (1891)
The River Plate American (later Anglo-American Review) (1924) (151572)
The River Plate Magazine (January 1864) (30114)
River Plate Railway News (November 1891)
River Plate Sport and Pastime (August 1891) (30572)
The Southern Cross (1875) (30744/74)
The Southern Star (May 1807–July 1807) Facsimile: Instituto Histórico y Geográfico del Uruguay. (258159) (30517)
South American Bulletin (January 1933) (201090)

The Standard (1861) (30421)
The Standard News Bulletin (1900) (30712)
The Weekly Standard (1866–1874) (30587)
The Times of Argentina (1900) (200326)
La Nación
La Prensa
Todo es Historia magazine

Documents relating to the British Invasions, 1806–7 (at the Biblioteca Mitre, Buenos Aires)

Trial of Lieut.-Gen. John Whitelocke, commander in chief of the expedition against Buenos Ayres, by Court Martial, held in Chelsea College, 28 January 1808 and succeeding days. Tipper, London, 1808.

A narrative of the expedition to and the storming of Buenos Ayres by the British army, commanded by Lieut.-General Whitelocke, by an Officer attached to the expedition. Printed by W. Meyler, Bath 1807.

An authentic narrative of the proceedings of the expedition under the command of Brig. Gen. Craufurd, until its arrival at Monte Video, with an account of the operations against Buenos Ayres under the command of Lieut.-General Whitelocke, By an Officer of the expedition. Printed for the author, London 1808.

Carta de despedida de los oficiales ingleses destinados a Catamarca, testificando su gratitud y reconocimiento por el buen trato y acogida que en esta ciudad experimentaron. Catamarca, 1* de agosto de 1807. Buenos Aires, Real Imprenta de los Niños Expósitos, 1807.

Authentic and complete trial of Lieut.-General Whitelocke, late commander of the attack on Buenos Aires, by a court martial, assembled in the Great Hall, Chelsea College, from Thursday, January 28, to Tuesday, March 15, 1808, including a complete copy of the defence. Taken in shorthand by a barrister. To which is added a sketch of the life and campaigns of General Whitelocke accompanied with a correct likeness, also an authentic narrative from his departure from England in March 1807. London.

Buenos Aires. Truth and reason versus calumny and folly, in which the leading circumstances of General Whitelocke's conduct in South America are explained. With an appendix in answer to an expressive publication of last week, refuting every personality therein advanced. London, 1807.

Documentos relativos a la expedición del Almirante Popham. Vol. I, Biblioteca Federal, Buenos Aires, 1852.

Invasiones inglesas al Río de la Plata. Documentos impresos, 1* época, 1806–1807, 2 vols.

Minutes of a court, held on board His Majesty's ship 'Gladiator' in Portsmouth harbour on Friday, the 6th day of March 1807, and continued by adjournment till Wednesday, March 11 following, for the trial of Capt. Sir Home Popham; including a complete copy of his defence, taken from the original. London, 1807.

Narrative of the expedition to and the storming of Buenos Aires, by the British army commanded by Lieutenant General Whitelocke, printed by an officer of the expedition. William Meyler, Orange Grove, London, 1807 (see also previous account, dated in Bath).

Narrative of the operations of a small British force, under the command of Brigadier General Sir Samuel Auchmuty employed in the reduction of Montevideo in the River Plate, 1807. By a field officer of the staff. Illustrated with a plan of operations. London, 1807.

Notes on the Viceroyalty of La Plata in South America, with a sketch of the manner and character of the inhabitants, collected during a residence in the city of Montevideo, by a gentleman recently returned from it. To which is added a history of the operations of the British troops in that country and biographical and military anecdotes of the principal officers employed in the different expeditions. Illustrated with a portrait, map and plans. London, 1808.

Proceedings of the general court martial held at Chelsea Hospital, January 28, 1808, and continued by adjournment, till Tuesday, March 15, for the trial of Lieut.-General Whitelocke, late commander in chief of the forces in South America. Taken in shorthand by Mr Gurney. With the defence copied from the original, by permission of General Whitelocke, also all the documents produced on the trial. London, 1808.

Trial at large of Lieutenant General Whitelocke, late commander in chief of the forces in South America, by a general court martial held at Chelsea Hospital, on Thursday, January 28, 1808, and continued by adjournment to Tuesday, March 15. Taken by Blanchard and Rensey, shorthand writers of the court, and published from their notes with a corrected copy of the defence, as delivered into the court and the Right Honourable judges' advocates' reply, also all the documents produced in evidence. London, 1808.

La Reconquista y Defensa de Buenos Aires, 1806–1807. Instituto de Estudios Históricos sobre la Reconquista y la Defensa de Buenos Aires, Peuser, 1947.

Miscellaneous

Los ferrocarriles británicos en la República Argentina. (A pamphlet produced in 1941 for British public-relations purposes.)

El comercio británico en la Argentina. (As above.)

Nueva Era. Tandil. Suplemento Bodas de Oro, 1919–1969. (Special supplement.)

Record of the British community in the River Plate, Vol. I. South American Bank Note Co., Buenos Ayres, 1902.

Informe anual del Comisario general de inmigración de la República Argentina. 1873/75/76. (National Library, Buenos Aires, 60441.)

Monarchical projects to place a Bourbon king on the throne of Buenos Aires, in opposition to British interests, being the proceedings instituted against the late congress and directory, for the crime of High Treason, with preliminary remarks illustrative of the subject in question, and explanatory of the causes which led to the recent revolution in that country, from authentic sources. London 1820 (Copy found at the Mitre Library, Buenos Aires).

Reports of H.M.'s secretaries of Embassy and Legation of the manufactures, commerce of the countries in which they reside. Report by Mr Ford on the financial condition of the Argentine Republic. London, 1867. (Copy at the Mitre Library, Buenos Aires.)

River Plate Handbook, guide, directory and almanac for 1863. Comprising the city and province of Buenos Aires, the other Argentine provinces, Montevideo, etc. Printed in Buenos Aires, 1863. (Copy at Mitre Library, Buenos Aires.)

River Plate correspondence respecting the hostilities in the River Plate. 1865–1868. Presented to the House of Commons. (Copy at Mitre Library.)

Summary account of the Viceroyalty of Buenos Aires on the Rio de la Plata, including its geographical position, climate, aspect of the country, national productions, commerce, government and state of society and manners. Extracted from the best authorities. London.

Asociación Argentina de Cultura Inglesa. Breve Historia de sus primeros diez años, 1927–1937. Buenos Aires, 1937.

Antología Histórica de Británicos Vistos por Ojos Argentinos. Nucleo Argentino de Estudios Históricos. Buenos Aires 1941. (This anthology gives a favourable view of British in Argentina. Published by people sympathetic to the British war cause, among them the British Society, it was aimed at countering pro-Axis leanings by reminding the public of Argentina's traditional links with Britain.)

Index

UTA Sempf
05151
15041
⊖

Wolfgang + Sara Köller
Kölnstr. 72
5300 Bonn 1
West-Germany
Tel: 0228-630053

Stephen Gansky
P.O. Box 351
Narberth, PA 19072
(215) 664-0648 (office)
293-0644 (home)